Notable Speeches in Contemporary Presidential Campaigns

Recent Titles in the
Praeger Series in Political Communication
Robert E. Denton, Jr., *General Editor*

With Malice Toward All?: The Media and Public Confidence in Democratic Institutions
Patricia Moy and Michael Pfau

Making "Pictures in Our Heads": Government Advertising in Canada
Jonathan W. Rose

Videostyle in Presidential Campaigns: Style and Content of Televised Political Advertising
Lynda L. Kaid

Political Communication Ethics: An Oxymoron?
Robert E. Denton, Jr., editor

Navigating Boundaries: The Rhetoric of Women Governors
Brenda DeVore Marshall and Molly A. Mayhead, editors

Talk of Power, Power of Talk: The 1994 Health Care Reform Debate and Beyond
Michael W. Shelton

When Congress Debates: A Bakhtinian Paradigm
Theodore F. Sheckels

The Rhetoric of First Lady Hillary Rodham Clinton: Crisis Management Discourse
Colleen Elizabeth Kelley

The Clinton Scandals and the Politics of Image Restoration
Joseph R. Blaney and William L. Benoit

Campaign Craft: The Strategies, Tactics, and Art of Political Campaign Management
Daniel M. Shea and Michael John Burton

The Idea of Political Marketing
Nicholas J. O'Shaughnessy, editor, and Stephan C. M. Henneberg, associate editor

The Primary Decision: A Functional Analysis of Debates in Presidential Primaries
William L. Benoit, P.M. Pier, LeAnn M. Brazeal, John P. McHale, Andrew Klyukovski, and David Airne

Notable Speeches in Contemporary Presidential Campaigns

Robert V. Friedenberg

Praeger Series in Political Communication

Westport, Connecticut
London

Library of Congress Cataloging-in-Publication Data

Friedenberg, Robert V.
Notable speeches in contemporary presidential campaigns / Robert V. Friedenberg.
p. cm.—(Praeger series in political communication, ISSN 1062–5623)
Includes bibliographical references and index.

1. United States—Politics and government—1945–1989—Sources. 2. United States—Politics and government—1989—Sources. 3. Presidents—United States—Election—History—20th century—Sources. 4. Campaign speeches—United States. 5. Speeches, addresses, etc., American. I. Title. II. Series.
E838.3.F75 2002
324.973′092—dc21 2001133086

British Library Cataloguing in Publication Data is available.

Library of Congress Catalog Card Number: 2001133086

ISBN 978-0-275-97573-9

ISSN: 1062–5623

First published in 2002

Praeger Publishers, 88 Post Road West, Westport, CT 06881
An imprint of Greenwood Publishing Group, Inc.
www.praeger.com

Printed in the United States of America

The paper used in this book complies with the Permanent Paper Standard issued by the National Information Standards Organization (Z39.48–1984).

10 9 8 7 6 5 4 3 2 1

Contents

Series Foreword

Those of us from the discipline of communication studies have long believed that communication is prior to all other fields of inquiry. In several other forums I have argued that the essence of politics is "talk" or human interaction.[1] Such interaction may be formal or informal, verbal or nonverbal, public or private, but it is always persuasive, forcing us consciously or subconsciously to interpret, to evaluate, and to act. Communication is the vehicle for human action.

From this perspective, it is not surprising that Aristotle recognized the natural kinship of politics and communication in his writings *Politics* and *Rhetoric*. In the former, he established that humans are "political beings, [who] alone of the animals [are] furnished with the faculty of language."[2] In the latter, he began his systematic analysis of discourse by proclaiming that "rhetorical study, in its strict sense, is concerned with the modes of persuasion."[3] Thus, it was recognized over twenty-three hundred years ago that politics and communication go hand in hand because they are essential parts of human nature.

In 1981, Dan Nimmo and Keith Sanders proclaimed that political communication was an emerging field.[4] Although its origin, as noted, dates back centuries, a "self-consciously cross-disciplinary" focus began in the late 1950s. Thousands of books and articles later, colleges and universities offer a variety of graduate and undergraduate coursework in the area in such diverse departments as communication, mass communication, journalism, political science, and sociology.[5] In Nimmo and Sanders's early assessment, the "key areas of inquiry" included rhetorical analysis, propaganda analysis, attitude change studies, voting studies, government and the news media, functional and systems analyses, technological changes, media technologies, campaign techniques, and research techniques.[6] In a survey of the state of the field in 1983, the same authors and Lynda Kaid found additional, more specific areas of concerns such as the presidency polls, public opinion, debates, and advertising.[7] Since the first study, they have also noted a shift away from the rather strict behavioral approach.

A decade later, Dan Nimmo and David Swanson argued that "political communication has developed some identity as a more or less distinct domain of scholarly work."[8] The scope and concerns of the area have further expanded to include critical theories and cultural studies. Although there is no precise definition, method, or disciplinary home of the area of conflict, its primary domain comprises the role, processes, and effect of communication within the context of politics broadly defined.

In 1985, the editors of *Political Communication Yearbook: 1984* noted that "more things are happening in the study, teaching, and practice of political communication than can be captured within the space limitations of the relatively few publication available."[9] In addition, they argued that the backgrounds of "those involved in the field [are] so varied and pluralist in outlook and approach, . . . it [is] a mistake to adhere slavishly to any set format in shaping the content."[10] More recently, Nimmo and Swanson have called for "ways of overcoming the unhappy consequences of fragmentation within a framework that respects, encourages, and benefits from diverse scholarly commitments, agendas, and approaches,"[11]

In agreement with these assessments of the area and with gentle encouragement, in 1988 Praeger established the series entitled "Praeger Series in Political Communication." The series is open to all qualitative and quantitative methodologies as well as contemporary and historical studies. The key to characterizing the studies in the series is the focus on communication variables or activities within a political context or dimension. As of this writing, over eighty volumes have been published and numerous impressive works are forthcoming. Scholars from the disciplines of communication, history, journalism, political science, and sociology have participated in the series.

I am, without shame or modesty, a fan of the series. The joy of serving as its editor is in participating in the dialogue of the field of political communication and in reading the contributors' works. I invite you to join me.

Robert E. Denton, Jr.

NOTES

1. See Robert E. Denton, Jr., *The Symbolic Dimensions of the American Presidency* (Prospect Heights, IL: Waveland Press, 1982); Robert E. Denton, Jr., and Gary Woodward, *Political Communication in America* (New York: Praeger, 1985; 2d ed., 1990); Robert E. Denton, Jr., and Dan Hahn, *Presidential Communication* (New York: Praeger, 1986); and Robert E. Denton, Jr., *The Primetime Presidency of Ronald Reagan* (New York: Praeger, 1988).

2. Aristotle, *The Politics of Aristotle*, trans. Ernest Barker (New York: Oxford University Press, 1970), p. 5

3. Aristotle, *Rhetoric*, trans. W. Rhys Roberts (New York: The Modrrn Library, 1954), p. 22.

4. Dan Nimmo and Keith Sanders, "Introduction: The Emergence of Political Communication as a Field," in *Handbook of Political Communication*, eds. Dan Nimmo and Keith Sanders (Beverly Hills, CA: Sage Publications, 1981), pp. 11–36.

5. Ibid., p. 15.

6. Ibid., pp. 17–27.

7. Keith Sanders, Lynda Kaid, and Dan Nimmo, eds. *Political Communication Yearbook: 1984* (Carbondale, IL: Southern Illinois Univeristy, 1985), pp. 283–308.

8. Dan Nimmo and David Swanson, "The Field of Political Communication: Beyond the Voter Persuasion Paradigm," in *New Directions in Political Communication*, eds. David Swanson and Dan Nimmo (Beverly Hills, CA: Sage Publications, 1990), p. 8.

9. Sanders, Kaid, and Nimmo, *Political Communication Yearbook: 1984*, p. xiv

10. Ibid.

11. Nimmo and Swanson, "The Field of Political Communication," p. 11.

Acknowledgments

I am indebted to a wide variety of individuals for their help in writing this book. Foremost among them are the Miami University librarians, particularly Rebecca Zartner and Christa Branson. As I have with each of my prior books, I continually find myself in the debt of these and many other hard-working and dedicated library staff members who have served so many Miami University faculty and students so well.

Moreover, I would be remiss without also thanking many of those students, particularly those in my most recent political campaign communication classes, who had to bear with some of my preliminary observations about the importance of many of the speeches examined in this volume. Their insights were often most helpful.

Over the years Miami University has frequently provided me support for my writing endeavors. The continued support of the university in the form of grants for clerical support and travel associated with this book are most appreciated.

When I wrote my first book it was dedicated in part to my two children. At the time, I observed that when the tedium of research and writing grew too great, no author could have asked for more enjoyable breaks than those I had with them playing baseball, checkers, ticktacktoe and reading all about *Pat the Bunny* and the *Cat in the Hat*. Now I would like to thank them for more tangible support. Our discussions about politics, their help in proof-reading, and their help with the Internet are all most appreciated. Finally, as with all my prior books, my most heartfelt thanks go to my wife, Emmy. Her patience and support, as well as her proofreading and indexing skills, grow with each book I write.

Introduction

Any attempt to identify notable addresses in contemporary presidential campaigns will no doubt be subject to question. Certainly this attempt is by no means definitive. Rather, it represents the judgment of one critic. That judgment was informed by several guidelines.

The first guideline, as the title of this book indicates, was that the speeches studied would be drawn from contemporary campaigns. One exception, to be discussed shortly, was made to that guideline. Since many students of political campaigning think of the 1960 Kennedy vs. Nixon contest as the first contemporary campaign, involving as it did extensive polling, extensive use of television, and political debates, the focus on contemporary campaigns was limited to campaigns since 1960.

Since presidential debates have been studied extensively, the second guideline was to limit this volume to studies of speeches, not remarks made in the context of presidential debates. Third, this critic made the assumption that in elections in which one candidate started with a commanding lead and remained clearly ahead throughout the campaign, no single speech was exceptionally notable, perhaps affecting the election outcome dramatically. On that basis, no speeches from the Nixon vs. McGovern campaign of 1972, the Reagan vs. Mondale campaign of 1984, or the Clinton vs. Dole campaign of 1996 were selected. Though the 1988 Bush vs. Dukakis campaign required Bush to come from behind after the conventions, he did so largely as a consequence of his political advertising. Moreover, he did so quickly and held a commanding lead through most of the campaign. Hence, to this critic, no speech in that campaign seemed to be unusually notable.

It is often said that events, not speeches, determine the outcome of elections. Though one could make that claim about many elections, it seems unusually true of the 1976 campaign between Jimmy Carter and Gerald Ford. Public dismay with the Watergate scandal had caused Richard Nixon to resign the presidency and Gerald Ford to succeed him. Though widely perceived as an honorable man, Ford was tainted by the Nixon scandals and by his own pardoning of Nixon. Carter campaigned as an outsider, never involved in Washington corruption, who would never lie to the American public. Though both men gave fine acceptance addresses to their respective conventions, the circumstances surrounding Ford's assumption of the presidency presented a barrier to his election that he seemed unable to surmount. Hence, to this critic, no speech in that campaign seemed to be exceptionally notable.

If the preceding helps to explain the absence of many speeches from this volume, a few words may help to explain the inclusion of those that are here studied.

The 1960 campaign was noteworthy for a host of reasons. Certainly one of them was the fact that a Roman Catholic, John F. Kennedy, won the presidency. Kennedy best addressed the issue of his Catholicism in his speech to the Greater Houston Ministerial Association. That speech was widely utilized during the campaign. It likely helped Kennedy, more than any other single speech he gave, to overcome what some perceived to be his most formidable obstacle to election.

The only speech in this collection delivered by a losing candidate is Barry M. Goldwater's acceptance address to the 1964 Republican National Convention. It is also the only speech in this group which was delivered in a campaign where one candidate, in this case Lyndon Johnson, had a big lead at the outset that never appreciably diminished as the campaign progressed. Nevertheless, Barry Goldwater's 1964 acceptance address seems to warrant inclusion as a notable speech. Goldwater's uncompromising speech failed to broaden his base of support beyond his own party and, indeed, may have narrowed it within his own party. Hence, it clearly had an immediate consequence on the 1964 election.

But if its short-term effect was negative, the long-term effect of this speech may well have been positive. The Goldwater campaign attracted many younger conservatives and may well have paved the path for the subsequent success of Ronald Reagan and conservative Republicanism in the 1980s and forward. Perhaps it is for reasons such as these that, along with John F. Kennedy's Houston address, Goldwater's acceptance address is the only speech by a major presidential candidate, delivered during the general election, that the Medhurst and Lucas national survey of rhetoricians ranked among the top 100 speeches of the twentieth century.[1]

Richard Nixon's 1968 acceptance address to the Republican National Convention introduced the nation to a new, presumably more mature, more statesmanlike, candidate. Nixon had been on the national stage since 1952. His career had been marked by controversy from his earliest elections. Having lost the presidency in 1960, and the California governorship in 1962, he seemed unlikely to ever win the presidency. However, he spent 1963–1968 recasting his image. Thus, for many Americans, his 1968 acceptance address, given at a time of national turmoil, was their first opportunity for an extended look at "the New Nixon." It was a critical moment for Nixon and his campaign.

From the moment he burst onto the national scene with his 1964 address in support of the candidacy of Barry M. Goldwater, Ronald Reagan had been a favorite of conservative Americans. With Goldwater's defeat, he became the champion of the conservative wing of his party. But though he came close to defeating an incumbent president of his own party in the 1976 Republican primaries, it was not until 1980 that Ronald Reagan was able to secure the presidential nomination of his party. Though the election day outcome of the 1980 election was not close, up to the very closing hours of the campaign it appeared as though it might prove to be a very close election. On election eve, with many pundits claiming the election was doubtful, both Ronald Reagan and Jimmy Carter addressed the American public. Hence, Ronald Reagan's Election Eve Address in 1980 was unusually notable.

In 1992 William Jefferson Clinton defeated an incumbent president, who a year earlier had appeared headed toward overwhelming reelection. But Clinton would have never been the nominee of his party had he not had success in the primaries. Perhaps the most significant moment of his campaign came during the New Hampshire primary when he and his wife Hillary Rodham Clinton were interviewed on the television show *60 Minutes* in response to accusations about his marital infidelity. Had this interview been poorly received, it is hard to imagine that Clinton would have survived the New Hampshire primary, much less gone on to win the nomination of his party and the general election. Though this was an interview and involved two speakers, the reader will find the Clintons treated it as though it was a speech.

The 2000 presidential election will likely be long remembered for the unprecedented way it ended. Earlier in the campaign George W. Bush and his staff determined that there would be two critical rhetorical challenges he had to meet. The first was to be well received by the American public on the basis of a strong acceptance address. The second was to debate well. Few major party candidates are as unknown to the public at large as was George W. Bush. Hence, he and his staff well realized the potential consequence of his acceptance address.

The original plan for this book included a brief introduction that would set the stage for a book about contemporary presidential campaign speeches by examining the first real campaign speech by a U.S. presidential candidate. However, the significance of the campaign of William Henry Harrison, recognized by relatively few communication scholars with the conspicuous exception of Robert Gunderson, and the lack of any readily available analysis of Harrison's speaking, caused me to believe that Harrison's 11 June 1840 speech at Fort Meigs warranted a full chapter. The circumstances that gave rise to that speech and the timeliness of Harrison's themes are a fitting prelude to an examination of more contemporary presidential campaign speeches.

I began by observing that any attempt to identify notable speeches in presidential campaigns is certainly likely to generate questions. With all our focus on the techniques and technology of contemporary politics, it is easy to forget that the definitive statements of most candidates are still made in public speeches. To the extent that this attempt at identifying and studying a group of significant speeches stimulates discussion and thought about speeches and speaking in political campaigns it will have been successful.

NOTE

1. Martin Medhurst and Steve Lucas, "Top 100 American Speeches of the Twentieth Century" (Paper presented at the National Communication Association annual meeting, Denver, CO, Nov. 2001). Full results of the survey can be found at http://www.news.wisc.edu/misc/speeches.

Prologue: 1840—William Henry Harrison

> No pledge should be made by an individual when in nomination for any office in the gift of the people. And why? Once adopt it, and the battle will no longer be to the strong—to the virtuous—or the sincere lover of the country; but to him who is prepared to tell the greatest number of lies, and to proffer the largest number of pledges which he never intends to carry out.

Most contemporary presidential candidates seek the office after long careers in public service. Typically, they have served in a variety of lesser positions, gradually attaining a position of considerable prominence, from that position then launching their presidential bids. George W. Bush, Albert Gore, Bill Clinton, Robert Dole, George Bush, Michael Dukakis, Ronald Reagan, Walter Mondale, Jimmy Carter, Gerald Ford, Richard Nixon, George McGovern, Hubert Humphrey, Lyndon Johnson, Barry Goldwater, and John Kennedy are individuals who have initiated their presidential campaigns after long careers in public service, culminating in such prominent positions as vice president of the United States, state governor, or U.S. senator.

It was not always so. In the mid 1830s a serious major party candidate for the U.S. presidency launched his campaign while serving as Hamilton County, Ohio, clerk of courts.

Most contemporary political parties are composed of individuals who share a relatively similar political philosophy. Currently, most Democrats can be characterized as believing in an activist federal government that best serves the people by expanding the scope of its activities to respond to a wide variety of national concerns. Most Republicans can be characterized as believing in a passive federal government that best serves the people by limiting the scope of its activities to those that a strict interpretation of the Constitution would allow and relying upon the states and individual citizens to address the remaining wide variety of national concerns. Typically, the leaders of these parties vie for the presidential nomination of the party. After a host of primaries and other activities, each party nominates a single presidential candidate and a single vice presidential candidate.

It was not always so. In the 1830s a major national party, the Whigs, had no discernable unifying political philosophy. Moreover, in 1836 the Whig party nominated no less than three presidential candidates. One of those candidates was the Hamilton County, Ohio, clerk of courts. The clerk of courts ran so surprisingly well that between 1836 and 1840, the Whig party turned its back on its two most accomplished national leaders, Senators Daniel Webster and Henry Clay. Rather, between 1836 and 1840 the Whigs gradually consolidated their political activities behind the Hamilton County, Ohio, clerk of courts.

Most contemporary presidential candidates campaign vigorously for the office. The centerpiece of their campaigns is their speaking. They tour the country addressing audience after audience. They engage in political debates. They speak hundreds, if not thousands, of times in their pursuit of the presidency.[1] Their speeches are widely reported in the press. Portions of their speeches are commonly turned into political commercials and aired thousands of times by the nation's radio and television stations.

It was not always so. George Washington had set a different precedent. Running unopposed, he did not deem it necessary to campaign for the presidency. In the decades that followed, it was considered unseemly, unpresidential, to ask the public for their support. The office would seek the man. The man would never be seen seeking the office. Though candidates would work behind the scenes in private meetings and correspondence, and though others might speak on the candidate's behalf, presidential candidates would not deliver a speech seeking public support. Thus, for almost the first half-century of our national life, presidential candidates did not engage in public speaking. That precedent was forever shattered in 1840 by the Whig candidate, the Hamilton County, Ohio, clerk of courts—William Henry Harrison.

THE SPEAKER

William Henry Harrison was born on February 9, 1773, the youngest child of Benjamin Harrison, a prominent member of Virginia's revolutionary generation. William was born in the family manor house, Berkeley, on the James River, midway between Richmond and Williamsburg. The Harrisons were among the famous first families of Virginia. William was a member of the sixth generation of Harrisons to have lived in Virginia. His ancestors had immigrated in 1632. His father was a large landholder, a member of the Virginia House of Burgesses, a member of the Continental Congress who helped smooth the way for Washingon's assumption of the command of the Revolutionary Army, a signer of the Declaration of Independence, and a member of the Continental Congress. Harrison grew up in a house where the issues of the Revolution were commonly discussed over meals and visitors included Washington and the marquis de Lafayette. His father served in the Virginia militia and fought at Yorktown.[2]

Harrison's father had hopes that his youngest son would become a doctor. Hence, though Harrison's older brothers had attended William and Mary, his father sent William Henry to Hampden Sidney College, then recognized as the primary medical educational institution in Virginia. Harrison soon found that his interests were more literary and historical than medical. At Hampden Sidney he became particularly interested in military history. He was also active in the literary society and studied rhetoric.[3]

Harrison's study of rhetoric at Hampden Sidney centered on Hugh Blair's textbook, *Lectures on Rhetoric and Belles Lettres*. Apparently Harrison greatly admired Blair's work. Several years later, when Harrison took his first military position and moved to Ohio, Blair's rhetoric was one of the very few books that Harrison was able to take in his saddlebags when he traveled across the Alleghenies.[4]

Due to a Methodist revival that swept over Hampden Sidney, the Episcopalian Harrison chose to transfer to the University of Pennsylvania Medical School in Philadelphia. Shortly after starting his studies, Harrison's father died. Though his father had expressed his desire that Harrison finish his studies, Harrison had never been strongly interested in medicine. Hence, with his father's death, and his love of military history, Harrison decided to pursue a military career. Robert Morris, the Revolutionary era financier, was a friend of Harrison's father, who had taken Harrison under his wing while the Virginian was in Philadelphia. Morris attempted to dissuade the young Harrison from his intention. However, Morris soon recognized that Harrison was determined to join the army. Harrison sought out Governor Richard Henry Lee of Virginia when the governor visited Philadephia. Harrison asked Lee, another old family friend, to help Harrison get a commission from yet another family friend, President Washington.

HARRISON'S MILITARY AND PUBLIC SERVICE CAREERS: PRECURSORS TO 1840

On September 20, 1791, the newly commissioned Harrison joined a group of eighty infantrymen and started overland for Fort Pitt. From Fort Pitt they took riverboats down the Ohio to Fort Washington, on the Ohio River at Cincinnati. Within a year Harrison was promoted to lieutenant and became an aide-de-camp to General Anthony Wayne. Wayne was an excellent military leader and at the Battle of Fallen Timber he defeated a coalition of Indians. Wayne commended Harrison's valor at Fallen Timber. In his official report on the battle to the secretary of war, Wayne wrote that Harrison "rendered the most essential service by communicating my orders in every direction" and by his "conduct and bravery exciting the troops to press for victory."[5]

By 1795 Harrison had been promoted to captain and put in command of a small outpost at North Bend, Ohio, fourteen miles downstream from Cincinnati and Fort Washington. In North Bend he met and married Anna Symmes. Anna was the daughter of Judge John Cleves Symmes, one of the largest land speculators in the Northwest Territory. In 1796 Harrison became the commanding officer at Fort Washington. But Harrison was growing dissatisfied with a military career. Wayne's victory at the Battle of Fallen Timbers and the treaty of Greenville that resulted from it had seemingly resolved America's difficulties with the Indians, at least in that part of the frontier. The opportunity to distinguish himself in the army seemed limited. Hence, in 1798 he resigned from the army.

Harrison had married Anna at North Bend, in what at the time might have been fairly described as a log cabin. He and Anna quickly began their family and made the first of many additions to what eventually became their 18-room home. Like so many generations of his Virginia ancestors, Harrison began to farm. However, his farm and several investments, including one in a distillery, were not satisfying to him. Again following in his family tradition, he turned to public service, and shortly after leaving the army, Harrison was appointed secretary of the Northwest Territory. President John Adams appointed Harrison for a variety of reasons. Adams knew Harrison's father, Benjamin, from their joint service in the Continental Congress. Moreover, Washington had recommended Harrison to him. While his family connections no doubt helped Harrison secure these appointments, his qualifications should not be overlooked. He had served with distinction in the West. He had spent much of his young adult life in the west and he was respected by both military and civilian leaders in the west.

By 1799 the population of the Northwest territory had grown and it was allowed to elect a delegate to Congress. Harrison was elected. While serving in Congress, Harrison represented his constituency effectively. His most notable accomplishment was to head the Committee on Public Lands, which made a host of recommendations that were ultimately embodied in the Land Act of 1800. Prior to this act, the smallest parcel of western land that could be bought was a 640-acre plot. Moreover, the land could be bought only at Pittsburgh and Cincinnati. These provisions worked hardships on the poor who sought to settle in the West but often could not afford to purchase such a large parcel of land and who did not want to have to endure the hardships of a long trip simply to purchase land. Harrison's influence caused the Land Act of 1800 to reduce the minimum purchase to 320 acres and to establish additional purchasing offices in Marietta, Chillicothe, and Steubenville.[6]

In 1801, Ohio entered the union as the first state from the Northwest Territory. President Adams appointed Harrison governor of the Indiana Territory. Though the battle of Fallen Timber and the resulting treaty of Greenville had temporarily reduced the Indian threat to the settlers, particularly in Ohio, that threat remained a constant source of concern for Harrison as the territorial governor of Indiana. Moreover, Harrison perceived that the British were working to win the friendship of the Indians and turn them against the United States. From 1806 and the emergence of the Shawnee leaders the Prophet and his brother Tecumseh until the Battle of Tippecanoe five years later, relations between the American settlers and government and the Indians, including the Delawares, the Potawatomi, the Miami, and the Shawnee, were often strained. Nevertheless, by 1809, though the British attempted to discourage the Indians from selling land, Harrison had negotiated treaties with most of the tribes. Harrison immediately requested that the army establish a new post on the Wabash River in the newly acquired territory and that the recently acquired land be surveyed.

Meanwhile, though Harrison had negotiated with individual tribes, Tecumseh and the Prophet proclaimed that Indian lands were held in common by all the tribes. Hence, they argued that no one tribe could negotiate away Indian land and that the treaties that Harrison had negotiated were not valid. By the spring of 1811 violence erupted on both sides, with sporadic raids and killing, and rumors that the Prophet was organizing for a massive Indian attack and was seeking British help. In August, Harrison and Tecumseh met. Tecumseh announced that he was going south for a few months. Having successfully formed a confederation of northern Indians, he hoped to do the same among the southern tribes. Tecumseh indicated that when he returned he wished to meet with the American president. Harrison informed him that the president, James Madison, would never give up the lands that the United States had acquired from the Indians.

Harrison believed that Tecumseh was a superior military leader. Hence, in Tecumseh's absence, Harrison determined to strike at the Indians. He sought permission and help from Secretary of War William Eustis. Eustis, acting on President Madison's behalf, instructed Harrison to try to deal with the Prophet peacefully but authorized him to attack if the Indians resisted his efforts to settle and survey the newly purchased lands. Eustis also provided Harrison with several companies of regular army troops, which Harrison supplemented with Indiana militia and volunteers from Kentucky. The regular army forces under Harrison's command were led by Colonel John P. Boyd.

Harrison's forces moved to the banks of the Wabash and built what later became known as Fort Harrison. While the army established this outpost in the newly acquired territories, Harrison negotiated with the Delaware and Shawnee Indians, attempting to persuade them to leave. The Indians refused. By the end of October, Fort Harrison was completed. During the first week of November, Harrison's force moved up the Wabash to within two miles of what was called the Prophet's town. At 4 A.M. on the morning of November 7, the Indians attacked.

The Battle of Tippecanoe raged for three hours. Harrison's leadership was critical. He moved troops from strong to weak spots with the ebb and flow of battle. He was almost killed when a bullet passed through his hat and grazed his head. The Prophet had hoped to utilize surprise and darkness to offset the fact that he was badly outnumbered. While Harrison's force suffered far more casualties than the Indians, thus creating some criticism of his leadership, ultimately they won.[7] The Prophet fled from his town and the new outpost at Fort Harrison was firmly established.

However, the frontier was still not safe. Tecumseh's influence likely prevented another major clash, but throughout the following months the Indians frequently raided the frontier settlements. In the spring of 1812, Tecumseh again attempted to unify the Indians. Moreover, by now it was clear that war with England was likely. Concern about the west was no longer centered on the western frontier, Tippecanoe, and the Wabash. Rather, it was focused on Detroit and Fort Malden, the British fort facing it.

With war clearly in the air, Harrison sought an appointment in the army. But others sought appointments as well. As Harrison awaited word from Washington, the news for the United States was bad. The British captured most of the western forts, including those at Detroit, Mackinac, and what is now Chicago, often with help from the Indians. On September 17 Harrison received word that Madison had placed him in full command of the Army of the Northwest and that he was assigned to recover Detroit and invade Canada. The Army of the Northwest, composed of both regular army units and militia from Kentucky, Ohio, and Indiana, numbered approximately 10,000.

Though this is not the place to closely examine Harrison's war record, it should be noted that he was successful in resisting the British siege at Fort Meigs and that he won the Battle of the Thames. British general Henry Proctor, after capturing Detroit, had eventually moved south to Ohio, where he engaged the Americans at Fort Meigs. Harrison was in a strong position within the well-armed and well-supplied fort. Moreover, he knew that help was on the way. Proctor soon found his Indian allies deserting and was forced to retreat. In light of the controversies that arose during the campaign of 1840, it is sufficient here simply to note that while neither Harrison nor Proctor distinguished himself in the four-day siege of Fort Meigs and the related skirmishes, Harrison did in fact successfully defend the fort against the British and their Indian allies.

Though Fort Meigs was not a major triumph for Harrison, such a triumph was not long in coming. Commodore Oliver Perry's destruction of the British fleet in the Great Lakes had made General Proctor's position at Fort Malden a difficult one. Lacking the reinforcements he had been requesting, Proctor abandoned Fort Malden. On October 5, 1813, after forced marches to catch the fleeing British, Harrison's forces overtook the British on the banks of the Thames River. Tecumseh had marshaled 1,200 Indians to help the badly outnumbered British. The battle was over quickly. The Americans captured virtually all 600 British regular troops under Proctor's command, though Proctor himself escaped. Tecumseh was killed and virtually all the British artillery pieces and small arms were also captured. Harrison's victory, along with that of Perry, effectively eliminated the British threat to the upper northwest. Moreover, the death of Tecumseh, and the dispersal of his supporters, dramatically reduced the fear of the Indians throughout the territories. Nine days after the battle, Harrison concluded an armistice with the Miami, Potawatomi, Wyandot, Wea, Eel River, Ottawa, and Chippewa Indians. The Battle of the Thames was of major importance to the Northwest Territory.[8]

In the election of 1840 the Whigs trumpeted "Tippecanoe and Tyler too." But it is likely that the Battle of the Thames, twenty-seven years earlier, had a substantially greater impact on the development of the Northwest Territory, which ultimately became the states of Michigan, Ohio, Indiana, Illinois, and Wisconsin, than did the battle of Tippecanoe. The Battle of the Thames was of major importance to William Henry Harrison, who was lauded throughout the country. But, with the war in the northwest over, six months later Harrison resigned from the army and returned to his family home in North Bend, Ohio. He now had a wife and eight children for whom he was responsible.

Harrison briefly farmed in North Bend, but he was soon again active in public affairs and in 1816 he was elected to Congress. In Congress his activities centered on military affairs. He spoke on behalf of relief for the widows and children of soldiers killed in the War of 1812 and spoke against legislation that would limit the compensation citizens would receive for property damage or injuries suffered during the war. He also worked on behalf of legislation that would provide for a stronger militia. His congressional speeches were generally well received. He often made classical allusions in his speeches. In addition to his concern with military matters, he spoke on behalf of the interests of his Cincinnati area constituency, particularly for internal improvements that would increase travel between the East Coast and the western frontier.

In 1822 Harrison lost his seat in Congress by 342 votes. Harrison likely lost because of his support for the Missouri Compromise and his support for the Bank of the United States.[9] However, that loss proved to be a blessing in disguise, for now unemployed, the Ohio legislature quickly elected him to the U.S. Senate.[10] Harrison compiled an undistinguished record as a U.S. Senator, but in 1828, after six months of lobbying by Harrison, John Quincy Adams followed the recommendation of his cabinet and appointed Harrison envoy extraordinary and minister plenipotentiary to Colombia. Harrison's interest in the position likely resulted from three factors. First, a close friend, General Charles Todd, had served in military and diplomatic positions in Colombia since 1820 and painted a bright picture of Colombia to Harrison. Todd stressed that Colombia was a developing democracy and the nation's leaders were selflessly dedicated to their country. Second, the appointment represented a substantial increase in salary. Third, the appointment offered an adventure for Harrison, who had virtually never traveled out of the country, much less to a dramatically different climate and culture.[11]

Harrison returned after three years in Colombia. He resumed his life as a farmer in North Bend, Ohio, winning election as the clerk of courts of Hamilton County, Ohio. He was immediately mentioned for more prominent offices, including both governor and U.S. senator. Though Ohio turned elsewhere to fill these offices, Harrison remained a well-respected public figure, often invited to speak at major celebrations and public meetings throughout the state.

HARRISON AND THE ELECTION OF 1836

In 1832 Andrew Jackson had won reelection with ease over Henry Clay, candidate of the National Republicans, and William Wirt, candidate of the Anti-Masonic party. That election effectively marked the end of both the National Republicans and the Anti-Masons. Their supporters formed what became known as the Whig party. In 1836 the Whig party was composed of disparate groups unified only by their dislike of Jackson and his policies. Given the nature of the Whig party, it is not surprising that the party had little concern about the beliefs or policies of its nominee. Rather, in 1836, after two terms of Jackson, and facing a unified Democratic party that was supporting Jackson's vice president, Martin Van Buren, electability became the Whigs' principal criterion for selecting a candidate.

Southerners had given the party its name.[12] In the South, the Whigs were the party of plantations and slavery. Two-thirds of all slaves were owned by Whigs. Jackson had opposed the nullification theories of South Carolina senator John C. Calhoun and other states' rights advocates, which threatened the southern defense of slavery. Southern states' rights advocates perceived themselves to be in the tradition of Britain's Whigs. They took the name Whig in part because it seemed to characterize their positions as more democratic than those of the Jacksonians. Like the British Whigs, who sought to curb the power of the king, their American counterparts perceived themselves as attempting to curb the powers of a dictatorial executive. Moreover, if they were Whigs, that suggested that the term *Tory,* the British party opposed by the British Whigs, would best describe the Jacksonians. *Tory* was a term of disparagement, as during the Revolutionary era it had been frequently used to describe those who resisted American independence and were supportive of the monarchy, an association relished by the many Whigs who perceived Jackson as attempting to create a strong central government with many of his policies, including his opposition to the southern nullifiers.

In the North the Whig party was dominated by Massachusetts Senator Daniel Webster. Northern Whigs carried on the traditions of Alexander Hamilton. The principal Whig constituencies in the North were the merchants who wanted protective tariffs and the bankers who disliked Jackson's financial policies. In addition, the Anti-Masonic party was, by 1836, largely absorbed by the Whigs. The Anti-Masonic feeling that had given rise to the party had largely dissipated as early as 1832. In upstate New York and parts of Pennsylvania where the Anti-Masons maintained a following, by 1836 they had come to stand primarily for internal improvements to the

New York canal system and protective tariffs. Hence, they too found a ready home in the new Whig party.

In the West, the Whig party was built around the large personal following of Henry Clay and advocacy of his "American System" of internal improvements, particularly roads and canals, and protective tariffs. Whigs in this part of the country favored internal improvement, particularily roads and canals that would enable them to get their crops to market cheaply and allow them to purchase manufactured goods inexpensively. Moreover, they were concerned with the distribution of western lands. Thus, in 1836 there was little that unified the newly emerged Whig party, though to some degree they all disliked what they would characterize as Jackson's "executive tyranny."[13]

As those who opposed Jackson searched for a winning candidate, it is not unreasonable to imagine that they might have looked to Jackson himself as a model of an electable candidate. For whatever reasons, at the end of 1834 the *Pennsylvania Intelligencer* proposed General William Henry Harrison for the presidency.[14] Pennsylvania Whigs were looking for a candidate who could win. Harrison, some Whigs imagined, could be portrayed as another Jackson, a war hero with a long career in public service. Harrison, they argued, had served as governor of the Northwest Territory and of Indiana. He had served in both houses of the national legislature. He had served as a diplomat. He started with an unusually strong base, since he was looked upon as virtually a native son by both Indiana (by now a state) and Ohio. If the hero of the Battle of New Orleans could be elected president, why not the hero of the battles of Tippecanoe and of the Thames?

Prophetically, Nicholas Biddle, the Philadelphia banker who wielded great power among Pennsylvania Whigs, observed that

> if General Harrison is taken up as a candidate, it will be on account of the past, not on the future. Let him then rely entirely on the past. Let him say not one single word about his principles, or his creed, let him say nothing, promise nothing. Let no committee, nor convention, no town meeting even extract from him a single word about what he thinks now or what he will do hereafter. Let the use of pen and ink be wholly forbidden as if he were a mad poet in Bedlam. General Harrison can speak well and write well, but on this occasion he should neither speak nor write—but be silent—absolutely and inflexibly silent.[15]

Within months Henry Clay and a host of other Whig leaders were speaking about Harrison "as the most available candidate."[16]

Henry Clay had been beaten badly in 1832 and he perceived 1836 as another Democratic year. For both political and personal reasons, Clay did not want to run.[17] Moreover, a variety of candidates was being mentioned.

Among them were South Carolina's brilliant senator, John C. Calhoun, and Tennessee congressman Hugh L. White. White, a one-time Jackson ally, had broken with the president and garnered considerable support for doing so. The other potentially serious Whig candidate was Daniel Webster. But most of Webster's supporters recognized that he would be unable to attract many votes outside his native New England. A federalist in Congress, Webster had opposed the War of 1812 and forever won the enmity of the West.

In December 1835 a Whig convention at Indianapolis nominated Harrison for the presidency. Whig conventions in Pennsylvania and Maryland quickly followed suit. In February 1836 the Kentucky legislature nominated him and at the end of that month, in one of the largest political rallies ever held in the western states, the Ohio Whigs lauded both Henry Clay and Daniel Webster as "godlike men" but voted to nominate Harrison.[18] In 1836 the Whig party was scarcely three years old. It did not hold a national nominating convention. It was a party without a political philosophy. Thus, when various groups of Whigs or Whig-controlled legislatures nominated a candidate, the remainder of the party did nothing. Hence, in 1836, the Whig party fielded three candidates. White, Webster, and Harrison were all regional candidates. Many Whigs hoped that they would prevent Van Buren from obtaining an electoral college majority and throw the election into the House of Representatives, where the Whigs could unify behind a single candidate.

William Henry Harrison received 549,000 popular votes and 73 electoral votes. Tennessee's Hugh White received 145,000 popular votes and 26 electoral votes. The "godlike Daniel" received 41,000 popular votes and 14 electoral votes. Combined, the Whig candidates fell slightly short of Van Buren's 763,000 popular votes, and well short of the New Yorker's 170 electoral votes.[19] Though Van Buren's victory in the electoral college was decisive, the Whigs had found a candidate with national appeal in the old general from North Bend.

THE WHIG PARTY NOMINATES HARRISON IN 1840

William Henry Harrison had been the one Whig candidate in 1836 who illustrated the potential for a national constituency. Whigs had hoped that Harrison would do well in the West. He did, carrying Ohio, Indiana, and Kentucky and running strongly elsewhere in the West as well. But what most impressed Whigs was his vote-getting in other regions of the country. Harrison carried Vermont, New Jersey, Delaware, and Maryland. Expected to run well in the West, Harrison had also exceeded most expectations elsewhere in the country.

During the 1836 campaign, Harrison had traveled throughout the mid-Atlantic states. He had visited Washington, Baltimore, Wilmington (Delaware), Philadephia, Princeton, New Brunswick, Trenton, and New York City. His return trip brought him through Harrisburg and Pittsburgh. In Pittsburgh he boarded a river steamer and returned to Cincinnati. In each city he was greeted as a conquering hero. Large public demonstrations of welcome greeted him. Local dignitaries praised him. Bands, flags, and cheering Whigs lined the streets he traveled. Typically, Harrison responded with nothing more than a wave of his hand or hat and a brief speech of thanks that incorporated local and personal references. For example, Harrison concluded his brief speech at Philadelphia's Independence Hall by recalling his father.

> And here before these sacred walls—walls rendered doubly sacred to me by the memory of one more dear to me than any other, who here pledged his life, his fortune and his sacred honor in the cause of his country, and from whom I imbibed the same feelings of devotion to American Liberty, I offer you the same pledge, rigidly and to the uttermost extent of my power to maintain the honor, glory and dignity of my native land.[20]

Whether he was aware of the advice Nicholas Biddle had so freely offered him in 1835 or not, he nevertheless seemed to follow that advice. He spoke infrequently, only when not to do so would have been rude. He never made direct references to the impending election or any issues. His remarks were nonpartisan and might have been made by virtually any individual in his situation.

If Harrison had showed surprising popular appeal in the 1836 election, that same election had illustrated that Daniel Webster was not a viable national candidate. Webster had carried Massachussetts but demonstrated no popularity beyond his home state. In 1837 Webster took a page out of Harrison's campaign book and decided to travel west, perhaps hoping to revive his presidential ambitions. During his tour of the west, the steamboat *Albany* made a special run for him between Cincinnati and North Bend so that he might have breakfast with Harrison and his family.[21]

Webster was moderately well received. The crowds listened politely to him. His speeches consistently attacked Jackson's bank and other economic policies. He lauded the accomplishments of the West. All the same, his speeches generated no enthusiasm and his tour did little to revive him as a viable national candidate.[22] Recognizing the unlikelihood of his nomination, Webster ultimately withdrew before the Whig convention.

Meanwhile, Van Buren's administration was presiding over a growing depression. The financial panic of 1837 guaranteed that the Whig nomination to challenge Van Buren would be valuable. Van Buren's policies were widely believed to have contributed to the nation's financial woes. In 1840 the Whigs would hold a national nominating convention to unify around one candidate. Harrison readily recognized that 1840 could well be his year. In personal correspondence he observed that not only Whigs, but also many of the same people who had elected Jackson, might now turn to him.[23]

By 1838 it was clear that Harrison had the inside track on the Whig nomination, but his path was not without obstacles. The biggest of them was Henry Clay. Another challenger was General Winfield Scott. Like Harrison, Clay recognized that 1840 could well be a Whig year. Clay was the party's congressional leader and the most eloquent Whig spokesman. At the same time, New York Whigs, following the lead of Albany newspaper publisher and party boss Thurlow Weed, began to tout the candidacy of General Winfield Scott. Scott had won the admiration of many New Yorkers in 1838 when he was sent to upstate New York to deal with a band of Canadian revolutionaries who briefly threatened several New York towns.

Throughout 1838 and 1839 supporters of Scott, Clay, and Harrison maneuvered in anticipation of the Whig national convention that would open on December 4, 1839, in Harrisburg, Pennsylvania. It took the Whig convention only two ballots to nominate Harrison. His nomination was the result of both his strength and Clay's weakness. Ever since 1836, Harrison had been perceived as the Whig candidate who might best attract voters. Moreover, Harrison had said and done nothing since 1836 that might create opponents. He was the truly available man. In contrast, during Clay's long and distinguished public career he had created enemies. Moreover, by 1840 a new force was emerging. The abolitionists were becoming a political force with which candidates had to deal. Harrison had said little about slavery.[24] Clay, in contrast, was a slaveholder. Northern Whigs, such as Thurlow Weed, were fearful that Clay could not win in their states. Between the first and second ballots in the Whig convention, Weed swung the Scott support in the New York, Michigan, and Vermont delegations to Harrison. Harrison and Scott both had military backgrounds, but Weed likely felt Harrison a more proven vote-getter. Sensing a bandwagon, the Illinois delegation shifted from Clay to Harrison, and the Hamilton County, Ohio, clerk of courts—William Henry Harrison—became the presidential candidate of the Whig party.[25]

WHY THE GENERAL SPOKE

The Whig convention attempted to accommodate Henry Clay and his supporters by nominating John Tyler of Virginia as Harrison's running mate. Then, again no doubt seeking to avoid any controversy, the convention adjourned without even considering, much less writing, a platform for its candidates to run upon. As expected, the Democrats nominated Van Buren. The Whigs were determined to run an issue-free campaign. They had observed how Andrew Jackson had beaten them in 1828 and again in 1832, running campaigns that were based on images of Old Hickory and his personal qualities, rather than on issues. They would turn the tables with their own military hero, Harrison, in 1840.

Within days of the Whig convention, the Democrats inadvertently gave the Whigs just what they needed to run an image-oriented campaign. The *Baltimore Republican* reported that Democrats were scornfully dismissing Harrison's candidacy, mockingly claiming that if he were given a barrel of hard cider and a pension, Harrison would be delighted to spend the rest of his days reading philosophy in a log cabin. The Whigs immediately latched onto the imagery this remark provoked. Harrison quickly became the log cabin, hard cider candidate. Cider flowed freely at his rallies, and log cabins were pictured on all his campaign literature.[26] In contrast, the Whigs attempted to portray Van Buren as an elitist aristocrat often indulging himself and his friends with the taxpayers' money.[27] Whigs claimed that Van Buren had more in common with the wine-drinking royalty of Europe than with the hard cider drinkers of America. By 1840 it was not a wise electoral strategy to scorn the common man.

When voters did ask about the ideas of the comparatively unknown Harrison, he claimed that his ideas could be found by reading several of his letters, which had been widely published. The most widely circulated and reprinted of these letters had been written in November 1838. At that time an anti-Masonic convention representing six northern states had nominated Harrison. Harrison responded with a letter in which he discussed the policies he would follow if he was elected president. He ignored controversial issues such as the desirability of nationally financed internal improvements, high protective tariffs, a national bank, and the abolitionist movement. Treating any such issues would likely generate a position that would offend some voters. Rather, Harrison provided a succinct statement of the principles he would follow in governing the nation:

1. A Harrison presidency would be limited to one term.
2. A Harrison presidency would exert no influence over the public treasury.

3. A Harrison presidency would exert no influence to affect elections.
4. A Harrison presidency would honor the laws passed by the people's representatives and make exceedingly little use of the veto.
5. A Harrison presidency would never use the office for partisian political purposes.
6. A Harrison presidency would provide a rationale to the Senate every time it removed an individual from public office.
7. A Harrison presidency would never initiate or be the source of new legislation.[28]

Clearly, many of these broad guidelines for a Harrison administration were responses to what Harrison and other Whigs perceived to be the excesses of the Jackson and Van Buren administrations. In sum, what Harrison was suggesting was that his would be a passive presidency. In a Harrison administration, the people's representatives in Congress, not the nation's chief executive, would take the lead in setting the policies by which the nation would be governed. Harrison avoided specific issues. Rather, he presented general principles that reinforced his image as the champion of the common man.

This approach blended well with the history and tradition of American presidential campaigning. By 1840 candidates might discreetly campaign, but the overt act of soliciting votes, such as by a public speech, was not considered "presidential." However, at least four circumstances conspired to cause Harrison to ultimately break with tradition and deliver a series of public speeches throughout the campaign.

First, from 1824 forward, the number of voters had increased dramatically. For that reason, by as early as 1828, and most assuredly by 1840, a presidential candidate had to appeal to a large number of voters. Candidates could no longer rely on personal correspondence, word of mouth, and private meetings to influence a sufficient number of voters. If those methods had ever been possible, they surely were no longer possible by 1840.

The cries of "bargain and corruption" that had characterized the 1824 election—in which the House of Representatives selected John Quincy Adams although Andrew Jackson had won the popular vote—gave impetus to lowering the property, income, and other qualifications for voting in many states. Between 1824 and 1828, the total number of eligible voters had tripled, from 350,000 to slightly over a million. In 1840 more than 1,200,000 citizens would vote for Harrison alone.[29]

The massive numbers of voters now required were often persuaded through political rallies, which involved public speeches. As the popularity and importance of such rallies grew, the demand for speakers grew. It seemed only a matter of time before that demand was satisfied not simply by surrogates, but by candidates themselves.

As political rallies began to draw literally thousands of participants, speeches by candidates had the potential to energize and persuade large audiences.

Second, Harrison had seen the potential effect of campaign speaking in his own activities during the campaign of 1836. Though Harrison had not delivered any overt political speeches, he had traveled to the East Coast and often delivered very brief, nonpolitical addresses. Harrison was likely aware that three of the eastern states that he had carried in 1836 were ones where he had appeared and given brief speeches. While many factors likely contributed to his winning these states, certainly his activities in them could not be totally dismissed.

Third, by 1840 the very nature of presidential campaigning called for public speeches. As noted earlier, the Jackson campaign of 1828, and to some extent virtually all those that followed, was built in part around large political rallies. Such rallies typically included displays of banners, signs, and a wide variety of other symbols such as Jackson's hickory sticks and Harrison's log cabins. Often prominent were cheers and chants of political slogans, such as "Tippecanoe and Tyler Too." The rallies often distributed food and drink, such as Harrison's hard cider, and often included parades, which featured appearances by bands and other musical groups. The music was largely composed of patriotic songs and campaign songs. Typical was "Harrison and Liberty."

> From Mississippi's utmost shore to New Hampshire's piney hills
> From broad Atlantic's sullen roar to where the Western Ocean swells
> How loud the notes of joy arise from every bosom warm and free
> How strains triumphant fill the skies, for Harrison and Liberty.[30]

But more than the banners, posters, food, drink, and songs, these rallies involved speeches. Well-known candidate advocates toured the country speaking at such rallies. Local leaders also spoke at rallies for the national candidate. Harrison benefited from the advocacy of many of his former comrades in arms.[31] Certainly, with everyone but the candidate speaking by 1840, it was not hard to imagine that eventually the candidates themselves would be featured at political rallies.

Finally, and perhaps most important, in 1840, William Henry Harrison and Martin Van Buren were both subjected to negative attacks. It is impossible to judge whether the attacks on Harrison were more negative than those on Van Buren, or on Adams and Jackson before them. However, they were certainly more personal. The attacks on Harrison ultimately prompted a response. Moreover, the very nature of many of those attacks dictated that Harrison respond through speaking, rather than through the press.

The Whigs attacked Van Buren as an aristocrat who used the taxpayers' money to indulge in extravagant food and drink, while he turned the White House into a virtual palace, replete with unnecessarily gilt chandeliers, candelabras, bronze lamps, and ornate mirrors and pictures. Van Buren was accused of lavish and wasteful spending. For example, he was charged with providing the White House gardener with a higher salary than that of the governor of Ohio.[32]

Though the Whig's negative assult on Van Buren may have been unwarranted and excessive, it was not marked by the highly personal tone of the Democratic attack on Harrison. Sixty-eight years old, Harrison was called senile, and both his physical and mental abilities were repeatedly questioned. Throughout the campaign, Democrats mocked him as "Granny Harrison." He was called an imbecile. It was alleged that the Whigs kept him caged, for fear that he would be seen and disgrace himself. Democrats charged that Harrison had slept with Indian women during his early years in the army. His military record was attacked. Democrats claimed that others were responsible for the victories attributed to Harrison, and that indeed he was a coward. The Whigs had attacked Van Buren's foibles. The Democrats attacked the very essence of Harrison the man.

Moreover, the Democrats attacked Harrison's avoidance of the issues. Van Buren's positions and his party platform were clear. The Whigs had no platform and their standard bearer was silent on the issues. The Democrats derided "General Mum." They claimed that in contrast, Van Buren's positions were well known. Moreover, the Democrats claimed that Harrison remained mum because their charges about his senility, his stupidty, and all the rest were accurate. Clearly, if Harrison had remained silent, he would have been playing right into the hands of Van Buren and the Democrats.

For Harrison, the best way to effectively refute the Democratic charges would be to speak in public. He was the first presidential candidate who was likely to really suffer by not speaking. Though he might write to the press and to individuals, and though his writings might be published, the authorship of his writings might be questioned. There was no way he could decisively illustrate that they were his and not the work of others. However, if Harrison were to take to the public platform, particularly if he did so by delivering a great many relatively long speeches, he would be illustrating his health, his stamina, and his intelligence. His very presence on the platform would graphically demonstrate the gross exaggerations of the Democrats. Moreover, if what he said proved persuasive with his audiences, that would be icing on the cake. We will never know how much Harrison's personal pride also entered into his decision. Certainly, though, it is hard to imagine that this man who had held positions of command and responsibility throughout his life, who had received the nomination of a major party for the highest office in the nation, could have heard the highly personal attacks on his competence and integrity without anger and frustration.[33] It is reasonable to surmise that the nature of the Democratic attack on Harrison made the general anxious to respond.

In sum, a combination of factors no doubt were at play as William Henry Harrison considered how to deal with his opponents. He knew that his message needed to be presented to a large number of people. He likely sensed that his public appearances and brief nonpartisian speeches four years earlier had been effective. He recognized that the very nature of presidential campaigning had become such that major efforts went into political rallies that built to a climax that was reached when a featured speaker delivered an address. Finally, he likely recognized that his continued silence was giving his opponents a weapon to use against him, and he no doubt felt frustrated by his inability to disprove what he knew to be the greatly exaggerated personal charges against him. It is probable that all these reasons contributed to Harrison's decision to speak.

GENERAL MUM SPEAKS: WILLIAM HENRY HARRISON AT FORT MEIGS—JUNE 11, 1840

On June 11, 1813, British general Henry Proctor had lifted the brief siege of Fort Meigs, located just outside Perrysburg, Ohio. In 1840 Perrysburg, no doubt with the enthusiastic support of the local Whig establishment, decided to celebrate the anniversary of the victory at Fort Meigs. Naturally, the celebration's organizers extended an invitation to the fort's defenders, including its commanding officer, William Henry Harrison. Harrison accepted. Harrison's address at Fort Meigs was to be the first of many addresses Harrison delivered during the campaign.

By June 1840, the Whig campaign was well under way, and Harrison, particularly in his home state, was becoming a major celebrity. As would happen throughout the campaign, when Harrison traveled, he was warmly greeted and frequently urged to speak. Traveling from North Bend to Perrysburg, Harrison found himself spending the evening of Friday, June 5, and the morning of Saturday, June 6, in Columbus. The sympathetic *Ohio State Journal* tells us what happened:

> The people's favorite arrived in this city on Friday evening last on his way to Ft. Meigs. He came down upon us without giving the citizens any time to prepare for

his reception—yet his welcome was warm and enthusiastic such as befitted a free and intelligent people to give and an unostentatious Republican to receive. He was waited on at his quarters at the National Hotel by a large proportion of our population and was enthusiastically cheered by the crowd.

Before his departure on Saturday morning, in answer to repeated calls made upon him, he addressed the assembled citizens from the steps of the hotel in a speech of an hour's length. We were not in town and can therefore only speak the opinion of others which assign to this off hand performance of the old Hero a high order of merit. Like all his work it was well done, as his enemies will long have occasion to remember, many of whom were present and listened to his remarks.

At 10 O'Clock he left for the north, escorted several miles on his way by a large calvalcade of citizens headed by the Mayor. On taking leave, his honor made a short address in behalf of the citizens, which was responded to by the General in the happiest manner. The band struck up "Hail Columbia" and with three harty [*sic*] cheers his friends bid him God speed.[34]

Thus, William Henry Harrison delivered the first overt political campaign speech by a presidential candidate from the steps of the National Hotel, in Columbus, Ohio, on June 6, 1840. However, because it was spontaneous, like many other such speeches he gave that summer, we have no record of what was said.[35]

Though the spontaneity of the Columbus address has deprived us of a clear record of what Harrison said, we do have speech texts for many of the addresses he delivered that summer, including Harrison's first major speech, delivered on June 11, at Fort Meigs.[36] There are similarities between the Fort Meigs speech and many others Harrison delivered. However, this speech differs markedly from later speeches, for it is composed primarily of Harrison's recollections of the siege at Fort Meigs and the men with whom he served. The similarities between his later speeches suggest that eventually Harrison began to use what today we would call a "stock speech."[37]

Harrison's major addresses were delivered as the climaxes to major rallies. Such was the case at Fort Meigs. Approximately three months of planning had preceded the Fort Meigs rally.[38] We do not have an account of Harrison's arrival at Perrysburg and Fort Meigs, but he was the centerpiece in parades that were held all along the route as he traveled to many of his major addresses. Near the outset of one such trip, the order of procession was as follows:

1. Band of music
2. Canoe bearing national flag
3. Farm wagons drawn by 4 horses

4. Farm wagons drawn by 2 horses
5. Coaches drawn by 4 horses
6. Band of music
7. Coaches and barouches drawn by 2 horses
8. Buggies drawn by 1 horse
9. Tippecanoe men on horseback

Harrison is reported to have ridden to many of his speeches in an open barouche, a four-wheeled carriage with a collapsible top, two double seats facing one another, and a raised seat outside the carriage for the driver.[39] Such a vehicle would make him readily visible to the public, particularly if he occasionally stood up and waved. Normally the coaches and barouches were found, as in this case, in the last third of the parade. Parades such as this also featured a large number of men carrying canoes and log cabins. Moreover, slogans and banners abounded. In this case at the rear of the parade several men were carrying a giant banner inscribed "The Patriot and Hero, William Henry Harrison."[40]

At Fort Meigs Harrison found an audience estimated at 40,000. Countless banners, bands, and military companies were scattered through the audience. In anticipation of Harrison and the other speakers, church bells were rung, bands played, and muskets and cannons were fired. After an opening prayer delivered by the Reverend Joseph Badger, who had been the military chaplain at Fort Meigs in 1813, fifteen speakers preceded Harrison. They included several officers who had served under Harrison in 1813.[41] Finally, Harrison spoke.

As he did in virtually all his major addresses, Harrison opened his speech by dealing with the very fact that he was speaking.

> Fellow citizens—I am not, upon this occasion, before you in accordance with my own individual views or wishes. It has ever appeared to me that the office of President of the United States should not be sought after by any individual, but that the people should spontaneously and with their own free will, accord the distinguished honor to the man whom they believed would best perform its important duties. Entertaining these views, I should, fellow citizens, have remained at home, but for the pressing and friendly invitation which I have received from the citizens of Perrysburg and the earnestness with which its acceptance was urged upon me by friends in whom I trusted, and whom I am now proud to see around me.[42]

Harrison continues, justifying his speaking by means of the special meaning that this place and the many men who served with him at Fort Meigs hold for him.

Harrison often opened his speeches by attempting to justify the fact that he was a presidential candidate speaking in public during a presidential campaign. He typically did so in two ways. First, as at Fort Meigs, he made references to the location and the date. He claimed that the events being commemorated evoked considerable personal feelings and memories, which justified his speaking. When he spoke at Dayton on the anniversary of Admiral Perry's victory, he spoke about his memories of the War of 1812; and when he spoke in Greenville, Ohio, he recalled his service at Fort Greenville. In these instances he would claim that these locales or dates brought to mind wonderful memories and he wanted to share those memories so that his audience could appreciate the history of the nation. Invariably, as at Fort Meigs, his memories centered on the men he commanded.

> The soldiers who fought and bled and triumphed here were lawyers who had thrown up their briefs—physicians who had laid aside their instruments—mechanics, who had put by their tools—and, in far the largest proportion, agriculturalists who had left their ploughs in the furrow, although their families depended for their bread upon their exertations, and who hastened to the battle field to give their life to their country if it were necessary, to maintain her rights.

Harrison continued, indirectly addressing his Democratic critics who claimed that he was an ineffective military leader.

> I personally supervised and directed the arrangement of the army under my command. I trusted no colonel or other officer. No person had any hand in the disposition of the army. Every step of warfare, whether for good or for ill, was taken under my own direction and of none other, as many who now hear me know.

Thus, as he did on other occasions during the campaign, Harrison justified his speaking in the midst of a presidential campaign by claiming that this was an exceptional event that had a great deal of personal meaning for him. The nature of the event itself, the commemoration of a military victory, allowed Harrison to respond to some of his critics. He did so in the presence of many of the very men who served with him. Their cheers and applause effectively rebutted those Democrats who questioned his military exploits.

On those occasions when Harrison could not justify speaking because he was speaking at an exceptional event, he justified his speaking because he felt it was necessary to respond to his critics. "I am not with you today, fellow citizens," Harrison told his audience at Chillicothe, "in accordance with my own sense of propriety." Prophetically, he continued:

> Indeed I sometimes fear that upon me will fall the responsiblity of establishing a dangerous precedent to be followed in future times. Much more consonant would it be with my feelings to remain at the domestic fireside than to be harassed by the cares, the difficulties, the anxieties of a struggle like this. . . . I am here because I am the most persecuted and calumniated individual now living; because I have been slandered by reckless opponents to the extent that I am devoid of every qualification, physical, mental, moral for the high place to which a respectable portion, at least, of my fellow citizens have nominated me. I am here at the urgent solicitation of my friends, and because to appear among my fellow citizens was the only way to disapprove one, at least, of the many allegations that unscrupulous enemies have laid against me. And this much you must have already perceived, that I am not CAGED, that I am not the old man on crutches, nor the imbecile they accuse me of being, nor the prey to disease my enemies would have it believed.[43]

Thus, Harrison was clearly aware of the precedent-setting nature of his speaking and spent a considerable amount of time at the outset of each of his speeches justifying his actions.

Throughout the body of his Fort Meigs speech, Harrison continues to reminisce about his military career. He spends a considerable amount of time discussing the valor of the troops he served with under the command of General "Mad Anthony" Wayne. He laments the fact that the government has not treated these men, who helped to open the west to settlement, as well as it has other veterans. He discusses his efforts on their behalf while he served in Congress. He concludes this section by observing that "I can only say that if it should ever be in my power to pay the debt which is due these brave but neglected men, that debt shall first of all be paid." Harrison's long discussion of the failure of the government to help these old soldiers properly serves two important purposes. First, it helps to ingratiate him with those soldiers and their families. Second, it allows Harrison to avoid controversy.

Ironically, in the very moments after having made this campaign pledge to help the veterns of the Indian wars, Harrison then claims that "it is my opinion that no pledge should be made by an individual when in nomination for any office in the gift of the people." Harrison goes on to decry campaign pledges or promises because if they become widespread, the winning of elections "will no longer be to the strong—to the virtuous—or the sincere lover of the country; but to him who is prepared to tell the greatest number of lies, and to proffer the largest number of pledges which he never intends to carry out." Presumably Harrison's pledge to help the veterans of Indian wars differed from those he criticized by virtue of his determination to carry them out. There is no evidence that his audience perceived the irony of his having made a campaign promise and then moments later denouncing the practice of making such promises.

At this point, approximately halfway through his speech, Harrison has not treated any major controversial issue. Having perhaps utilized his military career as much as he could, Harrison turns to his civilian career. First, Harrison sets up a straw man, claiming that some have accused him of being a federalist, one who would increase the power of the federal government "at the expense of the separate states." Harrison reviews his past to refute this charge. Rather, Harrison claims that if his audience examined the policies advocated by Van Buren, they would recognize him as a federalist who wants to enlarge the power of the federal government, particularly the executive branch. This is as close to discussing issues or policies as Harrison comes in the course of this speech. Significantly, even when he claims that Van Buren seeks to enlarge the federal government, Harrison does not provide specific examples.

Second, Harrison suggests that all governments, but most especially the current administration, should be watched closely. For, claims Harrison, we must "see that the government does not acquire too much power." Essentially, this is simply a variation of Harrion's first point. In this instance he speaks about the importance of being vigilant and observes that our vigilance must be directed at the current officeholders, not those who oppose them. At the very end of this section, which immediately precedes the brief conclusion, Harrison finally mentions a specific policy of Van Buren's with which he disagrees. He suggests that "the sub-treasury bill will give to the President an accumulation of power that the constitution withholds from him, a monarch. This catastrophe to freedom would be and can be prevented by vigilance, union and perseverance."

Harrison concludes by reaffirming the need to watch the federal government. "Do that," he claims, "and your children's children, to the latest posterity, will be so happy and as free as you and your fathers have been." In sum, Harrison avoids dealing with controversial issues throughout his speech. Rather, he utilizes a series of platitudes that often generate applause from his friendly audiences but do not meaningfully indicate what a President Harrison would do and how that might differ from what a President Van Buren would do.

EFFECTS OF HARRISON'S 1840 CAMPAIGN SPEAKING

Prior to 1840, presidential candidates campaigned gingerly, if at all. Mindful of the tradition set by Washington, they were generally careful to avoid the appearance of actively seeking the office. In 1840, for a variety of reasons, General William Henry Harrison broke with that tradition and aggressively campaigned for the presidency. He did so primarily by delivering more than twenty major public speeches and a much larger number of brief, spontaneous speeches. Response to this change in presidential campaigning was predictably partisan. Democrats attacked Harrison for his active campaign. As Robert Gunderson has illustrated, they characterized Harrison's campaign as "a spectacle" and attacked his speaking as "a rare specimen of electioneering slang."[44]

Harrison's speaking no doubt contributed to his landslide victory. Harrison carried every state save seven. He won 234 votes in the electoral college to Van Buren's 49.[45] Harrison spoke to huge crowds. His audience of 40,000 at Ft. Meigs was characterized by supporters as a "monster demonstration," and "the mightiest assembly of people" that had ever existed in that part of the country.[46] His major speeches were often the climax of political rallies that lasted a full day.[47] Given the modes of travel in that day and age, many of his audience members devoted a minimum of two days to attending the rally. The Whig campaign of 1840 resulted in transforming the Old General, on the verge of living out his life as a gentleman farmer and the Hamilton County, Ohio, clerk of courts, into a "mythical personality, a symbol of virtue and American patriotism."[48]

Harrison's speech commemorating the siege of Fort Meigs was the first of his major addresses and evidences characteristics that were typical of Harrison's speaking. Most important, Harrison avoided controversy. He did not address the major issues of the day, such as the nation's financial problems and slavery. Rather, he treated issues that were not controversial. Few could argue, for example, with his claim that he would rarely use the veto because he wanted to honor the wishes of the people as expressed through their elected congressional representatives. Rather than seriously treat issues, Harrison devoted much of his speaking to discussing his early military successes. Though the very occasion of the Fort Meigs speech allowed Harrison to spend a disproportionate amount of time on his personal military recollections, he consistently dwelt on his prior accomplishments to such an extent that critics called him "a prodigy of garrulous egotism."[49]

Harrison was not an inspiring speaker. However, he did not have to be. Rather, the very fact that he did speak was often enough to illustrate the exaggerations of the claims being made about him. A member of the Fort Meigs audience observed that Harrison spoke "without notes, exhibiting a mind thoroughly disciplined in all the rules necessary to form a good public speaker, fully versed in the history of his country and capable of great and continued exertation. . . . His language is strikingly simple . . . bringing out clearly and fully the idea."[50] Following another address, one admirer observed that "not a man left the place without the fullest conviction of his

[Harrison's] strength of intellect, and that the talk about imbecility and decrepitude which their papers have so long spread abroad, is a shameful slander."[51] However, the fact that even his admirers seemed unable to say much more than that he had given the lie to claims that he was an imbecile hardly seems like great praise of Harrison's speaking. Similarly, much of the reaction to Harrison's speaking seems to center on his ability to project well and his physical condition. Harrison's health had become an issue in the campaign, and his speaking was taken as an indication of his good health.[52] Hence, the Whig press stressed that Harrison had a "clear, firm, and distinct voice which could be heard further than any other one [of the other speakers] who addressed the people."[53] One audience member, who wrote that he was in the middle of the crowd at Fort Meigs, claimed that "I never heard a voice of such variety and compass. I heard distinctly every word. He spoke with great vigor for more than an hour without any sign of faltering or fatigue."[54]

The approach that Harrison followed in his speeches, focusing on his personal qualities and history while minimizing his comments about the issues of the day, was consistent with the entire Whig campaign being waged on his behalf. Campaign biographies of Harrison, for example, consistently stressed his family and its support of the Revolution, his personal qualities as a down-to-earth farmer, and his military exploits.[55] Similarly, even extensive campaign documents gloss over the issues and stress Harrison's personal history and qualities.[56]

Harrison's speeches were marked by classical allusions and rhetorical questions. He tended to use topical organization. Within the topics he developed he frequently followed chronological order. There was little in Harrison's speeches to inspire his audiences. The fact that they apparently engendered a strong positive reaction likely speaks more to the rhetorical situations in which they were delivered than to Harrison's speaking itself. At Fort Meigs, for example, the crowd was celebrating a great military victory. The audience included many of the men who had fought at Fort Meigs, or their family members. As with his other major addresses, the audience had, in all probability, been looking forward to hearing from Harrison throughout a day that began with parades, songs, prayers, and speeches. All the preceding activities in these Whig rallies was designed in some fashion or another to laud Harrison. The entire rhetorical situation was planned to enhance the audience's reaction to Harrison.

Harrison's speeches seemed to be sufficient to disarm his severest critics, and the situations in which they were delivered helped enhance the public perception of him as well. While we cannot be precise in establishing the effect of Harrison's speaking, it likely contributed to his election. In addition,

Harrison had not only broken with tradition by aggressively speaking on his own behalf, but he won. His victory seemed to legitimize presidential campaign addresses. From 1840 forward, presidential candidates would much more actively and openly campaign for the office. Today, we cannot even imagine a campaign in which the candidates do not travel throughout the country speaking about the issues of the day. But in 1840, William Henry Harrison dramatically broke with tradition to become the first presidential candidate to speak aggresively on his own behalf. In so doing, he overturned the precedent set by another general and helped to set the stage for contemporary campaigns.

NOTES

1. See Judith S. Trent and Robert V. Friedenberg, *Political Campaign Communication: Principles and Practices* (Westport, CT: Praeger, 2000), pp. 190–91, for an indication of the amount of speaking in which political candidates engage.

2. Harrison has not been the subject of any recent biographies. The best biographies are Dorothy Goebel, *William Henry Harrison: A Political Biography* (Indianapolis: Indiana Library and Historical Department, 1926); Freeman Cleaves, *Old Tippecanoe: William Henry Harrison and His Time* (New York: Charles Scribner's Sons, 1939); and James A. Green, *William Henry Harrison: His Life and Times* (Richmond, VA: Garrett and Massie, 1941). The biographical information in this and subsequent paragraphs is drawn primarily from Cleaves, pp. 1–9, Goebel, pp. 1–19, and Green, pp. 1–17.

3. See Cleaves, pp. 6–7.

4. Harrison's biographer, James A. Green, donated a copy of Blair to the Harrison collection of the Cincinnati Historical Society. The copy of Blair donated by Green accompanied a cover letter from Green remarking on the importance of Blair to Harrison. See the introductory commentary, dated 26 Apr. 1928, to the copy of Hugh Blair, *Lectures on Rhetoric and Belles Lettres,* in the William Henry Harrison Collection of the Cincinnati Historical Society.

5. Wayne's report is quoted in Goebel, p. 34.

6. The best account of Harrison's service in Congress is in Goebel, pp. 43–52.

7. Harrison's force suffered 185 casualties. The Prophet's force suffered approximately 30. Some critics claimed that Harrison had virtually lost the battle and only the actions of the regular army troops and Colonel Boyd had saved the day. However, Harrison was vindicated by both the War Department and by his own officers, who praised his strategy and personal courage.

8. For details of the Battle of the Thames and its importance, see Cleaves, pp. 194–212, and Goebel, pp. 172–84.

9. Southern Ohio, particularly the area around Cincinnati, was a stronghold of the abolitionist movement and a major stop on the underground railroad. Harri-

son had straddled the slavery issue during his years in Congress, but in voting for the Missouri Compromise Harrison was voting for a policy that was guaranteeing the continuation of slavery. The bank was almost uniformly opposed by the Cincinnati business community. See Green, pp. 245–46.

10. Until the ratification of the Seventeenth Amendment in 1913, U.S. senators were elected by state legislatures.

11. See particularly Green, p. 262, on Harrison's interest in the Colombia appointment.

12. The discussion of the Whig party found in this and the next few paragraphs is based primarily upon Wilfred E. Binkley, *American Political Parties* (New York: Alfred A. Knopf, 1967), pp. 152–72. On the evolution of the Whigs, also see Theodore Cousens, *Politics and Political Organizations in America* (New York: Macmillan, 1942), pp. 117–44.

13. Binkley, *American Political Parties*, p. 152.

14. There have been suggestions that Ohio admirers of Harrison first brought him to the attention of the Whig-oriented *Intelligencer.*

15. Biddle is quoted in Green, pp. 294–95.

16. Ibid. See p. 295 for Clay's statement.

17. In addition, Clay had become the congressional leader of the opposition to Jackson and as such he found that Jackson had taken criticism very personally. In 1835–1836 Clay was exceedingly troubled by what he perceived to be the very personal tone politics had taken in the United States. Moreover, he was discouraged by what he perceived to be the emotional campaigning that seemed successful, as opposed to the intellectual campaigning in which he wished to engage. In late 1835, Clay wrote that he was "truly sick of Congress," and during this same period, Clay's daughter died. All these feelings no doubt contributed to Clay's reluctance to run in 1836. See Clement Eaton, *Henry Clay and the Art of American Politics* (Boston: Little, Brown, 1957), pp. 109–14.

18. Cleaves, p. 302.

19. These statistics are from Cousens, *Politics and Political Organizations in America*, p. 129.

20. Green, p. 305.

21. Ibid., pp. 308–9.

22. Ibid.

23. Harrison's letters are quoted in Binkley, *American Political Parties*, pp. 174–75.

24. The statements that Harrison had made, primarily upon being questioned during the 1836 campaign, were ambiguous. See Goebel, pp. 316–18.

25. For details on the convention see Cleaves, *Old Tippecanoe*, pp. 316–19, and Goebel, pp. 341–43.

26. Horace Greeley edited the principal campaign newspaper of the Whigs. It was called the *Log Cabin.* Local Whig campaign papers also often used that name. The Dayton, Ohio, *Log Cabin* had a border around the pages that was com-

posed of logs. See that publication in the Ohio newspaper collection of the Ohio Historical Society, Columbus, Ohio.

27. For examples of Van Buren's supposed extravagance, see Paul F. Boller, Jr., *Presidential Campaigns* (New York: Oxford University Press, 1985), pp. 68–69.

28. This letter, addressed to Harmar Denny, was widely reprinted in the Whig press. See, for example, the *Harrison Democrat* (Butler County, Ohio), 14 July 1840, pp. 3–4. A more convenient summary is in Cleaves, p. 312.

29. For the causes of this growth, see Robert V. Friedenberg, *Communication Consultants in Political Campaigns: Ballot Box Warriors* (Westport, CT: Praeger, 1997), pp. 5–13. The specific numbers are in Cousens, *Politics and Political Organizations in America*, pp. 114, 120, and 134.

30. The *Cincinnati Gazette*, 1 Oct. 1840, p. 2.

31. Harrison's best-known advocate in 1840, and according to his reputation the most talented, was Daniel Webster. On many occasions when his military abilities were questioned, Harrison was defended by those with whom he served.

32. Boller, *Presidential Campaigns*, pp. 68–69, and Glydon G. Van Dueson, *The Jacksonian Era: 1828–1848* (New York: Harper and Row: 1959), pp. 146–147, will provide the reader with a good feel for the nature of the Whig attacks on Van Buren.

33. The highly personal nature of the attack on Harrison is, in some respects, similar to that faced by Barry Goldwater in 1964. Goldwater's very sanity, it will be remembered, was questioned by a major national magazine, as a result of their survey of a large number of psychologists. Goldwater's frustration and disdain for this type of criticism, which he considered well beyond the bounds of fair play, may have contributed to the harsh and uncompromising language in his acceptance address. Similar frustration and disdain may have strongly motivated Harrison to take the unprecedented act of speaking out on his own behalf. See chapter 2, on Goldwater.

34. *Ohio State Journal* (Columbus), 9 June 1840, p. 3.

35. Robert Gunderson, *The Log-Cabin Campaign* (Westport, CT: Greenwood Press, 1977), p. 165, claims that Harrison delivered twenty-three major addresses. At least one of his major speeches, scheduled for Springfield, Ohio, on June 18, was canceled, due to the death of Harrison's son Benjamin. Though Harrison delivered approximately twenty major addresses, he delivered scores of other addresses, often like the one in Columbus, as he was traveling to the site of a scheduled major address. For example, the *Harrison Democrat* reported that on his way from North Bend to a major address scheduled for 28 July in Greenville, Ohio, Harrison delivered "numerous speeches at various points along the way." That paper goes on to report that "General Harrison did not intend to address the people at the intermediary points on his way; but they were determined to hear him." The *Democrat* account of his trip to Greenville claims that Harrison traveled "150 miles in six days of July amidst clouds of dust with thousands thronged around him making no less than TEN speeches in the open air, to immense multi-

tudes." Once having delivered his major address, Harrison was not finished. On his return, he spoke at Twinsborough, Lewisville, West Alexander, Winchester, Germantown, Franklin, and Middletown. See "Greenville Celebration," *Harrison Democrat*, 14 Aug. 1840, p. 2. Major addresses are distinguished by the fact that they were scheduled and publicized well in advance. Hence, they routinely drew crowds of 5,000 or more, on several occassions reportedly attracting 60,000 to 75,000. Typically they were given at the end of a long campaign rally and were well reported in the press.

36. The most readily available source of Harrison's Fort Meigs speech text is that found in "Harrison's Great Speech: At the Wonderful 'Log Cabin' Campaign Meeting at Ft. Meigs, in 1840," *Ohio Archaeological and Historical Publications* 17 (Columbus, Ohio, 1908): 197–224. No author is indicated for this article, though the editor indicates it is reprinted from the *Toledo Blade* of 8 May 1908. This verision of the text coincides with versions published contemporanously with its delivery in the Whig press. See, for example, *Harrison Democrat,* 9 July 1840.

37. For examples, see the text of Harrison's speech at Greenville, Ohio, 28 July 1840, in *The Whig* (Jonesboro, Tennessee), 9 Sept. 1840, p. 1; Harrison address at Dayton, Ohio, 10 Sept. 1840, in the *Log Cabin* (Dayton, Ohio), 18 Sept. 1840; and the text of Harrison's speech at Chillicothe, Ohio, 17 Sept. 1840, in the *Calumet Tippecanoe and War Club* (Springfield, Ohio), 6 Oct. 1840, p. 1. Harrison's major addresses were delivered in Ohio, and the newspaper collection at the Ohio Historical Association in Columbus is the best repository for the state's daily and weekly papers, as well as the many campaign papers that were published by Whigs and Democrats in 1840.

38. See "Harrison's Great Speech," p. 199.

39. See, for example, the account of Harrison's arrival in the suburbs of Dayton the night before his address of September 10 in the *Log Cabin* (Dayton, Ohio), 18 Sept. 1840, p. 1. On the procession order see *Harrison Democrat*, 9 June, 1840, p. 1.

40. This description is of the parade between Hamilton, Ohio, and Eaton, Ohio, major county seats about 25 and 50 miles north of Harrison's residence. This account of the Harrison parade does not make clear his final destination, though the date and location suggest that this parade took place at the outset of his travels from North Bend to Fort Meigs. *Harrison Democrat*, 9 June 1840, p. 1.

41. "Harrison's Great Speech," p. 199.

42. This and all subsequent quotes are drawn from the text as found in "Harrison's Great Speech," pp. 200–206.

43. The text of Harrison's Chillicothe address can be found in the *Calumet Tippecanoe and War Club* (Springfield, Ohio), 6 Oct. 1840, p. 1.

44. Robert Gunderson, "A Political and Rhetorical Study of the 1840 Presidential Campaign" (Unpublished Ph.D. dissertation, Univ. of Wisconsin, 1948), p. 280. Gunderson quotes representative Democratic papers, including the *Cleveland Advertiser* and the *Louisville Public Advertiser*.

45. Cousens, *Politics and Political Organizations*, pp. 134–35.

46. "Harrison's Great Speech," p. 206, and the *Harrison Democrat*, 25 June 1840, p. 4.

47. Perhaps the best, most readily available, account of such a rally is in the *Cincinnati Gazette*, 3 Oct. 1840, p. 2. The *Gazette* provides readers with details of Harrison's 1 October rally and speech in Cincinnati. This rally attracted 60,000. Preparations for the rally started at 8 A.M. and the parade that was part of the rally began at 10 A.M. The rally lasted the entire day.

48. Gunderson, "A Political and Rhetorical Study," p. 284.

49. Ibid. Gunderson attributes this phrase to the principal national Democratic paper, the *Washington (D.C.), Globe*.

50. The audience member is quoted in "General Harrison's Speech at Fort Meigs," *Harrison Democrat*, 9 July 1840, p. 1.

51. Dayton *Log Cabin*, 8 Aug. 1840, p. 2.

52. At the time this issue was somewhat of a tempest in a teapot. There was no evidence that Harrison suffered any health problems beyond those that might be associated with his age of 68. Daniel Drake, a prominent Cincinnati doctor who had known Harrison for twenty-eight years testified to his excellent mental and physical health in a widely reprinted letter, first published in the *Louisville Journal*, 30 May 1840. Drake claimed that his intellect is "unimpaired by age" and that his "constitution is as good as that of most men half of his age." See the *Cincinnati Daily Chronicle*, 5 June 1840, p. 2. In retrospect, given Harrison's untimely death, the charges of ill health may be perceived differently.

53. Dayton *Log Cabin*, 5 Sept. 1840, p. 4.

54. The audience member is quoted in "General Harrison's Speech at Fort Meigs," *Harrison Democrat*, 9 July 1840, p. 1.

55. See *A Brief History of the Public Service of General William Henry Harrison* (no author or publisher) (Harrisonburg, PA, 1835). According to Harrison biographer, James Green, this was among the very first campaign biographies. It was a model for many that followed. See Green's cover letter found with this volume in the Harrison collection of the Cincinnati Historical Society.

56. See, for example, Old Democrat, "The Contrast: Or Plain Reasons Why William Henry Harison Should Be Elected President of the United States and Why Martin Van Buren Should Not Be Re-Elected" (New York: J.P. Giffing, 1840). This ten-page pamphlet, found in the Harrison Collection of the Cincinnati Historical Association, provides the reader with 43 reasons why Harrison should be elected, and a similar number why Van Buren should not be reelected. The largest single number, eight, deal with Harrison's military accomplishments. The next largest group treat his personal qualities. When Harrison's positions on issues are presented, they are presented in sweeping generalities with which few could disagree. For example, he should be elected "because General Harrison will be a President of the people, instead of a mere agent of a party."

Chapter One

1960—John F. Kennedy

> I am not the Catholic candidate for President. I am the Democratic Party's candidate for President, who happens also to be a Catholic.

In August 1943, the Japanese destroyer Amagiri sliced a U.S. PT boat in half. The U.S. boat's commander was eventually rescued, after he had heroically towed one of his crew to safety by gripping the end of a life jacket belt in his teeth. A year later, half a world away, Nazi Germany was on the verge of defeat. Airman Joseph P. Kennedy, Jr., the older brother of the heroic PT commander, volunteered for a dangerous mission against Nazi submarine bases in western Europe. Airman Kennedy, one of the youngest delegates to the 1940 Democratic convention, seemed destined for a bright political career. He was killed on that mission.

Young PT commander John F. Kennedy expected to become a writer and in June 1945, as the war ended, he attended the San Francisco meetings that helped to found the United Nations as a special correspondent for the Hearst papers. Though myth has it that Joseph P. Kennedy, Sr. "promoted" his second son John to replace his deceased son Joe, Jr., such was not the case. Politics had begun to intrigue John Kennedy. It offered him a way to serve. It offered him a way to improve a world that had taken the young lives of many of his friends as well as his brother. Years later Kennedy was asked, "Was it a conscious feeling on your part of taking Joe's place?" "No," he responded, adding "but I never would have run for office if he had lived. I never would have imagined before the war that I would become active in politics."[1]

Though it may well have taken the death of his older brother to cause Kennedy to enter politics, once he did so, he quickly became a skilled participant. But the Kennedys were Catholics. For many, that meant that they could be elected to congressional seats, governorships, even Senate seats, particularly from a state like Massachusetts with a large Catholic population. But in mid-twentieth century America, for many it still meant that Catholics could not aspire to the White House. Nevertheless, by the late 1950s, John Kennedy, who likely would have never run for public office had his brother not been killed, did aspire to the White House. In addition to the many obstacles every aspiring president faces, Kennedy's Catholicism seemed to stand in his way. Then he went to Houston.

THE SPEAKER

On 29 May 1917, Jack Kennedy was born in Brookline, Massachusetts, the second son of Joseph and Rose Kennedy. Joseph was an enormously successful businessman, often called unscrupulous, ruthless, and shrewd as he made his fortune in liquor, cheap movies, racetracks, the stock market, and real estate. Rose was the daughter of the legendary Boston political figure John Francis (Honey Fitz) Fitzgerald.

The Kennedy wealth enabled Jack to attend the best of schools. During Jack's junior year at the Choate School, Jack's headmaster, George St. John, wrote Kennedy's father. "I think we overestimate Jack's present academic ability. By and by, when Jack is in college, and especially when he can choose his own subjects, his academic output will correspond more nearly with his high I.Q."[2] A year later, Jack graduated sixty-fourth in his class of 112.[3]

Though he did not distinguish himself academically, Kennedy began to evidence traits at Choate that would prove important to his political career. Among them were his concern for athletics and physical accomplishment and his ability to make friends. Leaving Choate, and contrary to his father's desire that he attend Harvard where his older brother Joe was already a student, Jack enrolled at Princeton, where several of his closest Choate friends were continuing their education. However, he took ill, spent two months in a Boston hospital, and then spent four months recuperating in warm climates.[4]

In the fall of 1936 he took the entrance exams for Harvard. His scores in English and history were excellent, but his French and physics scores were low. Nevertheless, he was accepted and soon had made several good friends and was playing on the freshman football team. At Harvard, Jack's health continued to bother him. While at Harvard he traveled to Europe on several occasions and dated extensively. Curiously, it was not until 1939, that Kennedy ever dated a Catholic woman.[5] Kennedy is frequently called "casual" about his religious observance during this period of his life and that characterization would seem accurate given that Kennedy, who led an active social life in these years, dated his first Catholic when he was twenty-two years old.

Though he had started as a very average student, by his junior and senior years at Harvard, Kennedy had become a solid researcher and writer. He graduated with honors in political science, and his senior thesis, with help from his father's friends, was turned into a best-selling book, *Why England Slept*.

Graduating from Harvard in June 1940, the same summer that Congress passed the first peacetime draft in history, Kennedy, like many American men his age, faced a period of uncertainty. Kennedy decided to spend a year at Stanford. His year shrank to little more than a quarter in which he attended some classes and audited others. His stay was likely cut short in part by back ailments and other health problems. Kennedy spent much of the summer of 1940 in Europe with his family. He returned to find many of his friends going into military service. President Franklin Roosevelt had, while Kennedy was in Europe, declared a state of national emergency. Joe Kennedy was already receiving preliminary pilot training at the Squantum Naval Air Station near Boston.

Jack decided to join the navy. As Kennedy worked out to strengthen his back, his father sought to help by using his influence with several naval officers who had been attached to the U.S. embassy in Britain when Joseph senior had been ambassador to England. On 8 August 1941, Kennedy officially applied for a commission in the U.S. Navy, and on September 25, he was accepted.[6]

Kennedy's naval career has been well documented. In 1944 Kennedy was given a medical discharge from the navy. His back problems had been aggravated during his years in the navy, including the strain he put on it after his PT boat was sliced in half. In 1945 he briefly wrote for the Hearst news service, and his interest in politics began to grow. In 1946 he was elected to Congress from the eleventh congressional district of Massachusetts.

Winning the Democratic primary in this heavily Democratic district was the key to Kennedy's election. Kennedy went after victory with the "vigor" for which he later became famous. He spoke throughout the district and campaigned door-to-door continually.

However arduous Kennedy's campaigning, he also had other advantages. His father worked behind the scenes to help secure Kennedy's first electoral victory. Among other things that Joe Kennedy's money bought for the first Kennedy campaign were 100,000 reprints of a *Reader's Digest* article written by Jack's close friend, author John Hershey, on the PT 109 incident, as well as neighborhood meet-the-candidate socials that the Kennedy organization subsidized by providing host families with a case of liquor, the services of both a caterer and a cleaning women, and $100. Joseph Kennedy even attempted to buy off his son's principal competitor, former Cambridge mayor and state senator Mike Neville. The elder Kennedy offered him a lucrative $25,000-a-year job for the rest of his life. When Neville refused, Kennedy senior contacted his friend, William Randolph Hearst. *The Boston American*, Hearst's paper, refused to run a single Neville ad, print Neville's picture, or even mention Neville by name for the two months preceding the election. Vote buying was common in this district, but former Boston congressman Thomas P. (Tip) O'Neill, who succeeded Kennedy in the eleventh district, recalls that while other candidates offered $20, the Kennedy organization offered $50.[7]

After his initial victory in 1946, Kennedy was reelected in 1948 and 1950. In 1952 he won the Massachusetts Senate race by upsetting Henry Cabot Lodge. Kennedy, among the staunchest of the cold warriors during his years in Congress, attacked Lodge for failing to vigorously oppose global communism and for being overly conservative on domestic social issues.[8] Lodge spent much of late 1951 and early 1952 working not on his own election, but rather on that of General Dwight David Eisenhower. It could be argued that as much as any single individual, Lodge was responsible for helping to make Eisenhower president. However, Lodge's decision to aid Eisenhower was made at the expense of his own campaign. It indicates the confidence of an incumbent who did not take his challenger seriously. Indeed, when he first learned that Kennedy would run against him, Lodge predicted that he would win by 300,000 votes and sent word through a mutual friend to Joseph Kennedy that his son's race would be a waste of money.[9]

But Lodge underestimated Kennedy. Lodge had failed in his initial personal appeals in late 1951 to get Eisenhower to run for the presidency. Nevertheless, when an "Ike for President" organization headed by former Republican presidential candidate Thomas Dewey sought to draft the general, Lodge was named to manage the effort. Consequently, in January, February, and March 1952 Lodge was heading a write-in effort that would ultimately win Eisenhower the New Hampshire primary and turn him into an active presidential candidate. During those same months, Kennedy was finishing his characteristically systematic campaign to speak in every one of Massachusetts's thirty-nine cities at least twice and three hundred and twelve towns at least once. [10]

Lodge's work for Eisenhower not only limited his efforts on his own behalf but also gave Kennedy two issues on which to challenge him. First, Lodge's work for Eisenhower meant that he frequently missed Senate votes. Kennedy made Lodge's absence from the Senate an issue. Second, Lodge's support for Eisenhower had offended many conservative Republicans who had supported Ohio senator Robert Taft in the hotly contested battle for the Republican presidential nomination. Kennedy ran as an aggressive anti-Communist, which he based on his record in Congress, where he had been involved in exposing communists in the American labor movement. He attacked Lodge for supporting Harry Truman's policies that had "lost" China to the communists and derided Lodge for ignoring and minimizing Senator Joseph McCarthy's charges about communist influence in the State Department.

Late in the campaign, recognizing the effect of Kennedy's attacks, Lodge's organization attempted to get McCarthy to speak on Lodge's behalf. McCarthy refused, telling William F. Buckley that Lodge had consistently opposed him, while Democratic congressman Kennedy was among his covert supporters.[11] Prophetically, in light of the 1960 presidential campaign, Kennedy debated Lodge in Waltham, Massachusetts, and clearly defeated the more experienced Lodge.[12] Ironically, in 1952 Kennedy was taking positions with which Richard Nixon could and did readily agree. On election day, Eisenhower swept to victory throughout the nation and won decisively in Massachusetts. Nevertheless, the architect of his early campaign, U.S. Senator Henry Cabot Lodge, lost his Senate seat to Kennedy by 70,000 votes.

THE 1956 DEMOCRATIC CONVENTION: A CATHOLIC FOR HIGH NATIONAL OFFICE

John F. Kennedy's bid for the presidency really began at the 1956 Democratic National Convention. Before the convention Kennedy and his associates had considered making a bid for the vice-presidential nomination. It was clear that Adlai Stevenson would be his party's presidential candidate, and Kennedy had cordial relations with Stevenson. However, Joseph Kennedy was fearful that if his son went on the ticket and Stevenson lost, as almost everyone expected he would, it would be easy to blame the loss on a Catholic running mate. But other Kennedy associates argued that the distribution of Catholic voters in urban areas might make a Catholic running mate a real plus, and would provide Kennedy with a national stage from which he could gain exposure for any future endeavors. Kennedy decided to let his administrative assistant, Theodore Sorensen, test the waters by feeling out a variety of party leaders.

Sorensen found many party leaders receptive to Kennedy and his efforts to secure the vice presidential nomination. Stevenson was from Illinois, and Kennedy offered an element of geographic balance to the ticket. His youth and war record appealed to veterans around the nation. His 1955 book, *Profiles in Courage,* had made him one of the best-known Democrats in the country, and he had capitalized on that popularity with a heavy speaking schedule throughout much of late 1955 and 1956.

His Catholicism seemed to be perceived as a mixed blessing. It was perceived as a handicap insofar as it might cost him votes in parts of the country where there were strong anti-Catholic feelings. Al Smith's Catholicism had proven costly to him in his 1928 race against Herbert Hoover, and that campaign was well recalled by many party leaders. Smith lost such traditionally Democratic states in the South as Tennessee, Texas, Florida, North Carolina, and Virginia, states that had not been lost by a Democratic candidate since the Reconstruction days immediately after the Civil War.[13] There was little doubt that Smith's Catholicism contributed to his defeat in these states and elsewhere.

However, Kennedy's Catholicism would reinforce his strong anti-Communist positions and his presence on the ticket would help Stevenson deal with "soft on communism" charges that the Republicans might make. Moreover, Kennedy's Catholicism and family life would also help counter the effects of Stevenson's divorce. Kennedy's Catholicism, claimed his advocates, would help win back many of the urban Catholics who had voted for Eisenhower in 1952. Indeed, Sorensen prepared a detailed memorandum that suggested that a Catholic candidate would help in northern urban areas to such an extent that any losses in the South would be offset.

Sorensen's memo was written in 1956, but it supported many of the arguments used by Kennedy in 1960. Though it started as a private memo or talking paper that Sorensen would use in meeting Democratic leaders, it was ultimately leaked by the Kennedy organization and widely published. Because the memo provided Democrats with a rationale to overcome their legitimate concerns that a Catholic was not a viable national candidate, and hence opened a Catholic candidacy to serious consideration for the first time since Al Smith's disastrous defeat in 1928, Sorensen's memo played an important role in paving the way for Kennedy's 1960 nomination. For these reasons the memo warrants our close examination.

The memo studies voting patterns in the fourteen critical swing states where Catholics constitute 20 percent or more of the registered voters.[14] Sorensen notes that his study does not include seven other states where

Catholics constitute 20 percent or more of the registered voters primarily "because those states are not considered to be among the key swing states." Among the major conclusions drawn by Sorensen are:

1. These fourteen states represent 261 of the 266 electoral votes necessary for election. They include eight of the largest states: New York, California, Pennsylvania, Illinois, Ohio, Michigan, New Jersey, and Massachusetts.
2. Utilizing studies conducted by Gallup, Roper, and the University of Michigan Survey Research Center, Sorensen finds that Eisenhower has received a substantial share of the normally Democratic Catholic voters in these fourteen states. Each of the polling organizations cited had found that Eisenhower took 12–15 percent of the Catholic Democratic vote. Nationally, normally Democratic Catholic voters had rather consistently since 1928 given Democratic party candidates about 65 percent of their vote. In 1952 Catholic voters split evenly and the Democratic share of the Catholic vote declined to 50 percent.
3. In 1952 Catholic candidates for both houses of Congress and for governorships ran consistently ahead of their national tickets "in a striking example of ticket-splitting on the part of Catholic voters."
4. Recent polling indicated that 75 percent of American voters "would vote for a well-qualified Catholic nominated by their party for the presidency itself . . . and it is apparent that a Democratic Catholic vice-presidential nominee, though admittedly prejudice would be stirred, would lose no electoral votes for the ticket simply because a handful of Southerners or Republicans would not support him. Particularly in the key states and cities where he might be expected to concentrate his campaigning his religion would be irrelevant to most." Sorensen notes that Democratic margins in several southern states might be diminished, but the electoral vote impact would be negligible.
5. "The Al Smith myth is one of the falsest myths in politics." Sorensen argues that 1928 was a Republican year and offers evidence that Prohibition (Smith was a "wet," Hoover a "dry") was three times as important as religion. He further finds that Smith was the big-city "portly, cigar-smoking stereotype of the immigrant-base political boss" and that midwestern and southern voters reacted negatively to him on this basis, not on the basis of his religion. Sorensen concludes that "if Al Smith had been the Republican nominee and a Dry, he would have won the election regardless of his religion." He goes on to suggest that Smith actually helped the party more than he hurt it and quotes a variety of sources who conclude that it was Smith in 1928, not Franklin Roosevelt in 1932, who broke the Republican hold on cities.

Sorensen concludes by finding that if the Democrats were to nominate a Catholic for vice president and "he brought into the Democratic fold only those normally Democratic Catholics who voted for Ike, he would probably swing New York, Massachusetts, Rhode Island, Connecticut, Pennsylvania and Illinois, for 132 electoral votes. If he also wins the votes of Catholics who shifted to the Republicans in 1948 or earlier, he could also swing New Jersey, Minnesota, Michigan, California, Wisconsin, Ohio, Maryland, Montana and maybe even New Hampshire—for at total of 265 electoral votes." Thus, Sorensen concludes that the presence of a Catholic vice presidential nominee on the 1956 Democratic ticket could well be the key to defeating Eisenhower.

It is hard to estimate to what extent this memo assuaged the Democratic fear of nominating a Catholic. However, it clearly challenged the previously largely unchallenged belief that a Catholic could not win. The very fact that the Kennedy organization arranged for this information to be distributed by others suggests their concern that it would be perceived as self-serving. Though it obviously was just that, and Sorensen himself claimed that he was writing "a political answer" to Democratic fears of "an anti-Catholic vote by raising hopes of recapturing a greater share of the Catholic vote," the reliance on academic studies and voter statistics give this memo a sense of authorativeness.[15]

Meanwhile, in addition to thinking about the vice presidency, Stevenson and his staff were planning for the convention. Stevenson wanted to give the next generation of Democratic leaders prominence in the convention, and he considered Kennedy, with a growing reputation as a writer and speaker, "its most attractive spokesman."[16] However, many of his advisers, including former President Harry Truman, whom Kennedy had criticized four years earlier in winning his Senate seat, disliked the Massachusetts senator personally and were concerned that if he became Stevenson's running mate, his religion might hurt Stevenson's chances. Stevenson decided to give Kennedy exposure by inviting him to make the principal nominating address. Meanwhile, Stevenson remained silent about his plans for the vice presidency.

As the convention opened, speculation centered on who Stevenson would name as his running mate. Among those constantly mentioned were Tennessee senators Estes Kefauver and Albert Gore, Minnesota senator Hubert Humphrey, and two Catholics, New York City mayor Robert F. Wagner and Kennedy. Desirous of making a favorable impression on Stevenson with the nomination speech, Kennedy and Ted Sorensen reworked the speech draft that Stevenson's aides had provided to them. One observer of their collaboration recalls that "there was no question which was the dominant partner, but there was no question either that in Sorensen, Kennedy had found a remarkably intelligent, sensitive and faithful associate."[17]

After Kennedy's well-received address and Stevenson's subsequent nomination, Stevenson met with a key group of advisers, including House

Speaker Sam Rayburn and Senator Lyndon Johnson, both from Texas, Democratic National Committee Chairman Paul Butler, several governors, and several members of his own staff to discuss the vice presidency. A year earlier, President Eisenhower had suffered a heart attack. That event had sensitized the public to the importance of the vice presidency. Given Eisenhower's enormous popularity, and the fact that the country was both at peace and prosperous, much less the reality that Eisenhower had already defeated Stevenson once and now had the advantage of incumbency, it was clear that the respective vice presidential candidates would be one of the few areas where the Democrats might, with the right running mate for Stevenson, have an edge on the Republican ticket, which was to renominate Eisenhower and Richard Nixon.

Stevenson did not have a clear choice in mind. Several of his staff had argued that he should indicate that he would accept the choice of the convention. They claimed that by allowing the convention an open choice, the Democrats would draw a sharp contrast with the Republicans, who would no doubt renominate Vice President Richard Nixon without any opposition. A wide-open race for the vice presidency, Stevenson's aides argued, would add excitement to the convention. Though party leaders voiced their reservations, observing that Stevenson might end up with a weak running mate, Stevenson decided to follow the advice of his aides over that of the party leaders. Telling the country that seven of the thirty-four presidents had assumed office because of the death of the incumbent, Stevenson announced that this decision was too important for one man to make. Therefore, he wanted the entire party involved and would throw the choice open to the convention.

Stevenson made his announcement to the convention at 11 P.M. on Thursday evening. Balloting for the vice presidential nominee was scheduled for the following evening. The contenders had twenty-four hours to campaign.

There were two serious contenders. One was the New Englander, Kennedy. The other was Tennessee senator Estes Kefauver. Kefauver had challenged Stevenson in the primaries in both 1952 and 1956, having earlier come to national prominence by chairing the Senate Committee on Organized Crime, whose hearings were among the first congressional hearings to be nationally televised. An experienced campaigner, Kefauver was known throughout the country and the party from his earlier efforts to secure the presidential nomination. The other senator from Tennessee, Albert Gore, also had support, as did a large number of favorite sons.

In the weeks preceding the convention, as Sorensen explored a possible Kennedy vice presidential nomination with party leaders, he had found remarkable support for the personable New Englander. Kennedy's undeclared candidacy was endorsed almost immediately by governors Abraham Ribicoff of Connecticut and Dennis Roberts of Rhode Island. He quickly picked up support from the rest of New England. Prior to the convention, North Carolina governor Luther Hodges indicated his belief that Kennedy would be acceptable in the South, and members of the Texas, Louisiana, Mississippi, and other southern delegations expressed support for or interest in Kennedy.

At the end of the first ballot, Kefauver had 483.5 votes, Kennedy 304, and Gore 178.5. The remaining 407 votes were divided among a bevy of favorite son candidates. It would take 686.5 votes for nomination. As the Kennedy supporters worked the convention, they found unexpected support in the South and Midwest. But they were disappointed by the attitudes and voting of the party's Catholic leaders.

Many of the party's Catholic leaders, including Pittsburgh mayor David Lawrence, a key figure in his state's delegation, Ohio governor Mike DiSalle, and New York Democratic leader James Farley, were afraid of putting a Catholic on the ticket. Like Kennedy's father, they foresaw an Eisenhower victory. They feared that if Stevenson had a Catholic running mate, that individual, and his religion, would receive a considerable amount of the blame for a loss. Given the one-sided loss of Al Smith, and the likelihood of yet another landslide Eisenhower victory in November, they believed that an overwhelming loss in 1956 by a Democratic ticket with a Catholic on it would postpone by decades the consideration of another Catholic for the nation's highest offices.[18]

Nevertheless, the second ballot witnessed a rush to Kennedy. Favorite sons withdrew, and while both Kennedy and Kefauver gained votes, the New Englander was gaining more. In the middle of the alphabetical role call, New Jersey and New York gave Kennedy 126.5 more votes on the second ballot than he had received on the first. When Texas was called, Senator Lyndon Johnson announced that all of his state's 56 votes were "for that fighting sailor who wears the scars of battle."[19] Johnson and several Texas congressmen had beaten down the anti-Catholic sentiment within the delegation and the apprehensions of Speaker Rayburn. The Kennedy people knew who was responsible for those 56 votes and four years later they would remember.

At what might have been the end of the second ballot, Kennedy had 646 votes. He seemed on the verge of victory. But his victory was to be denied. Speaker of the House Sam Rayburn was presiding. A host of states were clamoring to be recognized so that they might switch their votes. Rayburn could have called a recess and reconvened for a third ballot. Instead, he continued the balloting.

Rather than recognize South Carolina, Illinois, or Alabama, all of which were ready to switch to Kennedy, Rayburn recognized Tennessee. Senator Albert Gore spoke for Tennessee and announced that he was withdrawing and urged those delegates who had supported him to support his Tennessee colleague, Kefauver. The next states recognized by Rayburn followed Gore's lead. The stampede to Kefauver was on. Though Rayburn was eventually to become a strong admirer and Kennedy partisan, in 1956 he was concerned that Kennedy's religion and youth would be major handicaps in a national campaign. Earlier in the convention he had told Stevenson "if we have to have a Catholic, I hope we don't have to take that little pissant Kennedy."[20]

Kennedy's experience in the 1956 convention was the true beginning of his 1960 campaign for the presidency. Had he won and gone down to defeat as Stevenson's Catholic running mate, it is hard to imagine Kennedy subsequently waging a successful race for the presidency. Theodore White claims that had Kennedy won the nomination and his ticket lost the general election, Kennedy

> would have been eliminated forever. Having lost, he could think about the future. In 1956 he had played his game for sport, as an overnight caprice between Thursday and Friday. But he had learned that the game might be played in the future for keeps: he would not be excluded from American leadership by his religion. Estes Kefauver had won out over him that night fairly and squarely, by showing his muscle to power brokers in primaries from coast to coast. Apparently what impressed bosses was the ability to pull support from ordinary voters in primaries that could coerce headlines and television attention.[21]

Though Kefauver had lost critical primaries in Florida and California to Stevenson, he had, in both 1952 and 1956, also demonstrated his ability to attract votes outside his home state. Kennedy had not. That lesson was not lost on Kennedy.

KENNEDY AND CATHOLICISM IN THE 1960 PRIMARIES

On the morning of 28 October 1959, sixteen people met in the living room of Robert F. Kennedy's home in Hyannisport, Massachusetts. They hoped to finalize the basic strategies for the campaign that would carry John F. Kennedy to the White House. John Kennedy opened the meeting and held the floor for three hours. He proceeded, according to the recollections of those who were there, "to survey the entire country without map or notes."

Interrupted "occasionally by a bit of information he might request of the staff," he displayed a "remarkable knowledge of every state, not just the party leaders, not just the Senators in Washington, but he knew all the factions and the key people in all the factions." Another participant recalled that "he knows the facts, who likes him and who doesn't, he knew where he should go and where he shouldn't, he has this incredible memory of places, names, dates, of who should be written to and who shouldn't." When Kennedy concluded and the group broke for lunch, the strategy had been clarified from the top down, as he saw it and meant to take it." [22]

Kennedy made it clear that he felt the nomination had to be won in the primaries. The country had never elected a Catholic. The country had never elected someone as young as Kennedy's forty-three years. The country had elected only one senator directly to the presidency in the preceding sixty years. Those patterns would not be broken in 1960 unless Kennedy could win in the primaries. If he could do that, he could then turn to the party bosses and deal with them from a position of strength. Moreover, Kennedy added, throughout the primary period the party leaders in nonprimary states had to be cultivated. He would need their votes, their loyalty, and the votes, loyalty, and efforts of those whom they commanded, after the primaries and in the general election. Thus, his route to the nomination would travel two roads. The more public road would be that which led him through the primary states. The private road would be that which he and the staff used to solidify the support of the leaders and organizations in the nonprimary states.

In 1960 primaries would be held in sixteen states. Kennedy made it clear that he would not enter all of them. To do so, in some cases, would offend favorite sons on whose support he would be counting later in the nomination and general election contests. Others were in small, relatively unimportant states that were not worth the time and resources of a primary campaign. But Kennedy insisted that the primaries selected had to be numerous enough and representative enough to give a national flavor to his efforts. They had to be selected not only for their own value, but because of the impact they might have on neighboring states and the impact they might have on the party's kingmakers. And, said Kennedy, every primary had to be won.

Kennedy's entire campaign was based on being able to convince the party leaders that he could win. One loss, in any primary, would be fatal. At this meeting the group agreed that he had to enter New Hampshire. It was the nation's first, and as such commanded great attention. Moreover, Oregon law required that all candidates be on the Oregon ballot. Candidates did not have a choice; whether they liked it or not, they would be on the Oregon ballot. Kennedy ran through the election laws and the pros and cons of entering each primary. Most of the discussion focused on Wisconsin, with little discussion of most other states, including West Virginia. Two major states, Ohio and California, presented special cases. Both had Catholic governors, Mike DiSalle and Pat Brown, who were expected to be favorite-son candidates. Ultimately Kennedy entered seven primaries. By doing so he not only afforded himself an opportunity to win, but he placed a burden on his competitors. Almost every other major candidate remained out of the primaries. Lyndon Johnson used his responsibilities as majority leader of the Senate as an excuse for avoiding the rigors of the primary season. But Kennedy believed that "Johnson had to prove that a Southerner could win in the North, just as I have to prove a Catholic can win in heavily Protestant states." Johnson's failure to enter any primaries was, in Kennedy's opinion, a fatal mistake. "When Lyndon said he could win in the North but could offer no concrete evidence, his claims couldn't be taken seriously," observed Kennedy.[23]

Kennedy also feared Adlai Stevenson and Missouri senator Stuart Symington. However, Stevenson had twice been his party's nominee and twice lost. He announced that he was not a candidate, but behind the scenes made his availability known, should the party deadlock. Symington, popular with conservative midwestern Democrats, was by his nature a compromiser. Kennedy had worked with him in the Senate and respected him but felt that he was unlikely to seek the clashes and confrontations that would be inherent in contesting the primaries.

Kennedy felt that had Symington organized early, he might have won primaries in several conservative states such as Nebraska and Indiana. But Symington, like Kennedy, could not afford to lose a primary and chose not to take the risk of doing so. He was not known well outside his home state, and an early defeat would likely prove fatal to his chances. In addition, unlike Kennedy, he had no ready sources for the money it would take to wage several strong primary campaigns. Perhaps most important, Symington's principal political mentor, former president Harry Truman, was strongly advising him to avoid the primaries. With Truman's help, Symington felt that he could secure the nomination if the convention deadlocked.[24]

Given the large number of favorite-son candidates—governors Brown of California, DiSalle of Ohio, G. Mennen Williams of Michigan, Robert Meyner of New Jersey, J. Millard Tawes of Maryland, Luther Hodges of North Carolina, David Lawrence of Pennsylvania, LeRoy Collings of Florida, and George Docking of Iowa—many Democrats were expecting a deadlock at the convention. Humphrey might well pick up some farm state votes. Johnson would likely have support from the South. Kennedy would be supported by New England. But none of these three would be close to having the support of a majority of delegates and the convention would deadlock. That was the scenario that Symington hoped for in staying out of the primaries, as did Stevenson and Johnson. All had reasons to feel that the party might well turn to them in the case of a deadlock.

With all three of what he perceived to be his principal challengers avoiding the primaries, Kennedy attacked his foes for attempting to win the nomination through back-room maneuvers. In his announcement of candidacy address, on 2 January 1960, he observed that "for fifty years no Republican or Democrat has reached the White House without entering and winning at least one contested primary." He went on to observe that every Democratic candidate should be willing to submit to the voters "his views, record and competence in a series of primary contests."[25]

One candidate did respond to Kennedy's challenge. Minnesota senator Hubert Humphrey announced that he would run in Wisconsin and West Virginia as well as his native state of South Dakota and the District of Columbia. Kennedy chose not to contest the latter two. Both were too small to have any impact on the nomination struggle, and Humphrey had the Democratic organizations in both strongly behind him.

Consistent with his original goal of entering a sufficient number of diverse primaries to give his campaign a national flavor, Kennedy and his organization had finally settled on which primaries to enter. He would run in New Hampshire, where there was no opposition. He would run in Wisconsin against Humphrey. He would run in Indiana—Symington's decision not to challenge him there meant that Kennedy would have little opposition. He would run against Humphrey in West Virginia. He would run in Nebraska, where again Symington's noncandidacy meant that Kennedy would have little opposition. He would run in his home state of Massachusetts. He would run in Maryland against Oregon senator Eugene Morse, whose candidacy Kennedy, and the rest of the nation, never took seriously. However, Maryland law mandated that an uncommitted delegation would be on the ballot. That delegation would be headed by Governor J. Millard Tawes. He would run in Oregon, where by law every candidate, including the state's favorite son, Senator Morse, was on the ballot. The two critical primaries were those of Wisconsin and West Virginia.

Kennedy had agonized over the decision to run in the Wisconsin primary. He would have much preferred to run in Ohio.[26] However, he did not have the resources to do both. Kennedy felt he could do well in Ohio and he feared that if Ohio governor Mike DiSalle, an old friend of Harry Truman, won the primary, as he surely would if unopposed, he would swing the delegation to Symington, or even Lyndon Johnson, before he would consider

Kennedy. DiSalle was one of the Catholic leaders who had opposed Kennedy in the 1956 vice-presidential fight. Moreover, if Kennedy opposed DiSalle in the primary, Kennedy would get the support of major elements of the state's Democratic party. Much of the Cleveland Democratic organization, headed by Kennedy's friend Ray Miller, was ready to battle Toledo native DiSalle, and Miller encouraged Kennedy to run.

It was an attractive option to running in Wisconsin, next door to Senator Humphrey's Minnesota, and where Humphrey was well known and respected. Moreover, Ohio would have more votes in the convention and had a winner-take-all primary. Wisconsin's primary laws awarded delegates by congressional district, a procedure that was likely to produce a split delegation.

But the Kennedy operatives knew that DiSalle did not want to go through a bitter primary fight simply to control his own delegation. Moreover, if he lost, his position within the state party would be dramatically diminished. In a series of secret meetings, DiSalle met with both John and Bobby Kennedy. He indicated that he would endorse Kennedy, but he did not want to be the first big state governor to do so. He argued that as a Catholic, it would be better for the Kennedys to have endorsements from others prior to his endorsement. He was also concerned that as the first big state governor to endorse Kennedy, he would particularly antagonize his old benefactor Truman. But the Kennedys were insistent. The deadline for their filling a slate of primary delegates was fast approaching. Bobby Kennedy and John Bailey met for one final time with DiSalle. They bluntly indicated that they would make every effort to destroy him in Ohio. They threatened to use the full weight of the Kennedy organizational skills and money to support a Kennedy-pledged delegation. It would be headed by DiSalle foe Ray Miller and the Cleveland organization. If Kennedy won in Ohio, Miller would effectively control the Democratic party in the state. DiSalle capitulated. He agreed to endorse Kennedy shortly after the New Englander announced his candidacy. Kennedy was now assured of Ohio's votes. Equally important, DiSalle's decision meant that Kennedy could now contest Humphrey in the Wisconsin primary.

As in his Massachusetts senatorial campaigns, the Kennedy campaign quickly organized for Wisconsin.[27] In short order the state was flooded with Kennedy partisans. As the candidate spoke throughout the state, members of his family, college friends, military friends, and other loyalists from Massachusetts poured into the state. The Kennedy organization quickly assigned each to a regional office, where they were employed going door to door, arranging house parties, telephoning, preparing mailings, and in similar activities. It was in this election that Kennedy's wife, Jackie, proved her merit as a campaigner.[28] Though both Humphrey and Kennedy spent about $150,000, chiefly on advertising, Kennedy had a far larger organization in the state. He opened offices in eight of the state's ten congressional districts. Humphrey could staff only two offices. Kennedy's people were working full time for him. Many were volunteers who had been able to get away from their normal pursuits and work full time for a week, a month, or the duration. Many of Humphrey's campaign workers were working on the weekends in Wisconsin and returning to Minnesota and their regular jobs during the week. Humphrey relied on his many friends in the Wisconsin Democratic party. For years he had spoken on their behalf, as their interests so often paralleled those of his Minnesota constituents. He also relied on the unions to provide manpower and money on his behalf.

The candidates took different approaches to the election. For Kennedy, running in the primary was a full-time job. For Humphrey, though his race was important, he was concerned about his Senate obligations. The tone set by the candidates pervaded their organizations. It was little wonder that Humphrey suggested the contrast was like a "corner grocer running against a chain store."[29]

More than 30 percent of Wisconsin's voters were Catholic. Though both Kennedy and Humphrey minimized the religious issue, the press consistently dwelled on it. Neither candidate spoke extensively about religion on his own. Rather, when religion was discussed, it was normally as a consequence of questions from the audience or the press. Nevertheless, Kennedy was bitter about the many personal attacks that he felt were made upon him. Not only his religion, but also his wealth, his early support of Wisconsin senator Joseph McCarthy, and his father's business dealings, womanizing, and alleged Nazi sympathies prior to World War II were all subjected to attacks that Kennedy strongly resented. However, outwardly Kennedy remained calm. He campaigned ceaselessly, speaking primarily about pollution in Wisconsin's rivers, the future of the St. Lawrence Seaway, taxes on farms, and the development of the timber industry. Though the press speculated endlessly on the effect Kennedy's religion would have, both candidates seemed to downplay the issue. Kennedy made no direct appeals for non-Catholic tolerance or for Catholic support.

On election day, Kennedy won. Or did he? He won 56 percent of the vote. Kennedy won more votes than Wisconsin had ever before given to a candidate in a primary election. He carried six of the ten congressional districts, and hence almost two-thirds of the state's delegates to the national convention would be pledged to him. In those four districts that Humphrey carried, a shift of less than 1 percent of the vote would have given two of them to Kennedy.

But Kennedy recognized that his was far from a total victory. He had chosen to run in the primaries to convince the party that a Catholic could win. But he had lost all four congressional districts that were predominantly Protestant. His entire popular vote margin had come from the four most heavily Catholic districts. Moreover, Wisconsin was a crossover primary state that allowed Republicans to vote in a Democratic primary if they wished. Humphrey could, and did, claim that many Republican Catholics had crossed over to vote in the Democratic primary for Kennedy. The voter statistics from portions of Green Bay, Sheboygan, and the Fox River Valley lent support to that claim.

Humphrey had expected defeat. Polls prior to the vote indicated he would lose. Yet he behaved like a winner. He claimed that he was encouraged by the results and said he was going back to Washington to tend to Senate business, and then on to West Virginia. He joked that "I was going to try to get a ride with Jack on his plane, but he thought I ought to catch the next bus."[30]

Both candidates understood that the Wisconsin primary would be read as a largely Catholic-Protestant split. Though he had won the popular vote and the majority of delegates, for Kennedy, Wisconsin was a hollow victory. The breakdown of the popular vote would not convince the skeptical leaders of his party that he was a winner. On election eve, when his sister Eunice saw Kennedy looking glumly at the results, she asked what the vote meant. Her brother responded, "It means that we have to do it all over again."[31] They would do it all over again in West Virginia.

Kennedy had chosen to enter the West Virginia primary for a variety of reasons. However, foremost among them was the polling work of Lou Harris, which showed that the state was surprisingly receptive to Kennedy.[32] Four months before the outset of serious campaigning in West Virginia, a Harris poll showed that Kennedy would carry 70 percent of the vote in a race with Humphrey.[33] Kennedy had been organizing in the state for almost a year before the Wisconsin primary. The day after the Wisconsin primary, his two principal organizers, Larry O'Brien and Dave Powers, flew with Bobby Kennedy to West Virginia to meet with the leaders of Kennedy's West Virginia organization.

They were shocked at the reception they received. Bob McDonough, a West Virginia printer active in Democratic state politics, was heading the Kennedy operation in the state. He introduced Bobby to a room filled with the precinct workers and others that McDonough had recruited for Kennedy and whom the three visitors had met during previous visits to the state. O'Brien and Powers recall that the room was strangely silent as the meeting opened.

McDonough introduced Bobby, whom many of the people had met before in our previous visits. "Well," Bobby said to them pleasantly, "what are our problems?" A man stood up and shouted, "There's only one problem. He's a Catholic. That's our God-damned problem!" The room broke into an uproar with everybody yelling at us that nobody in the state would vote for a Catholic in a contested presidential primary, or even in an election for dogcatcher. We were stunned by the suddenness of this wild emotional outburst from a group of people who had been working enthusiastically for Kennedy over the past several months and who had never shown much concern about the religious issue up to this time.[34]

Before the closing days of the Wisconsin primary, most residents of the Mountaineer State had not been aware of, or concerned about, Kennedy's Catholicism. However, in the days preceding the arrival of the Kennedy delegation, the press speculation on the impact Kennedy's Catholicism would have on the Wisconsin vote, and the analysis of that vote in light of his Catholicism, had made the entire state of West Virginia aware of Kennedy's Catholicism. Members of West Virginia's Kennedy organization reported that their neighbors and friends were ridiculing them for working on behalf of a Catholic. When Bobby notified Jack of the change in West Virginia, the candidate asked about the Harris poll of four months earlier. Bobby responded, "the people who voted for you in that poll have just found out that you're a Catholic."[35]

New Harris polls confirmed that Kennedy's Catholicism was having a clear negative impact on him in West Virginia.[36] Kennedy took a weekend vacation and returned believing that he had no alternative but to deal with the religious issue. As he opened his West Virginia campaign, Kennedy developed a basic rhetorical strategy to which he hewed throughout the primary. Rhetoricians Stephen Goldzwig and George Dionisopoulos describe the twofold nature of this strategy:

First, the candidate indicated that he would not be dismissing out-of-hand public concerns regarding his Catholicism. He would acknowledge that it was a genuine factor for some people, and that he did not consider all such concerns to be the product of bigotry or prejudice. As such, he would continue to answer not only all the reasonable questions but many unreasonable questions as well. . . . Of equal importance, Kennedy would address the issue publicly as often as necessary, proffering his definition of its only legitimate aspect—his independence of ecclesiastical pressure—proclaiming over and over that the Catholic hierarchy had no influence over him when it came to the weighty matters of American politics. He thus acknowledged the trepidation many felt, but would define the issue in such a way that legitimated only those concerns regarding the candidate—not the candidate's religion. In other words, he would only defend himself, not Catholic actions, doctrine, or history.[37]

On 13 April Kennedy first spoke about his Catholic faith in West Virginia. He observed that "nobody asked me if I was a Catholic when I joined the United States Navy and nobody asked my brother if he was a Catholic or a Protestant before he climbed into an American bomber plane to fly his last mission." He went on to add that "I don't think my religion is anyone's business but my business. Is anyone going to tell me that I lost this primary forty-two years ago when I was baptized?"[38] In addressing the issue, Kennedy was acknowledging that the public might have legitimate concerns. But, simultaneously, he was suggesting that religion was a private matter unless it impinged on the conduct of public office.

As the Kennedy organization swung into action and the candidate traveled the state, Kennedy decided that in order to fully articulate his position, he needed a more significant forum than those he was addressing on the campaign trail. So he asked his speechwriter, Ted Sorensen, to switch the subject of his impending address to the American Association of Newspaper Editors. Rather than discuss foreign aid, he would discuss the religious issue. In this speech, Kennedy indicated his views on education, birth control, and American relations with the Vatican. By implication, Kennedy was saying that these were legitimate concerns to be raised with a Catholic presidential candidate. As Goldzwig and Dionisopoulos indicated, he would not dismiss concerns about Catholicism out of hand. Men of good faith could have legitimate concerns about how a Catholic president might treat issues such as these, which were sensitive matters for the Catholic church.

But, Kennedy continued, when it came to his own personal religious beliefs,

> there is only one legitimate question. . . . Would you as President, be responsive in any way to ecclesiastical pressures or obligations of any kind that might in any fashion influence or interfere with your conduct of that office in the national interest?. . . My answer was—and is—no. I am not the Catholic candidate for President. I do not speak for the Catholic Church on issues of public policy, and no one in that Church speaks for me. . . . Are we to say that a Jew can be elected Mayor of Dublin, a Protestant can be named Foreign Minister of France, a Moslem can sit in the Israeli Parliament but a Catholic cannot be President of the United States?[39]

Delivered in Washington at the National Press Club, this speech generated considerable favorable publicity, and Kennedy was soon repeating this message throughout West Virginia.

But religion was not the only issue in economically depressed West Virginia. Kennedy addressed the economic concerns of West Virginia far more effectively than did Humphrey. He repeatedly visited the depressed mining areas of the state and made frequent references to his empathy with impoverished residents of the state. On 3 May Kennedy and Humphrey met in a widely televised debate. In his analysis of this debate, rhetorician Hermann Stelzner illustrates that Humphrey failed to focus as directly on the plight of West Virginia as did Kennedy. Stelzner likens Humphrey and Kennedy to suitors who wished to win the hand of the fair maiden, West Virginia. Stelzner finds that "a basic theme of this analysis is that Humphrey's inability to order his material consistent with his objective accounts for his poor performance. Contrariwise, Kennedy consistently structures his material so that it points to West Virginia."[40]

As Kennedy campaigned in West Virginia, Humphrey's campaign floundered. The Kennedy organization distributed 750,000 pieces of Kennedy literature to 400,00 West Virginia Democratic voters. Humphrey made no comparable effort. In the two largest media markets of West Virginia, Huntington and Charleston, Humphrey spent only 10 percent of what Kennedy spent on radio, TV, and newspapers. As in all Kennedy campaigns, many Kennedy family members and other surrogates spoke throughout the state.[41]

On the Sunday before the election, the Kennedy organization bought time for their candidate to speak to the people of West Virginia. For most of the program, Franklin Roosevelt, Jr., heir to what was still a potent political name in West Virginia, questioned Kennedy. Roosevelt had campaigned throughout the state for Kennedy. His questions helped Kennedy discuss the key issues of the campaign. At one point, Kennedy made a serious plea for religious tolerance. In response to Roosevelt's question, Kennedy spent ten minutes discussing the history of church–state relations. He concluded by looking directly at the camera and addressing the people of West Virginia:

> When any man stands on the steps of the Capitol and takes the oath of office as President, he is swearing to support the separation of church and state. He puts one hand on the Bible and raises the other hand to God as he takes the oath. And if he breaks his oath, he is not only committing a crime against the Constitution, for which the Congress can impeach him, and should impeach him, but he is committing a sin against God.[42]

On election day, West Virginia gave Kennedy a decisive victory. Kennedy won 61 percent of the vote. He carried all areas of the state, including 48 of West Virginia's 55 counties. Most important, he won decisively in precinct after precinct where the vast majority of the voters were Protestants.[43] In a state where 95 percent of the voters were Protestants, Kennedy swept every imaginable demographic group: women and men, urban and rural, black and white, and most important, Protestant and Catholic. Across the board, Kennedy prevailed. The victory that had eluded Kennedy in Wisconsin was his in West Virginia. On the same day that he won in West Virginia, Kennedy also won in Nebraska. A week later he won in Maryland. Regardless of whether he won in West Virginia because of his appealing persona, his thorough political organization, or his sensitivity to the economic issues of West Virginia, there could no longer be any reasonable doubt that Kennedy was an appealing candidate to millions of Democratic Protestant voters. After West Virginia he was on a fast track headed to the Democratic National Convention in Los Angeles and the presidential nomination of his party.

THE RHETORICAL SITUATION: KENNEDY COMES TO HOUSTON

Having won the West Virginia primary, Kennedy continued his string of primary victories. With seven primary wins, Kennedy was able to do what his campaign had first envisioned. They could deal with the party's leaders from a position of strength. Kennedy won a first-ballot victory at the Los Angeles Convention and selected Lyndon Johnson as his running mate, hoping to capitalize on Johnson's popularity in the South and Southwest.

Kennedy had hoped that his West Virginia victory would effectively eliminate the religious issue. Hence, in his acceptance address, he made only a brief effort to lessen anti-Catholic concerns, observing that his nomination indicated "confidence in the American people and in their ability to render a free, fair judgment—and in my ability to render a free fair judgment." This speech is best remembered for Kennedy's use of the phrase "New Frontier" to describe his goals and the programs he would initiate as president.[44]

Short weeks thereafter, the Republicans nominated Richard Nixon. Nixon anticipated stressing his foreign policy competence during the general election. To that end, he nominated Henry Cabot Lodge, then serving as ambassador to the United Nations, as his running mate. Nixon made a point of steadfastly refusing to discuss the religious issue and instructed his staff to also ignore it.

However, though the candidates wished to minimize the religious issue, others were also involved in setting the issue agenda. In late August a variety of religious groups expressed strong concerns about the possibility of a Catholic president. Among them were the Minnesota Baptist convention, the General Assembly of the Assemblies of God, which claimed to speak for over half a million members, and the Arkansas Baptist state convention. During the first week of September, a variety of major Protestant leaders and organizations continued to express their anxiety about a Catholic president. Perhaps most indicative of the worries of many Protestants was the concern expressed by the National Conference of Citizens for Religious Freedom, a group of 150 clergy and laity representing thirty-seven church groups. Norman Vincent Peale, arguably the nation's best-known religious leader, was the principal spokesman for this group of mainstream Protestant leaders.[45]

The essence of the concerns about Kennedy being expressed by these groups was captured in the statement of the Peale group, which observed that the critical question is

> whether it is in the best interests of our society for any church organization to attempt to exercise control of its members in political and civic affairs. While the current Roman Catholic contender for the Presidency states specifically that he would not be so influenced, his church insists that he is duty-bound to admit to its direction. This unresolved conflict leaves doubt in the minds of millions of our citizens.[46]

Similarly, other prominent clergy were raising what were perceived in many minds to be legitimate concerns about a Catholic president. Episcopal clergyman James A. Pike perceived that concern about a Roman Catholic president was not bigotry. "It is," said Pike, "the exercise of responsible citizenship." Pike claimed that such concern was legitimate because "it bears on what are in the life of the country certain basic questions on which voters may differ in terms of their individual conviction as the right direction of national policy." He claimed that foreign aid, birth control, aid to parochial schools, diplomatic representation of the Vatican, and the degree to which we encourage foreign governments which practice repressive measures against Christians, were examples of such questions.[47]

The statement of the National Conference of Citizens for Religious Freedom headed by one of the country's best-known clergymen indicated that Kennedy had not buried the religious issue in West Virginia, as he had hoped. The campaign organization had picked up concerns about Kennedy's religion almost from the moment the convention ended. The Peale group simply helped to quantify the extent of that concern, and perhaps to give it greater respectability. Clearly, it would have to be addressed forcefully again in the general election.[48]

Days before the National Conference of Citizens for Religious Freedom had issued their statement, Tim May, Kennedy's advance man in Houston, had notified the Kennedy organization that the Greater Houston Ministerial Association would be meeting during the period when Kennedy was scheduled to barnstorm in Texas, at the end of his first major campaign swing as the Democratic candidate. Moreover, they had invited both candidates to address them. Consistent with his policy never to make religion an issue, Nixon had refused the invitation.[49] The top command of the Kennedy organization, including Jack and Bobby, were skeptical of the invitation, feeling it was a trap that would result in embarrassing publicity . However, when Kennedy was informed of the Peale group's statement while campaigning in California, he reconsidered the invitation from Houston. Though many of his aides felt that Houston was not the place to address the issue, Kennedy believed otherwise. Ignoring the advice of his aides, Kennedy claimed that "This is as good a time as any to get it over with. I've got to face it sooner or later."[50] He agreed to "face it" with the Greater Houston Ministerial Association on the evening of 12 September.

Kennedy's Texas swing had already been considered crucial for his campaign; now the stakes were even higher. Texas was a key state in the Kennedy strategy. While Lyndon Johnson was being heavily relied upon to help carry his home state, Kennedy felt that he also had to campaign in Texas. Indeed, Kennedy was campaigning so ardently in California and Texas that by 12 September he was starting to lose his voice. Earlier that day he had spoken in El Paso, Lubbock, and San Antonio, as well as at a big Democratic rally earlier in the evening in Houston.[51]

Kennedy press secretary Pierre Salinger preceded Kennedy to the Rice Hotel, where the meeting with the ministerial association would take place. When Kennedy arrived, he asked Salinger, "What's the mood of the ministers?" Salinger answered, "They're tired of being called bigots."[52] If Kennedy was going to face a hostile audience, at least he would be utilizing ground rules that he had dictated.

Arrangements for the speech had been made by Kennedy aide James Wine, who had headed a five-person division of the campaign organization that had been working to neutralize the religious issue. Wine, who had previously worked for the National Council of Churches, had been primarily involved in responding to the 600–1,000 letters a week that the campaign was receiving about Kennedy's Catholicism. Wine was sent to Houston, where he made the speech arrangements. Kennedy, sensing the drama inherent in the situation, had instructed Wine that he wanted no one else on the platform; he wanted to stand alone. He also wanted an opportunity to make an opening statement, prior to accepting questions. Wine found that Johnson wanted to share the platform with Kennedy, and that the ministers did not want Kennedy to make an opening statement, but rather wanted him simply to respond to their questions.

Shortly before the speech, Wine made it clear to the ministers that Kennedy would make an opening statement. Moreover, Johnson associate Bill Moyers was enlisted to keep Johnson out.[53] Kennedy spoke from a lectern placed on a long head table in the Rice Hotel's Crystal Ballroom, which measured 63″ by 51″ and was decorated lavishly in pinks and greens. The audience members, numbering approximately 300, could see Kennedy from the chest up. The ministers were seated in front of the lectern with the press and spectators seated behind them.[54]

THE SPEECH

As with virtually all of Kennedy's major speeches, the candidate and Ted Sorensen were the principals who wrote the speech. Sorensen recalls that "the Senator's desire was to state his position so clearly and comprehensively that no reasonable man could doubt his adherence to the Constitution." With this goal in mind, Sorensen and Kennedy worked on the speech throughout the preceding weekend, as well as the night before, which Kennedy spent in El Paso. Sorensen recalls that "my chief source of material was Kennedy's own previous statements on religion to the American Association of Newspaper Editors, to the convention, to press conferences, and to *Look* magazine." Moreover, Sorensen also notes that he drew on "what I knew to be his views on the issue."[55] One of the additional facts desired by the senator "inasmuch as he was speaking at the Alamo in San Antonio on the way to Houston, was how many Catholics had died at that Shrine of Texas independence." [56] The Kennedy research staff in Washington could not give Sorensen a number, though they worked throughout the night. Rather, they provided him with a list of possible Irish-American names. Sorensen worked those names into the speech.

Sorensen wrote the drafts for this speech. Kennedy made editorial changes. The relationship between the two was one of the more remarkable principal-speechwriter relationships in the annals of the American presidency. Allen Otten, who reported on Kennedy both during the campaign and subsequently in the White House for the *Wall Street Journal,* claimed that they were two men "who sometimes give an eerie impression of blending into one person." Otten goes on to comment on Sorensen's speechwriting techniques. "Mr. Sorensen," observed Otten, "seemingly converted himself into the mirror image of the Senator while penning these addresses. Before locking himself into a hotel room for hours of composition, he would chat a while with Mr. Kennedy—a contact hardly sufficient to account for a strange transfusion of spirit." Many others have commented on Sorensen's incredible ability to mirror Kennedy's thinking and language.[57]

Given the press of writing the address during the campaign, it is understandable that Sorensen would do the drafting. Sorensen recalls that Kennedy "never just read a speech. He was the true author of his speeches. He worked over this one."[58] And well he might. For as at least one student of religion and the presidency has observed, this was likely as important a speech on church-state matters as ever was made by an American president.[59]

Sorensen, a Unitarian who had been dealing with this issue for the better part of four years, felt it was important to make sure Kennedy would not be offending any Catholics. Hence Sorensen read the speech to the Reverend John Courtney Murray, a Catholic scholar who dealt with church and state relations. It was also reviewed by a second Catholic scholar, John Cogley, as well as Kennedy staff members, including James Wine.[60]

Kennedy arrived in the ballroom a few moments before 9:00 P.M., the scheduled time for the speech to be broadcast throughout Texas. Ted Sorensen described the atmosphere in the room:

> The Senator, in black suit and black tie . . . flanked by the two ministers who presided, sat somewhat nervously behind the lectern. Glaring at him from the other side were the Protestant ministers of Houston. . . . Also on hand was a large number of national press pundits who had flown in for the great confrontation. A sense of tension and hostility hung in the air. The few minutes of waiting seemed endless.[61]

At 9:00, with the cameras rolling, Kennedy began to speak. Kennedy opened by observing that, while he would discuss religion, "I want to emphasize from the outset that I believe that we have far more critical issues in the 1960 election." After itemizing many of the critical issues, Kennedy acknowledged that "because I am a Catholic and no Catholic has ever been elected President . . . it is apparently necessary for me to state once again— not what kind of church I believe in, for that should be important only to me, but what kind of America I believe in."[62]

Kennedy's opening remarks served an important purpose. First, they reminded the audience, as Kennedy had been doing throughout the campaign, that his religion was a private matter and that there were far more important matters for presidential candidates to be discussing. Second, Kennedy acknowledged that there might be legitimate concerns about a Catholic president. However, Kennedy would resolve those concerns not by discussing his church, but rather by discussing his views of America. This approach allowed him to avoid defending every or any statement of the Roman Catholic

Church and its leaders. Rather, he would discuss only those aspects of the Church that might affect his views of America. Kennedy was limiting the scope of his remarks. He would defend himself. Those who attacked aspects of his church that did not impinge directly upon presidential responsibilities were, in effect, being defined as bigots.

At this point in the speech, Kennedy uses a series of paired statements that serve two imporant purposes. The first statement defines what Kennedy believes. These statements are conciliatory, they establish common ground between Kennedy and his audiences of ministers and voters. But each is paired with a second statement. The second statement placed his immediate audience, and indeed all who would oppose him on the basis of religion, on the defensive. The effect of each pair of statements was to suggest that Kennedy would more strongly uphold the separation of church and state than would those who questioned whether a Catholic could do this. For example, Kennedy claimed that

> I believe in an America where the separation of church and state is absolute—where no Catholic prelate would tell the President (should he be a Catholic) how to act and no Protestant minister would tell his parishioners for whom to vote—where no church or church school is granted any public funds or political preference—and where no man is denied public office merely because his religion differs from the President who might appoint him or the people who might elect him.

Kennedy is conciliatory and establishing common ground when he states that he believes "in an America where the separation of church and state is absolute—where no Catholic preplate would tell the President (should he be a Catholic) how to act." But, when Kennedy pairs that with his belief in an America where "no Protestant minister would tell his parishioners for whom to vote," he places his audience on the defensive. After all, were not many of the very ministers in the room likely guilty of this act? Indeed, if religion was thoroughly separated from voting, why would this meeting even be necessary? Neutral audience members might well surmise that Kennedy, more than his audience of ministers, was truly committed to the separation of church and state. Similarly, Kennedy is conciliatory when he states that he believes in an America where "no church or church school is granted any public funds or political preference." But he places his audience on the defensive when he pairs that with an America "where no man is denied public office merely because his religion differs from the President who might appoint him or the people who might elect him." After all, was not the entire controversy over Kennedy's religion a consequence of the fact that it differed from a large majority of the people who might elect him? Again, neutral audience members might well surmise that Kennedy, more than his audience of ministers, was committed to separation of church and state.

Kennedy continues his use of paired statements to describe the presidency in the America in which he believes. In Kennedy's America, the presidency would be "a great office that must be neither humbled by making it the instrument of any religious group, nor tarnished by arbitrarily withholding it, its occupancy, from the members of any religious group." Again, Kennedy continues to use paired statements to describe the presidency that he desires. As with his discussion of America, his discussion of the presidency utilizes paired statements. Each pair opens with a conciliatory statement, as when he says the presidency must not be "humbled by making it the instrument of any religious group." But then Kennedy places his immediate audience of ministers on the defensive when he also claims that the presidency must not be arbitrarily withheld from the members of any religious group. After all, were not many of the very ministers to whom Kennedy spoke that evening considering withholding the presidency from him on the basis of his Roman Catholicism? Again, neutral audience members might well perceive Kennedy as more committed to keeping the presidency out of the religious realm than were his audience of ministers. Kennedy continued in this vein, utilizing four paired statements to discuss the presidency in which he believed.

Kennedy had sensed the dramatic potential inherent in standing alone in front of a potentially hostile audience. He had also recognized that by utilizing an opening speech, he could set the tone of the meeting and control the agenda. The opening half of his address exploited the dramatic potential inherent in this rhetorical situation. Moreover, his remarks enabled Kennedy to avoid being placed on the defensive. He believed in a nation and a presidency where church and state were separate. Additionally, he structured his remarks in such a way as to suggest to objective viewers that his beliefs with respect to the separation of church and state were second to none, including his immediate audience of clergymen. The very situation itself, as well as Kennedy's deliberately paired statements, portrayed him as a sympathetic, conciliatory figure. They portrayed those who questioned his fitness for the office on the basis of his Roman Catholicism as unsympathetic, antagonistic, rancorous figures.

At this point Kennedy suggests the criteria upon which he should be judged. In this section of the speech Kennedy suggests that if his America and his conception of the presidency called for an absolute separation of church and state, then he should be judged on whether his life has reflected a commitment to that idea. Here he observes that as a Catholic his loyalty is not divided between his nation and his church. In what may well have been the most emotional portion of the speech, Kennedy observed that an America where separation of church and state was absolute

> was the kind of America I fought for in the South Pacific, and the kind my brother died for in Europe. No one suggested then that we might have a "divided loyalty," that we did "not believe in liberty" or that we belonged to a disloyal group that threatened, I quote, the "freedoms for which our forefathers died." And in fact this is the kind of America for which our forefathers did die—when they fled here to escape religious test oaths that denied office to members of less-favored churches—when they fought for the Constitution, the Bill of Rights, the Virginia Statute of Religious Freedom—and when they fought at the shrine I visited today, the Alamo. For side by side with Bowie and Crockett died Fuentes and McCafferty and Bailey and Bedillio and Carey—but no one knows whether they were Catholics or not. For there was no religious test there.

Kennedy was suggesting that he followed in the tradition of millions of American Catholics who went into harm's way when their nation called. Furthermore, he was suggesting that their willingness to do so was based in part on their recognition that church and state were absolutely separate in the United States.

Kennedy continued, illustrating that his voting record in Congress also illustrated his belief in the separation of church and state. He cited the relevant votes and suggested that he be judged on his personal record. He then claimed that it would not be appropriate to judge him on the basis of

> pamphlets and publications we have all seen that carefully select quotations out of context from the statements of Catholic church leaders, usually in other countries, frequently in other centuries, and rarely relevant to any situation here—and always omitting, of course, the statement of the American Bishops in 1948 which strongly endorsed church-state separation, and which more nearly reflects the views of almost every American Catholic.

As he had in the opening moments of his address, Kennedy was asking to be judged on his own merit, his own record, not that of his church. He was making it clear to his multiple audiences that he would defend his own actions, but he could not be held responsible for the actions of Catholics throughout the world, over centuries of time. By so doing, Kennedy was, as with his paired statements, placing himself in the mainstream of American values, which hold that each individual should be judged on his own merit. Moreover, he was placing his audience of ministers on the defensive, suggesting that they were attacking on the basis of statements made by foreign church leaders that had no real application in the United States, while deliberately ignoring the most critical statement issued by the American Catholic hierarchy. To the neutral observer, these passages might well seem to have placed Kennedy directly in the center of the American value system and placed his attackers on the fringes of that tradition, if not altogether outside it.

Kennedy concluded this portion of his address by observing that "these are my views—for contrary to common newspaper usage, I am not the Catholic candidate for President. I am the Democratic Party's candidate for President, who happens also to be a Catholic. I do not speak for my church on public matters—and the church does not speak for me." With these statements, Kennedy had effectively finished presenting his views.

The final four short paragraphs of Kennedy's speech to the Greater Houston Ministerial Association simply reiterated his dedication to the separation of church and state. However, two of those paragraphs warrant our attention. In the first, Kennedy observed that

> if the time should ever come—and I do not concede any conflict to be remotely possible—when my office would require me to either violate my conscience or violate the national interest, then I would resign the office; and I hope any other conscientious public servant would do likewise.

Theodore Sorensen claims that this paragraph was the one that Kennedy most deliberated over and the one that Kennedy himself had correctly predicted might be criticized. Sorensen claimed that this passage was meant to "still those Protestant critics who were certain he would succumb to pressure and those Catholic critics who were certain he would stifle his faith."[63] But, as rhetorical critic James Powell claims, "the inclusion of this argument raises (if only slightly) the very doubts that the speech had sought to dispel."[64] By observing that he would not even concede the possibility that such a conflict was remotely possible, Kennedy was in effect claiming that this passage was really unnecessary. In light of the fact that the passage does remind audiences of what had helped give rise to the entire issue involving Kennedy's Catholicism, it seems like an unnecessary risk to have included it.

If Kennedy erred with one paragraph near the end of his address, the final moments of the speech were exceptionally well conceived. Kennedy closed his address to the Houston ministers and the television audience by perceptively noting that if he should win the election he would "devote every effort of mind and spirit to fulfilling the oath of the Presidency." An oath, Kennedy significantly observed, practically identical I might add, with the oath I have taken for 14 years in the Congress. For without reservation, I can and I quote "solemnly swear that I will faithfully execute the office of the President of the United States and will to the best of my ability preserve, protect and defend the Constitution, so help me God."

Kennedy was finished with his prepared opening address. In contrast to Kennedy's delivery of the vast majority of his most significant campaign addresses, he never departed from his prepared text during his remarks to the Houston ministers.[65] Once the address was over, Kennedy fielded questions. Observers were almost unanimous in claiming that he handled the questions well. Kennedy was a talented speaker. As we have seen, he had been dealing with the issues raised by his faith for the better part of four years. As a result, he handled questions about his faith effectively.[66]

EFFECTS OF KENNEDY'S SPEECH TO THE GREATER HOUSTON MINISTERIAL ASSOCIATION

Kennedy's remarks to the Greater Houston Ministerial Association were designed to alleviate and lessen the fears many Americans might have about a Roman Catholic president. A first means of evaluating Kennedy's speech is to examine whether he provided sufficient substance to lessen those fears. Based primarily on a study of Southern Baptist newspapers, Beryl McClerren attempted to identify the principal fears of many who were concerned by Kennedy's Catholicism.[67] McClerren found that those who were concerned about a Catholic president had three primary fears. First, they were concerned that the Roman Catholic Church is a political-religious organization that does not believe in church-state separation. Second, they were concerned that the Roman Catholic Church does not believe in religious liberty. Finally, they were concerned that a president of the Roman Catholic faith would be influenced politically by the church.[68] These three concerns expressed repeatedly in Southern Baptist newspapers in 1960 exemplify the issues that Kennedy needed to address in his Houston speech.

Kennedy did not directly deny the first concern, that the Roman Catholic Church is a political-religious organization that does not believe in the separation of church and state. Rather he addressed this concern in two indirect fashions. First, he pointed out that it was a concern based on "selected quotations out of context from the statements of Catholic Church leaders, usually in other countries." He reinforced the "selectivity" of those who feared the church as a political-religious organization by reminding his audience that American bishops had, in 1948, strongly endorsed church-state separation. Again, Kennedy was putting his immediate audience on the defensive, questioning their objectivity and fairness.

Second, he clearly indicated that he strongly believed in the separation of church and state. He reiterated this belief throughout the speech. At one point he observed that "I am wholly opposed to the state being used by any religious group, Catholic or Protestant, to compel, prohibit or persecute the free exercise of any other religion." He also offered his audience evidence of largely Catholic countries where other religions flourished and had produced secular leaders. In this section of the speech he mentioned France, Ireland, "and the independence of such statesmen as de Gaulle and Adenauer." Kennedy had deliberately opened this speech by observing that he would state "not what kind of church I believe in, for that should be important only to me, but what kind of America I believe in." Though not directly addressing the fears of many audience members who perceived the Roman Catholic Church as rejecting the separation of church and state, he was responsive to those fears by suggesting that they were based on a selective reading of the statements of church leaders. Moreover, that selectivity seemed to deliberately ignore the most salient statement, that of America's Catholic bishops. And finally, he consistently indicated his strong personal belief in the sanctity of the separation of church and state.

The second concern that warranted Kennedy's attention was the fear of some audience members that the Catholic Church did not believe in religious liberty. Such fears were typically based on alleged examples of Catholic intolerance in nations such as Spain and Colombia.[69] Kennedy did not speak directly to the acts of the Catholic Church in other nations and at other times. Rather, he expressed his own beliefs and focused on religious liberty in America. He observed that he believed in an America where "no religious body seeks to impose its will directly or indirectly upon the general populace or the public acts of its officials—and where religious liberty is so indivisible that an act against one church is treated as an act against all."

Speaking in heavily Baptist Texas, Kennedy elaborated: "For while this year it may be a Catholic against whom the finger of suspicion is pointed, in other years it has been, and may someday be again, a Jew—or a Quaker—or a Unitarian—or a Baptist." Kennedy continued by noting that "It was Virginia's harassment of Baptist preachers, for example, that led to Jefferson's statute of religious freedom." Hence, he concluded, "today, I may be the victim—but tomorrow it may be you—until the whole fabric of our harmonious society is ripped apart at a time of great national peril." Kennedy kept his focus on that aspect of this concern that was likely the most salient to his large television audience, his own belief about religious liberty. In presenting his belief he attempted to establish common ground with many in his larger audience, which likely included Jews, Quakers, and Unitarians as well as Baptists. Though today it seemed as though the religious liberty of a Catholic was being violated, in the past the liberties of these religions had been attacked. Thus, Kennedy believed in an America where religious liberty was extended to all faiths.

Finally, Kennedy directly addressed the concern that a Roman Catholic president would be influenced politically by the church. In his discussion of the presidency in which he believed, Kennedy claimed that "I would not look with favor upon a President working to subvert the First Amendment's guarantee of religious liberty." He pointed to his record in Congress, citing three specific votes, to suggest that his political judgment would not be influenced by his church. Kennedy went on to claim that

> I do not speak for my church on public matters—and the church does not speak for me. Whatever issues may come before me as President, if I should be elected—on birth control, divorce, censorship, gambling, or any other subject—I will make my decision in accordance with these views [his previously stated perceptions of the presidency], in accordance with what my conscience tells me to be in the national interest and without regard to outside religious pressure or dictate.

Clearly, Kennedy was claiming that if elected his church would not exert political influence over him.

In sum, Kennedy had been dealing with this issue for years. He knew the fears of those who had sincere concerns about the election of a Roman Catholic president. In this speech he deliberately avoided being perceived as a defender of his church. Rather, he focused on defending his own personal beliefs. "For contrary to common newspaper usage, I am not the Catholic candidate for President. I am the Democratic Party's candidate for President, who happens also to be a Catholic."

Kennedy's rhetorical strategy was sound. It allowed him to avoid assuming an enormous burden of proof, that of defending church statements and policies made over centuries of time around the world. Rather, he asked to be judged as an individual, on his own record. Such an appeal was consistent with America's stress on individualism. Moreover, it facilitated his placing those who attacked the propriety of placing a Catholic in the White House in a defensive position. They seemed to be attacking his church, not him. They seemed to be basing that attack on a selective reading of the historical record. His paired statements early in the speech suggested that by focusing on Kennedy's Catholicism, his foes were guilty of the very actions they feared from a Catholic president; they were behaving as a political-religious organization, they seemed not to believe in religious liberty, they seemed to be politically influenced by their churches. Surely, Kennedy had provided his audience with sufficient substance to accept his position.

Contemporary evaluations of Kennedy's speech suggest that it helped to overcome resistance to his candidacy based upon his religion. The day after his Houston address, the National Conference of Citizens for Religious Freedom, the group whose initial concerns had caused the Kennedy organization to feel that they needed to address the religious issue yet again in the general election, issued a statement calling Kennedy's presentation "the most complete, unequivocal and reassuring statement which could be expected of any person in his position." Though the group still had reservations about whether the church hierarchy would agree with all that Kennedy stated, they were gratified by his remarks.[70] A variety of journalist accounts and informal samplings of the Texas clergy also suggested that Kennedy had helped himself with the speech.[71]

One of the clergymen in Kennedy's immediate audience, the Reverend John Turnbull, offered testimony to the effectiveness of Kennedy's strategies. He wrote

> there had been a strange feeling of tension, uncertainty, perhaps hostility in the air during the session. Doubtless it had many forms and stemmed from as many roots. . . . It was a strange kind of politico-religious event to be under the sponsorship of men who on the whole believe that religion and politics don't mix. . . . Was it really that the young senator from Massachusetts who was on trial, or was it we? . . . We could not but realize even if only somewhere in the remote recesses of our consciousness, that some deep and serious questions were being asked of us as well as of the candidate. It became increasingly clear that he was equal both intellectually and personally to whatever questions were asked of him. If we were not a very happy audience, it was perhaps because we were not sure that the same could be said of ourselves.[72]

A host of other clergymen, representing a wide variety of faiths, also reacted positively to Kennedy.[73] Press accounts of the speech stressed the tension in the room, the dramatic nature of the setting, and most important, the favorable impressions that Kennedy made on both his immediate and secondary television audiences.[74]

Perhaps especially noteworthy for their assessment of the effect on the large secondary audience that viewed the speech on television were the impressions of Texas political figures. Senator Ralph Yarborough's comments are characteristic of their reaction. Yarborough claimed that "I marveled at his intelligence. . . . He was supremely intelligent. He didn't convert all of them, but he converted enough that he won on that issue, put it to rest."[75]

Kennedy's advisers were also pleased by the speech. Sorensen claimed that "it was the turning point on the religious issue. It didn't stop the crazies but I think all of the responsible people who had reasonable questions felt that they were answered by the speech." Most Kennedy aides concurred with Sorensen's assessment.[76] Indeed, the pleasure of the Kennedy organization with this speech is perhaps best illustrated by the fact that they quickly began to circulate tapes of it.

The Kennedy organization subsequently used this speech in two ways. First, one-minute and five-minute advertising spots were cut from the tape of the complete speech. These ads were aired, primarily during the last two weeks of the campaign, where the campaign felt that anti-Catholicism was still an important issue. However, the campaign made use of the speech in yet another, more controversial fashion. They edited it into a thirty-minute tape. That tape was used heavily in the fourteen states that Sorensen's 1956 memo had identified as having a heavy Catholic urban vote that had defected from the Democratic party in 1952 and again in 1956 to vote for Eisenhower. The Kennedy organization aired their half-hour version of the speech in such heavily Catholic cities as Boston, Hartford, New York, Philadelphia, Baltimore, Pittsburgh, Chicago, and Milwaukee, as well as in states like Louisiana and New Mexico. As Kathleen Hall Jamieson has observed, the cities and states in which this tape was repeatedly aired suggest that it was being used to bring out the Catholic vote.[77] Kennedy spokespersons deny this motive, observing that communities where large numbers of Catholics reside and vote are also communities where there is often strong anti-Catholic feeling.[78]

The contemporary judgments of a wide variety of religious leaders, journalists, and political figures, as well as the behavior of the Kennedy campaign, all suggest that his speech was a success. In addition, polling data suggest that the speech was effective. Elmo Roper's polling organization found that in September 54 percent of the voters thought religion should have no importance in an election campaign. By late October, that figure had increased to 61 percent. Clearly, many factors may contribute to this shift. However, it would not be unreasonable, given the size of the shift and the publicity and exposure this speech received, to feel that the Houston address contributed to the increase in the number of people who felt that religion should have no importance in the campaign.[79]

Roper's polling also caused him to make a perhaps surprising conclusion about the religious issue as it played out in 1960:

> One thing is certain. If there was a net victim of religious prejudice it was Nixon more than Kennedy. All but one of the states most heavily populated by Catholics

went for Kennedy. Only one of the states most heavily populated by Protestants went for Nixon. This brings into sharp focus the fact that the term "religious bigot" has come to mean to liberals a White Protestant who doesn't like Catholics and Jews. Perhaps the concept, politically, can now be broadened to include anybody of *any* religious faith who votes for a coreligionist largely because he is a coreligionist.[80]

It is impossible to attribute findings such as these to one speech. But, as his definitive statement on the issue, and one which was subsequently well publicized, Kennedy's speech to the Greater Houston Ministerial Association may well have contributed to the heavy Catholic turnout for Kennedy.

The *New York Times* concurred with Roper. Reporter John Wicklein found that "a strong silent 'Protestant vote' cut into Senator John F. Kennedy's margin of victory, an analysis of election returns indicated yesterday. This was offset by a more strategically placed 'Catholic vote' which aided the Senator in large states he needed to win."[81] The *New York Times* went on to examine those states where Kennedy's religion may have hindered his efforts and those where it likely helped his efforts, and to examine the causes of Kennedy's success in 1960 compared to Al Smith's failure in 1928.

The 1960 election will be remembered for a variety of reasons. No doubt one of them will be that in a nation that was predominantly Protestant, for the first time, a Catholic was elected to the highest office the voters could bestow. Breaking that religious barrier not only opened the door for one religious minority, Catholics, but it also helped to open the door for many other minorities as they strove to take a more active role in the nation's political life. Though it is impossible to determine the precise effect of this speech, it has become a clarion call for tolerance in late twentieth century America. In a recent survey of communication scholars designed to determine the top hundred American speeches of the twentieth century, communication scholars ranked this speech higher than any other twentieth-century presidential campaign speech.[82] In the decades since it was delivered, Kennedy's "Address to the Greater Houston Ministerial Association" has transcended the immediate rhetorical situation in which it was delivered. It has become one of the most inspiring of American presidential campaign addresses.

NOTES

1. The preceding discussion of Kennedy's wartime experience and that of his brother is based on Arthur M. Schlesinger, Jr., *A Thousand Days: John F. Kennedy in the White House* (Greenwich, CT: Fawcett, 1965), pp. 79–89, and Kenneth P. O'Donnell and David F. Powers, *Johnny, We Hardly Knew Ye* (New

York: Pocket Books, 1972), pp. 47–53. Kennedy's comment about not entering politics had his brother lived can be found in O'Donnell and Powers, p. 49.

2. St. John is quoted in Joan Blair and Clay Blair, *The Search for JFK* (New York: Berkley, 1976), p. 30.

3. Ibid., p. 37.

4. See Blair and Blair, *The Search for JFK*, Chapters 2 and 3, for an account of Kennedy's pre-Harvard years.

5. Blair and Blair cite a letter from Kennedy to his father, evidently written in 1939, in which he makes reference to an impending date and calls it "my first date of a Catholic girl." He had previously dated extensively, and he had perhaps been rather serious with at least one woman who was not a Catholic. See Blair and Blair, *The Search for JFK,* pp. 68–71.

6. For an account of Kennedy's post-Harvard–pre-Navy days, see Blair and Blair, *The Search for JFK*, pp. 87–116.

7. Perhaps the best brief account of this race, which includes the comments of Tip O'Neill, is in Christopher Matthews, *Kennedy and Nixon—The Rivalry That Shaped Postwar America* (New York: Simon and Schuster, 1996), pp. 29–33. Also see O'Donnell and Powers, *Johnny, We Hardly Knew Ye,* pp. 47–81.

8. The account of Kennedy's 1952 Senate race that follows is based primarily on O'Donnell and Powers, *Johnny, We Hardly Knew Ye*, pp. 81–106; and Matthews, *Kennedy and Nixon*, pp. 76–77; 86–89.

9. On Lodge's confidence, see O'Donnell and Powers, *Johnny, We Hardly Knew Ye*, p. 102.

10. This systematic effort to gain exposure for Kennedy throughout the state was launched in 1951 and carried well into 1952. It was accomplished with considerable effort, for the travel involved took its toll on Kennedy's health. He was in frequent back pain.

11. See Matthews, *Kennedy and Nixon*, p. 87, on Lodge's vain effort to secure McCarthy's support.

12. See O'Donnell and Powers, *Johnny, We Hardly Knew Ye*, pp. 103–4.

13. Oscar Barck and Nelson Blake, *Since 1900: A History of the United States in Our Times* (New York: Macmillan, 1952), p. 429.

14. Sorensen states that in order to distance the memo from Kennedy, it was given to Connecticut Democratic state chairman John M. Bailey, who, along with others who received it, was encouraged to widely share it. Ultimately the press became aware of the memo and it was published in several magazines and newspapers. It became common knowledge when it was published under the headline "Can Catholic Vote Swing an Election?" *U.S. News and World Report,* 10 August 1956, 41–46. The remainder of this discussion and all quotes from the memo are based on the *U.S. News and World Report* version of what became widely known as the "Bailey Memo."

15. See Theodore C. Sorensen, *Kennedy* (New York: Harper and Row, 1965), pp. 82–83, for his personal reflections on the memo.

16. See Arthur Schlesinger, Jr., *A Thousand Days* (Greenwich, CT: Fawcett, 1965), p. 16.

17. Ibid., p. 16.

18. On Farley, Lawrence, and DiSalle, see O'Donnell and Powers, *Johnny, We Hardly Knew Ye*, pp. 136–37.

19. Quoted in Matthews, *Kennedy and Nixon*, p. 110.

20. Rayburn is quoted in Matthews, *Kennedy and Nixon*, p. 111. Schlesinger also quotes Rayburn, using a blank space to suggest a profanity where Matthews uses "pissant." Schlesinger adds that Rayburn felt that Congressman John McCormick of Massachusetts would be a better choice if Stevenson wished to nominate a Catholic vice president. See Schlesinger, *A Thousand Days*, p. 16.

21. Theodore White, *America in Search of Itself* (New York: Harper and Row, 1982), pp. 84–85.

22. The best account of this meeting is that found in Theodore White, *The Making of the President 1960* (New York: Pocket Books, 1961), pp. 64–69. White's account is based largely on his interviews, several months after the meeting, with Theodore Sorensen and Kenneth O'Brien. This paragraph and those that follow are based on White's account.

23. Sorensen, *Kennedy*, p. 129.

24. See White, *Making of the President 1960*, p. 47, on Symington's hopes.

25. Quoted in Sorensen, *Kennedy*, p. 129.

26. The details of the Kennedy-DiSalle negotiations discussed in the following paragraphs are drawn primarily from O'Donnell and Powers, *Johnny We Hardly Knew Ye*, pp. 170–75. Both authors participated in these meetings.

27. The following account of the Wisconsin primary is based on White, *Making of the President 1960*, pp. 93–114; Sorensen, *Kennedy*, pp. 133–38; and O'Donnell and Powers, *Johnny We Hardly Knew Ye*, 175–83.

28. O'Donnell and Powers, *Johnny We Hardly Knew Ye*, pp. 176–82.

29. Quoted in White, *Making of the President 1960*, p. 110.

30. Quoted in White, *Making of the President 1960*, p. 114.

31. Quoted in O'Donnell and Powers, *Johnny We Hardly Knew Ye*, p. 183.

32. Kennedy used the private polls of Lou Harris to a greater extent than any prior presidential candidate had ever used polls. One of the reasons that the 1960 Kennedy campaign is often perceived as the first "contemporary" campaign is Kennedy's recognition of the usefulness of polling.

33. O'Donnell and Powers, *Johnny We Hardly Knew Ye*, p. 183.

34. Ibid., pp. 183–84.

35. Ibid., p. 185.

36. Reported in Dan B. Flemming, Jr., *Kennedy vs. Humphrey, West Virginia 1960: The Pivotal Battle for the Democratic Presidential Nomination* (Jefferson, NC: McFarland, 1992), p. 37.

37. Stephen R. Goldzwig and George N. Dionisopoulos, *"In a Perilous Hour": The Public Addresses of John F. Kennedy* (Westport, CT: Greenwood Press, 1995), p. 23.

38. Quoted in Flemming, *Kennedy vs. Humphrey*, p. 33.

39. These speech excerpts can be found in Sorensen, *Kennedy*, pp. 142–43. All the elections to which Kennedy refers in this passage had taken place in the years immediately preceding this primary.

40. Hermann G. Stelzner, "Humphrey and Kennedy Court West Virginia, May 3, 1960," *Southern Speech Communication Journal* (Fall 1971): 30.

41. See Flemming, *Kennedy vs. Humphrey,* p. 47–49, for a discussion of the problems confronted by Humphrey.

42. Quoted in White, *Making of the President 1960*, p. 192.

43. For additional details on the scope of Kennedy's victory, see Sorensen, *Kennedy,* p. 146.

44. Kennedy and Sorensen worked on the text of this address during the convention. See Sorensen, *Kennedy*, pp. 166–67.

45. On the concerns of church groups with Kennedy's candidacy during this period, see Lawrence H. Fuchs, *John F. Kennedy and American Catholicism* (New York: Meredith Press, 1967), pp. 175–77; Goldzwig and Dionisopoulos, *In a Perilous Hour,* pp. 24–27; Sorensen, *Kennedy*, pp. 188–89; White, *The Making of the President 1960*, p. 311; and O'Donnell and Powers, *Johnny We Hardly Knew Ye,"* pp. 236–37.

46. Quoted in Goldzwig and Dionisopoulos, *In A Perilous Hour,* p. 25.

47. James A. Pike, *A Roman Catholic in the White House* (New York: Doubleday, 1960), pp. 132–33.

48. The Peale group statement made this clear to Kennedy and his advisers. Especially see Sorensen, *Kennedy*, p. 189. Sorensen notes that there was nothing new in any of these concerns. But the very fact that religious leaders of the prominence of Peale and other members of the Citizens for Religious Freedom, which included Billy Graham's father-in-law, among others, were expressing reservations about Kennedy's Catholicism indicated that this was not simply the concern of a small fringe group of religious bigots, but rather the concern of many Americans who warranted being reassured, yet again, by Kennedy. Also see White, *Making of the President 1960*, pp. 310–11, on the impact of the Peale group on Kennedy.

49. Nixon's campaign director, Robert Finch, recalls that Nixon "was dead serious" about not raising the religion issue. See Kathleen Hall Jamieson, *Packaging the Presidency: A History and Criticism of Presidential Campaign Advertising* (New York: Oxford University Press, 1984), p. 127.

50. Kennedy is quoted in O'Donnell and Powers, *Johnny We Hardly Knew Ye*, p. 236.

51. Perhaps the most complete account of Kennedy's campaigning earlier in the day can be found in Susan Dewine, "John Fitzgerald Kennedy Speaks on Catholicism September 12, 1960" (Unpublished M.A. thesis, Miami [Ohio] University, 1967).

52. See Dewine, "Kennedy Speaks on Catholicism," p. 105. Dewine cites *Time*, 26 Sept. 1960, p. 21, for the Kennedy-Salinger exchange. Ted Sorensen re-

ports the same exchange in his video *Ted Sorensen on Speechwriting*, Educational Video Group, 1995.

53. See James Wine's statement in Gerald S. Strober and Deborah H. Strober, *"Let Us Begin Anew": An Oral History of the Kennedy Presidency* (New York: HarperCollins, 1993), p. 44.

54. The best description of the physical setting is that found in Dewine, "Kennedy Speaks on Catholicism," p. 109. In addition to contemporary accounts, Dewine bases her description on her correspondence with officials of the Rice Hotel.

55. Sorensen's recollections about the preparation of this speech can be found both in Sorensen, *Ted Sorensen on Speechwriting,* and in his *Kennedy,* p. 189.

56. Sorensen, *Kennedy*, p. 189.

57. Otten is quoted in James Grant Powell, "An Analytical and Comparative Study of the Persuasion of Kennedy and Nixon in the 1960 Campaign," Unpublished Ph.D. diss., Univ. of Wisconsin, 1963, p. 203. Many have commented on the Kennedy-Sorensen relationship. See, for example, Schlesinger, *A Thousand Days*, pp. 16, 72; and Goldzwig and Dionisopoulos, *In a Perilous Hour,* pp. 9–10.

58. Sorensen, *Ted Sorensen on Speechwriting.*

59. Fuchs, *Kennedy and American Catholicism*, p. 179.

60. Sorensen, *Kennedy*, p. 190.

61. Ibid.

62. This and all subsequent quotations from Kennedy's speech are from Aaron Singer, ed., *Campaign Speeches of American Presidential Candidates, 1928–1972* (New York: Frederick Unger, 1976), pp. 303–7.

63. Sorensen, *Kennedy*, p. 191.

64. Powell, "An Analytical and Comparative Study," p. 428.

65. Ibid., p. 655. Powell studied thirteen of Kennedy's major 1960 campaign speeches. This was one of only two speeches in which Kennedy adhered faithfully to his text.

66. In making this observation, which is based on the claims of Sorensen, *Kennedy*, p. 191, and O'Donnell and Powers, *Johnny, We Hardly Knew Ye,* p. 240, and Kennedy TV adviser Leonard Reinsch, who is quoted in Jamieson, *Packaging the Presidency*, p. 133, it should be observed that the impressions of the ministers are not readily available. Certainly Kennedy's aides, such as these four, felt he answered the questions effectively.

67. Beryl McClerren, "Southern Baptists and the Religious Issue During the Presidential Campaigns of 1928 and 1960," *Central State Speech Journal* (May 1967): 103–12.

68. See McClerren, "Southern Baptists and the Religious Issue," pp. 106–9, on these three primary concerns of Southern Baptists and presumably others who feared a Roman Catholic president.

69. Ibid., pp. 108–9.

70. The statement of the National Conference of Citizens for Religious Freedom, or the "Peale Group," is quoted in Harold Barrett, "John F. Kennedy Before

the Greater Houston Ministerial Association," *Central States Speech Journal* (November 1964): 265.

71. See Barrett, "Kennedy Before the Greater Houston Ministerial Association," pp. 265–66, for a sampling of opinion from both clergymen and journalists.

72. John W. Turnbull, "The Clergy Faces Mr. Kennedy," *The Reporter*, 23 Oct. 1960, pp. 33–34.

73. For examples, see Fuchs, *Kennedy and American Catholicism*, p. 182.

74. For a survey of press reaction, see Powell, "An Analytical and Comparative Study," pp. 722–25.

75. Yarborough is quoted in Strober and Strober, *Let Us Begin Anew*, p. 44. Lyndon Johnson aides Jack Valenti and Bobby Baker and Speaker Sam Rayburn were all equally impressed. Rayburn told one associate, "As we say in my part of Texas, 'he ate 'em blood raw.' " See also Strober and Strober, pp. 45–46, and Sorensen, pp. 192–93.

76. For examples, see O'Donnell and Powers, *Johnny, We Hardly Knew Ye*, pp. 240–241 and Schlesinger, *A Thousand Days*, p. 78.

77. This paragraph is based on Jamieson, *Packaging the Presidency*, pp. 134–35.

78. Sorensen maintains this was the motive for running the speech tape in those areas where there were a large number of Catholic voters. See Jamieson, *Packaging the Presidency*, pp. 135–36.

79. Elmo Roper, "Polling Post-Mortem," *Saturday Review*, 26 Nov. 1960, p. 11.

80. Ibid., pp. 11–12.

81. John Wicklein, "Protestant and Catholic Votes Found to Offset Each Other In Kennedy's Victory," *New York Times*, 11 Nov. 1960, p. 23.

82. Martin Medhurst and Stephen Lucas, "Top 100 American Speeches of the Twentieth Century," paper delivered at the National Communication Association Annual Meetings, Seattle, WA, November 2000. The entire list can be found at www.news.wisc.edu/misc/speeches/.

Chapter Two

1964—Barry Goldwater

> I would remind you that extremism in the defense of liberty is no vice. And let me remind you also that moderation in the pursuit of justice is no virtue.

It is likely that the key event of the 1964 presidential election took place on 22 November 1963. The assassination of President John F. Kennedy totally upset the political circumstances that the supporters of Barry Goldwater had anticipated could result in his winning the presidency in 1964. The Goldwater candidacy was based, in large part, on the belief that a sharp philosophical clash between a liberal Democrat, such as Kennedy, and a conservative Republican, such as Goldwater, would work to the advantage of Goldwater. In sharp contrast to most candidates, who often run to the left or right in order to secure their party nomination and then move to the center for the general election, Barry Goldwater ran to the right to secure his party nomination and then, from his acceptance address forward, remained on the right. Goldwater hoped to move the nation to his conservative positions. He would not compromise nor move to the center in an effort to win the election.

Ultimately, history may record that his uncompromising stand made him the most influential defeated presidential candidate in the last half of the twentieth century. In the wake of Lyndon Johnson's landslide victory over Goldwater, many observers felt that the Arizona senator had badly crippled the Republican party. Yet within a decade, astute observers of the American political scene, such as Kevin Phillips and James Sundquist, were suggesting that the Goldwater debacle of 1964 might well be remembered as a realigning campaign.[1]

That judgment seems to have been borne out. Prior to Goldwater, the Democratic party base was in the South. Today, the South is considered part of the Republican base. Prior to Goldwater, Republican presidential candidates received upwards of a third of the black vote. Today, there is virtually no voter bloc that is more consistently supportive of Democrats on the national level than blacks.[2] The contemporary American political landscape is very different from that of the 1960s. Barry Goldwater's 1964 campaign seems to have set into motion many of the changes that followed.

THE SPEAKER

Barry Goldwater was born on 1 January 1909 in Phoenix, Arizona. He was raised in Phoenix, which still maintained a frontier flavor when Goldwater was a youth. Indeed, one of his earliest memories was of the celebration of Arizona's statehood.[3] Goldwater was the eldest son of a third-generation pioneer family. His grandfather had founded what was to become one of the leading department stores in Arizona. As a youth, Goldwater developed hobbies that stayed with him throughout his life. At the age of eleven, he owned one of the earliest radios in Arizona. He subsequently developed a serious interest in the history and customs of Arizona's Indians, became an outstanding photographer specializing in western landscapes, and in 1930 learned to fly. Goldwater was never an outstanding student, but during his years at Staunton Military Academy in Virginia, he became a student leader and excelled on the athletic field.

Goldwater's father, Baron, with whom Barry was never very close, had expanded the family business dramatically. In 1929, with the death of his father and the onset of the Great Depression, Goldwater left the University of Arizona after his first year to work in the family business. At the age of twenty Goldwater started at the bottom and worked in virtually every department of the family store. In 1934, after a courtship during which they were frequently separated by long distances, Goldwater married Margaret (Peggy) Johnson, daughter of a vice president of the Borg-Warner Company.

In 1937 Goldwater was named president of the family firm. He was an excellent merchandiser, and the stores grew under his leadership. One of his more curious business successes came when he designed and marketed men's boxer undershorts with an all-over pattern of red ants. "Antsy Pants" became a national fad. As his business prospered, Goldwater grew interested in civic affairs. Goldwater's interest in politics was first stimulated by his uncle Morris Goldwater, a founder of the Arizona Democratic party and the mayor of Prescott.

Goldwater began to read political theorists, including Locke, Burke, Jefferson, and Madison. With the outbreak of World War II, Goldwater sought to serve as a combat flyer. Old athletic injuries and poor vision prevented him from qualifying for such a position, though he enlisted the aid of both Arizona senators, Carl Hayden and Ernest McFarland, in his efforts to fly in combat. However, he was found suitable to ferry planes into combat theaters. He flew planes over the famous "hump" of the Himalayas for use in the Pacific theater and piloted fighter planes across the Atlantic for use in the European theater. He also served as a gunnery instructor, and by the end of the war he had risen from first lieutenant to the rank of lieutenant colonel.

The Emergence of a Conservative Spokesperson

With the end of the war, Goldwater turned his attention to the family business and became more involved in local Republican politics in Phoenix, serving on the Phoenix city council and managing the successful gubernatorial campaign of his friend Howard Pyle. In 1952 he ran for the U.S. Senate. Benefiting no doubt from the coattails of Dwight Eisenhower, he defeated the Senate majority leader, Ernest McFarland. Though an early admirer of Eisenhower, Goldwater soon began to question the new president's policies.

With the death of Ohio senator Robert Taft, Goldwater gradually began to fill the vacuum in conservative leadership. By 1957 he had sharply criticized the Eisenhower administration's spending levels. As Goldwater gradually distinguished himself from more moderate Republicans, his admirers grew. They perceived him as the one individual in public life who based his policy positions on his moral beliefs and would not compromise them for political expediency. In 1958 Goldwater decisively won reelection, this time without help from Eisenhower. Moreover, he became chairman of the Republican Senatorial Campaign Committee. This latter position put him in contact with major contributors, allowed him to travel throughout the country, and won him the praise and appreciation of countless Republicans.

Goldwater's speaking had constantly improved during the 1950s. In 1959, Washington lawyer and Goldwater friend Mike Bernstein encouraged and helped Goldwater to develop a stock speech summarizing his conservative beliefs. Goldwater's statement of conservative principles, which he called "The Forgotten America," was so well received by so many audiences that soon the senator's office was flooded with requests for copies.

In November 1959, Goldwater delivered a major address to the Western Republican Conference, held in Los Angeles. Goldwater, speaking after New York governor Nelson Rockefeller, took dead aim at the liberal New York governor and potential presidential candidate, claiming that

> for the past twenty-five years the apostles of the welfare state . . . have been busy transforming that stern old gentleman with the top hat, the cutaway coat, the red, white and blue trousers, from a symbol of dignity and freedom and justice for all men, into a national wet nurse, dispensing a cockeyed kind of patent medicine labeled "something for nothing," passing out the soothing syrup and rattles and pacifiers in return for grateful votes on election day.[4]

Goldwater went on to claim that he would like to see a Republican party committed to a free state, limited central power, a reduction in bureaucracy, and a balanced budget. Goldwater received a standing ovation from his audience.

Largely as a result of the exposure he received from this speech, the editors of the *Los Angeles Times* offered the Arizonan the opportunity to write a thrice-weekly column for their paper. Goldwater accepted. The *Los Angeles Times* quickly announced that they were about to introduce a column by Goldwater, "the leading conservative thinker in American public life."[5] Though the *Times* had its own self-interest at heart in such a description, they were not far from the truth. More and more, Goldwater was filling the vacuum left by the death of Robert Taft. After three months, the *Times* syndicated the column, and within a year it was appearing in 140 papers.

Goldwater's growing recognition as the preeminent spokesperson for conservatism caused another friend, Dean Clarence Manion of Notre Dame, to suggest that he write a book. Manion arranged for a small Kentucky firm, Victor Publishing Company, to print 10,000 copies. Working with ghostwriter Brent Bozell, Goldwater finished his book in about three months. "All I hoped to accomplish," he claimed, "was to awaken the American people to a realization of how far we had moved from the old constitutional concepts to the new welfare state."[6] Goldwater's *Conscience of a Conservative* was a national bestseller that went through eleven printings in the first year and ultimately sold 3.5 million copies.[7] Thus, by 1960, Senator Barry Goldwater was not only among the highest-ranking conservatives holding public office, but his speeches, newspaper column, and book had made him the preeminent advocate of a conservative philosophy of government.

Goldwater and the 1960 Republican Convention

Goldwater's stature as the leading Republican conservative was solidified at the 1960 Republican convention. As the platform committee of the Republican party labored to produce a party platform for Richard Nixon to run on, Nixon secretly met New York governor Nelson Rockefeller to discuss a variety of issues. What resulted soon became called the "Fourteen-Point Compact of Fifth Avenue." In effect, Rockefeller wrote the Republican platform on which Nixon would run. Clearly Nixon was seeking to unify a potentially divided party. But his effort to appease liberal Republicans like Rockefeller dismayed not only conservatives like Goldwater, but many other Republicans. In effect the Compact of Fifth Avenue was replacing the Republican platform, over which 103 delegates, headed by Illinois businessman Charles Percy, had labored intensively on and off throughout 1959 and early 1960. Percy, then president of Bell and Howell and soon to be elected to the Senate from Illinois, had been handpicked by Nixon to craft a platform for modern Republicans in the post-Eisenhower era. All of the platform committee's work seemed to be undone by the Compact of Fifth Avenue, which seemed to question the Eisenhower administration's national defense effort, particularly in the area of missile technology. The compact called for a substantial increase in government spending on defense, regardless of cost. Moreover, it called for massive increases in government spending on social welfare programs, particularly medical care for the aged, and aid to education. The compact favored much more government intervention into American life than did the Percy platform, or Eisenhower's policies.

Conservatives and party regulars were dismayed by the apparently high-handed manner in which Rockefeller and Nixon wished to circumvent the labor of the platform committee, as well as by a variety of provisions in the compact. Party regulars particularly resented portions of the compact that seemed to repudiate Eisenhower's management of national defense, in the wake of Russia's Sputnik launchings. Goldwater characterized the compact as "a surrender," the "Munich of the Republican Party," and the guarantee of "Republican defeat in November."[8]

Conservatives responded to Nixon's appeasement of the liberal wing of the party, in part, by offering Goldwater's name in nomination. They did so without the support of the Arizona senator. Governor Paul Fanning of Arizona gave the principal nominating speech and observed that

> the action I shall take here tonight is directly contrary to the wishes of a man who has been my friend since childhood. All of you know, at ten o'clock this morning the man whose name I shall place in nomination specifically recommended against

such action. In any other situation I would feel compelled to accept this decision without question, but his is not an ordinary situation. The Arizona delegation, after careful deliberation, was unanimous in its insistence that I carry out this responsibility.

Goldwater used the opportunity to withdraw his name from nomination to challenge his conservative supporters. In effect, his speech was the first of his campaign for the 1964 Republican nomination.

"We have lost election after election in this country in the last several years," claimed the Arizona senator, "because conservative Republicans got mad and stayed home." He called on conservatives to unite behind the Republican ticket, denouncing the Democratic party as one that had little faith in capitalism and little faith in the dignity of man and believed that the United States was a second-rate power. After claiming that he would make every effort to secure the election of Republicans from the top of the ticket to the bottom, Goldwater challenged conservatives. "Let's grow up, conservatives. Let's, if we want to take this party back—and I think we can some day—let's get to work."[9]

Goldwater was as good as his word. He spoke for Nixon throughout the campaign. He spoke for a host of Republican senatorial candidates. By early 1961, with Nixon defeated and Kennedy, the epitome of the liberal eastern establishment, in the White House, Goldwater was fast becoming the leading Republican in the country. By mid-1961 a *Time* poll of 1960 Republican convention delegates found that 49 percent favored Goldwater as their candidate in 1964. The combined Nixon and Rockefeller supporters numbered 44 percent.[10]

Will He or Won't He? The Decision to Run

Goldwater was perceived as the straight shooter. To his admirers, he was the down-to-earth westerner who disliked pomposity and evasiveness, so often found in political leaders. But to his detractors, he had a tendency to shoot from the hip. They derided what they perceived to be his careless and regrettable remarks, made, they claimed, without thinking them through. His uncompromising stands exhibited an inflexibility that won enemies as well as friends.

As Republicans began to look over the field of potential candidates for 1964, each was measured against President John F. Kennedy. At a time when American politics was becoming more and more a battle of image and charisma projected on television, Goldwater seemed well positioned to challenge Kennedy. By 1964 he would be a young-looking fifty-five years old. Tall and tan, with a rugged western look, wearing dark horn-rimmed glasses and with wavy gray-white hair, Goldwater might not have the movie-start handsomeness of Kennedy, but he surely looked like an actor Hollywood might cast as an American president. If Kennedy was identified with PT 109 and the navy, Goldwater was a general in the Air Force Reserve and an active jet plane pilot. If Kennedy was a Harvard scholar who wrote a best-selling popular history, Goldwater was a self-educated scholar who wrote best-selling political theory. But, if his image and charisma made Goldwater an attractive candidate, Goldwater's uncompromising conservatism scared off major elements of his own party. His road to the nomination was fraught with obstacles.

On 8 October 1961, twenty-two men met in a Chicago hotel. F. Clifton White, a skilled New York political operative, chaired their meeting. Most were veterans of local political campaigns who had been active in the Young Republican organizations of their states. The group agreed to attempt to recast the Republican party into a more conservative party. Though the group did not explicitly commit itself to a draft-Goldwater movement, it agreed to seriously consider how to turn the Republican party to the right, and to meet again in December.

A month later, on 17 November, Clif White and another member of the group, Charlie Throne, met with Goldwater. Throne had become friends with Goldwater during Throne's years as national president of the Young Republicans and as chairman of the Nebraska Republican party. They shared their hope that the Republican party could become more conservative and shared the aspirations of the group of twenty-two that had met earlier with Goldwater. White explicitly told Goldwater "that he had not formed the group to work for his candidacy, nor for the candidacy of any other individual." White and Throne went on to indicate to Goldwater that they believed no decisions should be made about potential candidates until after the 1962 elections. Rather, they wanted to find and encourage conservatives to take a more active role in the local, state, and national Republican party organizations. In effect, White and Throne were telling Goldwater that they were accepting the challenge he had issued to conservatives in the 1960 convention. They were working to secure control of the Republican party.

Goldwater responded favorably. "This is the best thing I've heard of since I became active in the Republican Party on the national scene. I wish you fellows a lot of luck," responded Goldwater, who also offered to do whatever he could. Goldwater agreed to White's request that he share his speaking itinerary for the next few months so that they might encourage key people in the areas Goldwater was visiting to contact him, and so that he might indicate people in those areas who he felt would also be sympathetic to moving the party to the right.[11]

As Goldwater spoke throughout the nation, White's group gradually began to recruit conservative activists to the Republican party. White headed the effort, operating out of Office Suite 3505 of the Chanin Building in New York. Since this attempt to build a national conservative movement had no name, its members simply referred to it as the 3505 project. Throughout 1962 White traveled the country, establishing relationships with local political operatives, lining up support from such groups as the Young Republicans and the National Federation of Republican Women, and learning about the delegate selection procedures.[12]

White's actions should be recalled in light of Republican party politics of this period. Like the Democrats, most Republican convention delegates who would serve in 1964 would be selected by local and state party organizations. The sixteen states that used primaries to select delegates to the 1964 Republican convention selected only 541 of the 1,308 delegates.

In December 1962, shortly after the November elections, the 3505 project again met in Chicago. However, on this occasion the press became aware of the meeting. Liberal Republicans were upset to learn that the conservative wing of their party was working to shift the basic nature of the party. Goldwater was equally upset at the exposure of the 3505 project. Press speculation centered on the project as a draft-Goldwater movement. The Arizona senator claimed that though he was aware of the group's efforts to build the conservative movement and help local conservative candidates, it was not working on his behalf. Moreover, he announced that he was not a presidential candidate and was opposed to any movement that sought to draft him.[13]

Nevertheless, three months later, on 8 April 1963, the 3505 project leaders, now fortified with such major party figures as Texas Republican party chairman Peter O'Donnell, U.S. Senators Carl Curtis of Nebraska and John Tower of Texas, and a growing number of congressmen, led by John Rhodes of Arizona, decided to gamble that Goldwater would eventually agree to become a candidate and announced a draft-Goldwater campaign without his consent. White, O'Donnell, and Goldwater's growing number of supporters perceived themselves to be taking an enormous chance, for if Goldwater chose to repudiate them at this date, it would be difficult for him to successfully launch a campaign later. Leaders of the draft-Goldwater movement waited anxiously throughout the day as the press attempted to get Goldwater's response to their morning announcement. The first response came from Goldwater's senate office, which refused comment. Goldwater was finally located at a reception being hosted by the District of Columbia

Republican Committee. Asked about the draft movement, he responded "I am not taking any position on this draft movement. It's their time and their money. But they are going to have to get along without any help from me."[14] The draft movement had what it needed. Though Goldwater avoided association with the movement, he did not repudiate it.[15]

Goldwater was not being coy. Rather, he had serious reservations about a run for the presidency. Later he recalled that

> my reluctance to seek the Republican nomination for the office of President in 1964 was, in part, purely personal. My life-style is casual, informal, spontaneous. The possibility of being a prisoner in the White House, my every move attended by the Secret Service, surrounded by a corps of sycophantic advisers, with every move I made, every word I spoke, interpreted and analyzed by the national press, was repulsive to me. Even though I had been in the public eye for twelve years, I fiercely resisted the thought of surrendering all my privacy to the job.[16]

Goldwater also observed that "There were other considerations." Among them, he recognized the difficulty in being elected and the difficulty he would face in dealing with government bureaucracies if he was elected. Moreover, he recognized that he would likely be sharply limited by a Democratic congress.[17]

Goldwater's advocates felt that he could win the Republican nomination, and the general election against Kennedy, by building a base of southern and western voters. Added to this base, they anticipated strong support from traditionally conservative midwestern Republican states such as Ohio and Indiana. This so-called "southern strategy" reflected the growing strength of the Republican party in the South during the early 1960s. Southern voters were responding to the Republicans, who were fielding more and better able candidates in the south than ever before. The influx of northerners and midwesterners with Republican sympathies into states like Texas, Virginia, and Florida were making such states more competitive for Republicans. The Republican defense of lower taxes and less government also resonated well in the New South. At the same time, underlying the southern strategy was what David Reinhard has called "the specter of racism." Republicans accurately pointed out that support for their party was concentrated in the fast-emerging progressive urban and suburban areas of the south, and that it was the Democratic rural areas where racism was strongest. Nevertheless, much of the newfound conservative Republican appeal in the south was based on the party's rejection of a large federal government and endorsement of states' rights. Though Republicans like Goldwater had consistently voted for civil rights prior to 1964, and had personally been leaders in the integration of their communities, their political philosophy allowed individual states to continue to discriminate and to interfere with federal efforts to end discrimination.[19]

Moreover, Goldwater's advocates felt that his potential competitors for the nomination were politically weak. Nixon's loss of the governorship of his home state had effectively weakened him. In November 1961 Governor Rockefeller announced his separation and probably divorce from his wife of thirty years and the mother of his five children. This situation was made more awkward by his wife Mary's decision to contest the divorce. When the Rockefeller divorce was final, the governor quickly married Margaretta, "Happy" Murphy, who had herself been divorced only a month earlier and was the mother of four young children. In 1963 these actions were serious political liabilities. Indeed, after Rockefeller's remarriage, his standing in public opinion polls dropped sharply. Thus, perhaps the two most formidable foes that Goldwater faced were both politically flawed. As liberal Republicans scrambled for potential candidates, those who were mentioned—such as Michigan governor George Romney and Pennsylvania governor William Scranton—were new to the national political scene and relatively unknown.[20] Thus, the draft-Goldwater forces were confident that if they could persuade the Arizona senator to join the race, he could be the party nominee.

With Goldwater not having rejected a possible candidacy, the draft-Goldwater movement increased it efforts. The pressure on Goldwater mounted as public opinion polls showed he and Rockefeller to be the party's two favorite candidates. Throughout 1963 Goldwater's popularity increased. The sharp ideological differences between the two men put Goldwater under increasing pressure from his fellow conservatives.

As 1963 progressed, a general election victory appeared feasible. Goldwater's second major bestseller, *Why Not Victory*, published in 1962, had served to illustrate his foreign policy differences with liberals. Kennedy's alleged failures to deal properly with Cuba and the Bay of Pigs fiasco, the brinkmanship of the Cuban missile crisis, and the apparent continued triumph of communism in other parts of the world, seemed to make Kennedy vulnerable. Moreover, Goldwater's ability to win the South and West would offset much of Kennedy's strength in the Northeast, perhaps making the real battleground states those of the traditionally Republican Midwest. In 1960, Kennedy's margin of victory—even in the midwestern states he won, such as Illinois—was often small.[21]

Then, on 22 November 1963, the news came from Dallas. Kennedy was dead. Goldwater immediately asked the draft-Goldwater movement to suspend its activities. The classic liberal versus conservative battle that

Goldwater wanted to make would not be. Goldwater accurately sensed that against him, Lyndon Johnson might prove to be a far more formidable candidate than Kennedy. Not only would Johnson be better able to hold the south, always at the heart of Goldwater's strategy, but he would be the recipient of the nation's sympathy and feelings for the slain Kennedy. Goldwater confided to his wife Peggy that he did not feel Johnson could be defeated.[22]

Moreover, Goldwater was genuinely depressed by the Kennedy killing. Goldwater characterized his personal relations with the president as "warm and friendly."[23] All Goldwater's close advisers during this period concur in their belief that Goldwater was changed by the Kennedy death. "There is an element of truth in the claim that Oswald's bullet struck down both the champion and the challenger," wrote Stephen Shadegg in summarizing Goldwater's reaction to Kennedy's death. Goldwater, Shadegg, continued, "was never quite the same. The Senator's heretofore unfailing good humor vanished."[24]

By 1963, Kennedy and Goldwater had spoken of campaigning against one another. Goldwater knew that beating an incumbent would be difficult, but in Kennedy, he felt he would meet an opponent who would keep the level of political debate high. The two had discussed joint appearances, such as those between Kennedy and Nixon in 1960. In sum, Kennedy's death deprived Goldwater of an opponent whom he perceived as offering the opportunity to conduct a national dialogue on major questions. With Kennedy, Goldwater felt that conservatism and liberalism would both get a fair hearing and the public would be well served.[25]

In contrast, Goldwater had served in the Senate while Johnson had been the majority leader. He respected Johnson for his efficiency, but according to one Goldwater intimate, "he despised the Johnson methods."[26] He perceived Johnson as devious, ponderous, dull, and lacking in principled beliefs.[27] Goldwater did not perceive a campaign against Johnson as one that would involve the clash of ideas that might take place had he been running against Kennedy.

Goldwater's initial reaction to Johnson's ascendancy to the presidency was to close down the draft-Goldwater movement and to end any speculation about his possible candidacy, but Goldwater's supporters would not give up. On 8 December Goldwater met with a group of friends and advisers. Though others argued that Kennedy's death had not changed the issues, it was New Hampshire senator Cotton Norris who made the most effective argument. Norris appealed to Goldwater's sense of duty. Norris claimed that Goldwater had a responsibility to the conservative movement and to the nation to run. His supporters, Norris indicated, had built an organization in state after state. His popularity was high and his supporters awaited only the word from him. In effect, Norris was arguing that Goldwater had allowed the draft movement to go too far to reject it.[28] As he listened to Norris and the others, Goldwater must have sensed that he could not turn his back on the efforts his supporters had made over the previous years and then expect them to rally to him in the future. Their disappointment and bitterness would no doubt diminish their future enthusiasm in a Goldwater campaign. Like it or not, if Goldwater ever expected to command the respect and admiration that he commanded at the end of 1963, he had to run in 1964.

On 3 January 1964, at his Phoenix home, Senator Barry M. Goldwater announced that he would be a candidate for the presidency. Using a phrase that would soon be heard throughout the nation, he claimed, "I will not change my beliefs to win votes. I will offer a choice, not an echo."[29]

Winning the Republican Nomination

Once he declared his candidacy, Goldwater and his organization went to work securing his nomination. The initial strategy of the draft-Goldwater organization was to use the conservative network to encourage conservatives sympathetic to Goldwater to seek low-visibility positions in the precinct, county, and state organizations. It was these groups that would select the convention delegates in over two-thirds of the states. Conservative activists were the most committed of the Republican party workers in 1964, and the organization headed by White, with six regional directors was successful in mobilizing local Goldwater supporters for precinct meetings and caucuses in state after state. In the typical state, these individuals elected representatives to congressional district conventions, who in turn elected representatives to statewide conventions, who in turn selected the state's delegation. White's organization had prepared well. They had planned and worked earlier and harder than virtually any candidate organization in Republican party history. As 1964 progressed, in state after state, working from the precinct level upward, delegations favorable to Goldwater were selected.[30]

Goldwater's organization dramatically altered the Republican party's way of financing campaigns as well. In 1952, 88 percent of Eisenhower's finances had come in large donations over $500. In 1964, Goldwater raised only 28 percent of his finances with large donations over $500. In contrast, he received contributions of $100 or less from 650,000 contributors. Never had a Republican candidate had such a broad contributor base. At the same time, while earlier Republican candidates had drawn most of their financial support from the East and secondarily from the Midwest, Goldwater drew on the new wealth of the Southwest, raising money in Houston, Dallas, Denver, Phoenix, and Los Angeles.

As the Goldwater organization went to work in the nonprimary states, Goldwater campaigned in the primary states. In New Hampshire, the nation's first primary, Goldwater was defeated by a write-in effort on behalf of Henry Cabot Lodge, then serving as the Johnson administration's ambassador to South Vietnam, and narrowly defeated Rockefeller. Lodge finished with 35 percent of the vote, Goldwater finished with 23 percent of the vote, and Rockefeller finished with 20 percent. A write-in effort on behalf of Richard Nixon won 16 percent of the vote for him.

Goldwater's difficulty in New Hampshire came from what critics called his "shooting from the hip." Goldwater gave few prepared speeches in New Hampshire. Rather, he responded to audience questions and talked about any issues raised by his audiences. He was roundly criticized for a variety of remarks. Most significant among them was his call to make Social Security voluntary, which the press interpreted as a move to end the program. He also supported existing policy that under some circumstances NATO commanders might be given control of nuclear weapons. The press interpreted this as granting a large number of NATO field commanders the authority to use nuclear weapons. He suggested that American missiles were not totally dependable. He indicated that it might be time for the government to sell the Tennessee Valley Authority.[31]

When a candidate such as Goldwater loses to an undeclared write-in such as Lodge in the nation's first primary, it might be the kiss of death. But though Goldwater lost in New Hampshire, his campaign was doing fine. Before the New Hampshire primary, both the Oklahoma and North Carolina Republican state conventions had given the Arizonan their entire delegations. The diligent work of White and others was paying dividends.

After New Hampshire, Goldwater altered his campaign style. He relied more on prepared speeches and avoided question-and-answer formats. He began to circumvent the press and speak directly to the people with radio and television advertisements. The changes worked. With token opposition, he took 64 percent of the vote in the Illinois primary. He won in Nebraska, South Carolina, Kansas, Nevada, Oklahoma, Wyoming, and Washington. As Goldwater won primaries in these states, his organization was scoring victories elsewhere. In Wisconsin, North Dakota, Kentucky, Arizona, and Louisiana, delegates pledged to Goldwater were elected.

By May, the Goldwater forces were on the verge of control. The senator had won decisive primary victories in Texas, which sent 56 delegates to the convention, and had picked up another 50 votes in the state conventions of Tennessee, Maine, and Georgia. By the end of May, Goldwater's chief delegate counter, Clif White, estimated that Goldwater had in excess of 400 of the 655 votes necessary for nomination. White had consistently estimated low, giving every benefit of the doubt to Goldwater's foes.[32]

As Goldwater approached nomination, his foes could not unify. Rockefeller had challenged Goldwater in some states but pulled out in others. A variety of favorite sons, some of whom might well prove favorable to Goldwater, had tied up other blocks of votes. While Pennsylvania's delegation was committed to their governor, William Scranton, who would challenge Goldwater in the convention, other favorite-son delegations were sympathetic to Goldwater. Ohio's delegation was pledged to Governor James Rhodes. Michigan, where Goldwater's organization had secured 8 delegates, was committed to its favorite son, Governor George Romney. In both states, the Goldwater forces had reason to believe that when the favorite sons released their delegates, Goldwater would be the big beneficiary.

As the 2 June California primary approached, it was clear that Goldwater was approaching the nomination. A sweep of the 86 votes from California and the bandwagon that might generate would likely carry Goldwater to the nomination. The California primary would be a contest between Goldwater and Rockefeller. The New Yorker had defeated both Lodge and Nixon in Oregon, where Goldwater had removed himself from the ballot early. Rockefeller's victory had effectively eliminated Lodge and Nixon and caused the liberal wing of the party to unify behind him.

The California primary became a battle between Goldwater's superior organization and Rockefeller's spending on television and radio advertising. Goldwater's organization mounted a massive get-out-the-vote effort and a direct-mail effort to supplement the senator's campaigning. In Los Angeles county alone, the Goldwater forces had 9,500 volunteers working to get out the vote on election day. In other Republican strongholds, their numbers were equally impressive. In Orange County and in the San Diego area, 10,000 Goldwater volunteers worked on election day. In the Republican strongholds of northern California 5,000 Goldwater volunteers were at work on election day. Goldwater won with 51.4 percent of the vote to Rockefeller's 48.6 percent. The difference was less than 60,000 votes among more than 2,100,000 cast. One of the campaign imponderables was the impact of the birth of Nelson Rockefeller, Jr., on the Saturday before the election. That birth raised the old issue of the governor's divorce and remarriage, largely forgotten for months.[33]

Scarcely noticed in the wake of the California primary was that on the day of the California victory, Goldwater picked up an additional 29 votes in state conventions. With those votes, the private vote tallies of the Goldwater forces showed their candidate with 665 total votes, ten more than needed for nomination.

Four days after Rockefeller was defeated in California, and as liberal Republicans scrambled to find an alternative to Goldwater, Pennsylvania governor William Scranton met with the one Republican who he felt could most help turn the tide against Goldwater, former president Dwight David Eisenhower. In a brief press conference after the meeting, Scranton announced that Eisenhower had requested that Scranton "make himself more available" for the nomination.[34] Scranton was scheduled to attend the National Governor's Conference the next day. The press speculated that he would use the Governor's Conference as a forum to announce his candidacy.

Scranton had come close to announcing his candidacy in 1963, but he declined to do so, largely because he felt that even if he had won the Republican nomination, his one term as a congressman and his year-and-a-half tenure as governor of Pennsylvania would not enable him to compete effectively against an incumbent president. But Kennedy's death changed the equation for him, as it did for others.

With Rockefeller's defeat, Scranton saw himself as the champion of the liberal wing of the party. Moreover, if he could secure the nomination, he might well win a general election against a relatively conservative southerner. Though Goldwater relished a race against Kennedy, Scranton found the prospect of confronting Johnson more appealing.

When Scranton arrived in Cleveland for the Governor's Conference, there was a message to call Eisenhower. Over the phone, the former president made it clear that if he had conveyed the impression that he would support Scranton in a last-minute struggle against Goldwater, this was not the case. Eisenhower apologized to Scranton if he had inadvertently misled him the previous day, but he made it clear that he would not be involved in any last minute "cabal" to stop Goldwater.[35]

Nevertheless, Scranton remained the most viable liberal alternative to Goldwater, who already in fact seemed to have sewn up the nomination. Scranton delayed announcing at the Governor's Conference, making a final unsuccessful attempt to gain Eisenhower's support. Without Eisenhower's backing, on 11 June he traveled to Baltimore to address the Maryland State Republican Convention. Here he announced his candidacy, claiming that "I have come here to offer our party a real choice. I reject the echo we have thus far been handed—the echo of fear and of reaction—the echo from the never-never land that puts our nation on the road backward to a lesser place in the world of free men."[36] As Scranton was announcing, the Associated Press was reporting that Goldwater had in excess of 600 of the 655 delegates necessary for nomination.[37] For the next five weeks Scranton campaigned among Republicans, utilizing two themes to attack Goldwater. Scranton argued first that Goldwater was too dangerous to trust with control of our nuclear arsenal. Second, he claimed that Goldwater would be so badly defeated by Johnson that other Republicans would also be defeated.

Scranton's pleas were largely ignored. He spoke to the uncommitted neighboring state delegation from New Jersey, hoping to secure the support of at least a portion of that large delegation. After his address, the New Jersey delegates voted to remain uncommitted and make their final decision in San Francisco. Their decision virtually guaranteed that more than half of New Jersey's 40 votes would be cast for Goldwater, whose organization had helped elect them to the state delegation. Scranton addressed the Republican State Convention in yet another neighboring state, Delaware. Afterward, Delaware's favorite son, Senator John Williams, dropped his candidacy, announcing for Goldwater, and bringing the entire 12-vote delegation with him. With the convention less than a month away, Goldwater was locking up state after state as the delegations met prior to traveling to San Francisco. Goldwater secured the unanimous support of the Montana delegation and the Utah delegation. Even in states such as Arkansas, whose governor, Winthrop Rockefeller, was Nelson's brother, and Hawaii, whose affection for favorite son Senator Hiram Fong had never been questioned, much less challenged, by Goldwater or any other candidate, Goldwater received 50 percent or more of the votes.

On 21 June the Goldwater campaign issued a statement providing the press with a state-by-state breakdown of Goldwater's support. Goldwater had more than 800 first-ballot votes. Scranton had spent five weeks winning some delegates who were formerly committed to Rockefeller or Lodge, but throughout Scranton's five-week campaign, Goldwater had been increasing his delegate strength. As the convention opened, it was clear that Goldwater would be its nominee, and the convention would follow his lead.

THE RHETORICAL SITUATION: THE 1964 REPUBLICAN NATIONAL CONVENTION

The liberal wing of the party clung to the hope that Scranton might yet defeat Goldwater in the convention. This faint hope assumed that if Goldwater could be stopped on the first ballot, the convention would recognize the merit of Scranton's candidacy and turn to him. Yet, for Scranton to stop Goldwater on the first ballot, some Goldwater delegates would have to abandon the Arizona senator. Furthermore, the votes that had been won by Rockefeller, Lodge, Nixon, and others in the primaries would have to remain committed to these candidates at least through the first ballot. In addition, the large blocs of votes that were pledged to favorite sons such as Congressman Melvin Laird in Wisconsin, Governor James Rhodes in Ohio, and Michigan governor George Romney, would have to remain firm.

Characteristic of its thoroughness throughout the campaign, the Goldwater organization was well prepared for the convention. As one veteran political reporter observed, "probably there were fewer of the hardened political types than had been seen at any national convention for many years" at the Republican's San Francisco gathering. To aid their new recruits, the Goldwater forces established an elaborate communications system that enabled them to contact anyone on the floor of the convention quickly and purchased time on a local San Francisco radio station, KFAX. In a memo distributed to Goldwater delegates, they were urged to take a portable radio to the convention floor so that they could tune in to the five-minute Goldwater programs that would be broadcast hourly throughout the convention.[38] This was yet another way in which the Goldwater campaign could quickly direct its delegates on the campaign floor.

The tone of the last-ditch Scranton effort was set by the tabloid newspaper they published and distributed to delegates as they arrived in San Francisco. In light of subsequent events, the intemperate language and charges being made about Goldwater by his fellow Republicans cannot be ignored. VICIOUS DRIVE FOR GOLDWATER OPENED BY RADICAL BACKERS headlined the Scranton tabloid whose second lead story claimed GOLDWATER WILL STRIKE OUT AT 623 VOTES: BILL SCRANTON BOOM PICKS UP AFTER COUNT. Readers found headline stories claiming BLACK NOVEMBER FOR GOP IF GOLDWATER CANDIDATE—BARRY WOULD LOSE ALL FIFTY STATES. In an article strikingly similar to what became the most famous television ad of the fall campaign, on an inner page readers found the headline GOLDWATER'S POST CONVENTION PLANS RAISE QUESTIONS OF NUCLEAR SANITY above a two-column-wide picture of the mushroom cloud of an atomic explosion.[39]

The run-up to the convention proceeded as scripted by the Goldwater forces. The platform committee, meeting in the days immediately preceding the convention to finish their work, had produced a document acceptable to the Goldwater forces. However, liberal Republicans were most distressed by the civil-rights plank in the platform. Shortly before the convention, Goldwater had voted against the Civil Rights Bill of 1964, claiming that two sections of the act, Title 2, the employment practices act, and Title 7, the public accommodations section, were unconstitutional and unenforceable. Goldwater's understanding of the constitutionality of the act was based at least in part on the legal advice he received from Robert Bork, later the Solicitor General of the United States and a conservative federal judge, and from future Supreme Court justice William Rehnquist.[40] Before casting his vote, Goldwater had told his fellow senators that

> I am unalterably opposed to discrimination of any sort, and I believe that though the problem is fundamentally one of the heart, some law can help, but not law that embodies features like these, provisions which fly in the face of the Constitution, and which require for their effective execution the creation of a police state. If my vote is misconstrued, let it be, and let me suffer the consequences. My concern extends beyond any single group in our society. My concern is for the entire nation, for the freedom of all who live in it and for all who were born in it. This is my concern and this is where I stand.[41]

Goldwater had previously voted for the Civil Rights Acts of 1956 and 1960. His store was among the first major businesses in Phoenix to hire blacks on an equal basis with whites and he was a long-time member of both the Urban League and NAACP. To imply, on the basis of this one vote, that Goldwater was a racist was highly questionable.

Though their candidate had opposed the act, the Goldwater forces felt they had made a conciliatory gesture toward the moderates by approving a platform that promised "full implementation and faithful execution of the Civil Rights Act of 1964, and all other civil rights statutes." The platform went on to endorse "improvements of civil rights statutes adequate to the changing needs of our times."[42] Moreover, during the convention, in his meetings with state delegations, Goldwater made it clear that if elected he would enforce the Civil Rights Act he had just opposed.[43] However, moderates wanted stronger language, and they wished to broaden the platform language to more explicitly denounce racial discrimination.

The liberals were thwarted in their attempt to include a platform plank denouncing extremism, particularly the John Birch Society. They were further thwarted in their attempt to reaffirm presidential control of nuclear weapons, a clear attempt to embarrass Goldwater in light of his alleged suggestions that field commanders might be given control of nuclear weapons. Liberals announced that they would take these issues to the floor of the convention when the platform came to a vote.

On the eve of the convention, one of the more remarkable documents in American campaign history was delivered to Senator Goldwater. A messenger arrived at the Goldwater headquarters with a white envelope marked "Personal." It proved to be a letter from Governor Scranton. It warrants being quoted at length.

Dear Senator:

As we move rapidly toward the climax of this convention, the Republican Party faces continuing struggle on two counts. The first involves, of course, selection of a candidate. Here the issue is extremely clear. It is simply this: will the convention choose the candidate overwhelmingly favored by the Republican voters, or will it choose you? Your oganization does not even argue the merits of the question. They admit that you are a minority candidate, but they feel they have bought, beaten and compromised enough delegate support to make the result a foregone conclusion. With open contempt for the dignity, integrity, and common sense of the convention, your managers say in effect that the delegates are little more than a flock of chickens whose necks will be wrung at will. [At this point Scranton claims that the true vote count in the convention gives Goldwater 620 votes.] . . . You have too often casually prescribed nuclear war as a solution to a troubled world. You have too often allowed the radical extremists to use you. You have too often stood for irresponsibility in the serious question of racial holocaust. You have too often read Taft and Eisenhower and Lincoln out of the Republican Party. . . .

Goldwaterism has come to stand for nuclear irresponsibility. Goldwaterism has come to stand for keeping the name of Eisenhower out of our platform. Goldwaterism has come to stand for being afraid to forthrightly condemn right-wing extremists. Goldwaterism has come to stand for refusing to stand for law and order in maintaining racial peace. In short, Goldwaterism has come to stand for a whole crazy quilt collection of absurd and dangerous positions that would be soundly repudiated by the American people in November.[44]

As might be expected, Goldwater and his staff were dismayed by both the tone and content of Scranton's letter.

Goldwater's reaction to this letter is revealing in light of his acceptance address. "I knew I wasn't overwhelmingly favored by Rockefeller, Lodge, Romney, Scranton, or Margaret Chase Smith [all of who had run against him in one or more primaries], but after seven months of campaigning I could count on the votes of at least 800 delegates. . . . Along with my other deficiencies, it was alleged that I had not mastered simple addition."[45] Goldwater went on to observe that in the introduction he was called a minority candidate, he was charged with buying votes, with beating up delegates, and with compromising delegates. Moreover, Scranton claimed Goldwater had no respect for the delegates.

Goldwater observed that "what followed [the introduction] became the basis of LBJ's campaign against me." Scranton's claim that Goldwater had "too often casually prescribed nuclear war as a solution to a troubled world" particularly disturbed the Senator.

I read that sentence twice. Never once in all my statements or writings on foreign policy had I ever advocated nuclear war as a solution to a troubled world. I have never believed the security interests of the United States required us to destroy communist Russia. Its doctrines are antithetical to human nature as I understand it and must ultimately be brought down by the weight of its own errors. . . . This charge wasn't being leveled by some pacifist, left-wing radical; this total distortion of my search for peace was coming from a fellow Republican.

To Scranton's emotionally loaded charge that Goldwater "stood for irresponsibility in the serious question of racial holocaust," the senator claimed that "I had voted for every civil rights measure except for the one in June, and my objections to that piece of legislation were on very solid constitutional ground." To Scranton's charge that Goldwater had read Taft, Eisenhower, and Lincoln out of the Republican party, "I had to wonder if Bill Scranton had taken leave of his senses."

The letter was as strong an attack on Goldwater as virtually any that were made on him by his more natural political enemies in the Democratic party. Moreover, it came not simply from any Republican, but rather, it came from a Republican whom Goldwater regarded as a friend. The two had served in the same Air Force Reserve unit. Goldwater had counseled Scranton, when the Pennsylvanian sought out his opinion, to run for the governorship of the Keystone State. Indeed, Goldwater later recalled that until he received Scranton's letter, Scranton was still under serious consideration for the vice presidency.[46]

An accurate reading of Goldwater's acceptance address, delivered seventy-two hours after he had received Scranton's intemperate letter, must consider the criticisms that had been leveled at Goldwater by his fellow Republicans throughout the spring and culminated in that letter. Clearly, the Goldwater organization felt that the liberal element of the party had been beaten. That element had dictated the Republican nominee throughout the 1940s and 1950s. After more than two decades of waiting, felt the conservatives, they had finally prevailed in a nominating process that they had won fairly. But now the liberal wing of the party, acting like a sore loser, was unnecessarily continuing the fight for no reason other than to splinter the party, perhaps making it easier for them to dominate in the future.

The Goldwater organization decided to simply distribute Scranton's letter to all the delegates. They quickly had it reproduced and attached a brief cover letter that noted that Governor Scranton's letter had "been read here with amazement. It has been returned to him." The cover letter suggested that "perhaps upon consideration the Governor will recognize the intemperate nature of his remarks." It closed with the text of a letter written by Abraham Lincoln to Horace Greeley:

I have just read yours of the 19th addressed to myself through the *New York Tribune*. If there be in it any statements or assumptions of fact which I may know to be erroneous, I do not, now and here, controvert them. If there be in it any inferences which I may believe to be falsely drawn, I do not, now, and here, argue against them. If there be perceptible in it an impatient and dictatorial tone, I waive it in deference to an old friend, whose heart I have always supposed to be right.[47]

Messengers were sent throughout the city to slip copies of Scranton's letter and Goldwater's rejoinder under the hotel doors of every convention delegate. As many journalists observed, it seemed that the liberals were practicing extremism and the extremists quoting Lincoln on forgiveness and restraint.[48]

With the Goldwater forces in control of the convention, it proceeded smoothly with two exceptions, both on Tuesday evening. First, former president Eisenhower addressed the convention. Eisenhower anticipated Goldwater's acceptance address by focusing heavily on morality, crime, and the liberal press criticism of the party's conservative movement. He drew his greatest applause when he asked his audience to unify in the face of press criticism. "Let us particularly scorn the divisive efforts of those outside our family," advised the party's former leader, "including sensation seeking columnists and commentators."[49]

One reporter described the reaction of the convention to Eisenhower's comment. "There was a roar, then a standing ovation, then a steady, sustained snarl that grew in intensity. Delegates shook their fists at the press section and at the television 'anchor men' in their glass penthouses. These people really were mad at us."[50] This spontaneous demonstration against the press continued for several minutes.

Eisenhower had not finished his sentence before the crowd response. When the spontaneous reaction died down, he continued, "because my friends, I assure you that these are people who couldn't care less about the good of our party." Again the convention exploded in applause. Later that evening, as the platform was being read, several NBC reporters were removed from the convention floor. There is some evidence to suggest that this might have been a deliberate ploy on the part of the press.[51] Nevertheless, the demonstrations of distaste for the media were clear to the nation, which viewed them through the very media with which Republican delegates were upset.

After Eisenhower's speech, the platform was read to the delegates. This effectively delayed the proceedings so that the liberal attempts to amend it would occur after much of the nation took itself to bed. As Nelson

Rockefeller took the podium to offer the first of three proposed amendments, it was approaching midnight on the East Coast. The Scranton forces had determined to offer amendments on extremism, civil rights, and nuclear responsibility. All these amendments constituted clearly implied criticisms of Goldwater.

As Rockefeller approached the lectern and began to speak, he was greeted by a growing chorus of boos. To the television audience that remained, it appeared as though the Goldwater delegates were drowning out the New York governor. However, virtually all the reports that followed indicated that the demonstration was not from the delegates. It served no purpose for the Goldwater forces to appear rude and hostile to the governor of the largest state in the union. Indeed, the moment the booing started the Goldwater high command trailer sent the word to the floor to stop. In moments it became clear that the booing was coming from the galleries. All the reports, both those of convention participants and those of reporters, agree that the Goldwater delegates were not booing, nor were those sections of the galleries where the Goldwater campaign had its allotment of tickets. Theodore White describes Rockefeller and the reaction he generated.

> Chairman Morton with difficulty gaveled the auditorium to silence and Rockefeller began. His five minutes were allotted to the topic of extremism—and as, with absolute zest in the first minute, he swung into his call, the audience exploded again. . . . The floor itself was comparatively quiet, Goldwater discipline holding firm, and here one had the full contrast that plagued all reporters throughout the year—the contrast between the Goldwater movement and the Goldwater organization. There is not, and was not, anywhere in the entire high command, in the brain trust or in the organizational structure of the Goldwater campaign anyone who remotely qualified for the title "kook." Nor was there evident any "kook" on the floor. But the "kooks" dominated the galleries, hating and screaming and reveling in their own frenzy. . . . And as the TV cameras translated their wrath and fury to the national audience, they pressed on the viewers that indelible impression of savagery which no Goldwater leader or wordsmith could later erase.[52]

Theodore White's distinction between the Goldwater organization and the Goldwater movement affords one explanation for the ugly scenes that much of the country saw that night. Clif White, in charge of the Goldwater convention floor operation, offers another. In light of Goldwater's subsequent speech, it too warrants our attention.

> When Rockefeller appeared on the rostrum the booing began before he could even speak. At the sound of the very first jeer, I flashed the signal, "*Cut it.*" Still the boos continued. With Rockefeller obviously relishing the role of martyr, smiling his

pleasure even as he spoke, . . . I ordered them [Goldwater regional directors, floor leaders, gallery leaders] to check each state delegation and gallery position individually and find out where the noise was coming from. The replies quickly came in from the floor, and were verified by a glance at our television sets. There was no booing there. . . . I quickly dispatched a platoon of workers to the galleries and within minutes the reports came back. "These are not our people." Jim Day, working the galleries with a team of volunteers, concurred. We knew the people we had given tickets to, and we knew where they were seated. The groups that were doing the booing were complete strangers. . . . The strangers kept right on, shouting, booing, jeering. In defying our orders, they were obviously carrying out someone else's. This then was the "incident" we had so painstakingly tried to prevent while some of the liberals were just as carefully plotting it. . . . This gigantic charade was being played out for the benefit of a larger audience—the millions of voters who would march to the polls in November. . . . How many votes Barry Goldwater lost on that one night alone could never be calculated. But I would wager they ran into the hundreds of thousands, perhaps millions, when his opponents were done branding him and his supporters by mistakable implication as extremists, anti–civil rights fanatics and nuclear warmongers.[53]

Whether Theodore White is correct and the nasty demonstration was the work of fringe Goldwater supporters, or whether Clif White's perception that the liberals had provoked an incident to discredit Goldwater on national TV is correct, may never be known. But Goldwater's speech the next evening must be put in the context of this convention. For twenty years, conservative Republicans had supported presidential candidates reflecting the liberal wing of their party. They had, like Goldwater himself in 1960, often worked vigorously for the ticket. Now, many of them, like Clif White, perceived the liberals as not simply sore losers, but as destructive losers, who were taking dead aim at Goldwater before the general election had even begun. Though the liberal amendments were readily defeated, the persistent efforts of the defeated liberals, which culminated, in the minds of many Goldwater supporters, in a platform fight and ugly demonstrations, did not bode well for the coming general election. It was in this environment that Barry Goldwater, the next night, would accept his party's nomination for the presidency of the United States.

GOLDWATER'S ACCEPTANCE ADDRESS

An early draft of Goldwater's acceptance address was composed largely by Goldwater braintruster Karl Hess. Hess was a conservative journalist who also worked for the American Enterprise Institute. However, William Baroody, who had over the years built the American Enterprise Institute into a major Washington public-policy think tank, quickly took over the supervision of preparing the acceptance address. The address itself resulted from a team effort of several close Goldwater advisers: Hess; Baroody; political science professor Henry Gaff of Claremont College; Washington lawyer Ed Macabre; and attorney Dennis Kitchel, a longtime trusted friend of Goldwater who had run the Goldwater for President Committee after the senator's announcement. Material on crime and lawlessness, supplied by Phoenix newspaper publisher Eugene Pullman, was also worked into the speech. Goldwater had seen the speech as it developed and had reacted particularly positively to what would prove to be the most controversial lines in the speech, those dealing with extremism.

Acceptance addresses have traditionally served four purposes. They allow the candidate to formally assume the role of party leader. They generate a strong positive response from the immediate audience. Presumably inspired, this audience will provide a core of dedicated workers. Third, if nomination has been contested, the acceptance address of the winner is an opportunity to unify the party and rally support, even from those elements of the party that had previously vied for the nomination. Finally, it allows the candidate to deliver a partisan political address, which in some instances may be the most widely reported and viewed speech of the campaign. Hence, it should also serve as a highly persuasive message.[54]

Over the years candidates have used a variety of rhetorical strategies to fulfill these purposes. By 1964, four such strategies were common in acceptance addresses of presidential candidates. First, candidates frequently used oversimplified partisan statements. Second, candidates tended to lament the present and celebrate the future. That is, candidates would speak of the terrible state of affairs that currently existed, attributing it to their opponent. They would then celebrate how wonderful the future would be, after they were elected and had made a variety of improvements. Third, candidates tended to stress the crucial nature of this election. The electorate is told that they stand at a crossroads. If they follow the candidate, the future will be bright. If they follow the opponent in this critical moment in history, the consequences will be severe. Finally, acceptance addresses are speeches in which candidates seek to move beyond the core group of supporters with whom they won the nomination and appeal to other constituent groups whose support will be necessary to win the general election. Having secured a base in their party, candidates use acceptance addresses as an opportunity to broaden their appeal.[55]

Goldwater utilized three of these four strategies. By doing so, he was able to satisfactorily accomplish two of the four goals of acceptance addresses. He was also able, at least for part of his audience, to satisfy a third goal. However, ultimately this speech is remembered not because of what Goldwater accomplished, but rather because of what Goldwater did not accomplish.

Like most candidates, Goldwater opened by assuming his role as party leader. After briefly acknowledging the convention's leaders and commending recent Republican presidents and candidates such as Hoover, Eisenhower, and Nixon, Goldwater accepted his party's nomination. In doing so, he seemed in the initial moments of his address to be reaching out to those he had defeated for his party's nomination. "From this moment, united and determined," claimed Goldwater, "we will go forward together dedicated to the ultimate and undeniable greatness of the whole man."

> Together we will win. I accept your nomination with a deep sense of humility. I accept too, the responsibility that goes with it, and I seek your continued help and your continued guidance. My fellow Republicans, our cause is too great for any man to feel worthy of it. Our task would be too great for any man did he not have with him the heart and the hands of this great Republican party.[56]

Goldwater began the speech as a man humbled by the responsibilities he was now assuming and seeking aid from all who would provide it.

Having assumed his role as the leader of his party, Goldwater quickly moved into an attack on the policies of the Kennedy-Johnson administration. Initially, he did so by labeling many of those policies, particularly those involving foreign affairs, as failures. "Now failure cements the wall of shame in Berlin; failures blot the sands of shame at the Bay of Pigs; failures marked the slow death of freedom in Laos; failures infest the jungles of Vietnam, and failures haunt the houses of our once great alliances and undermine the greatest bulwark ever erected by free nations, the NATO community." But Goldwater was just warming to his task. "Failures proclaim lost leadership, obscure purpose, weakening wills and the risk of inciting our sworn enemies to new aggressions and to new excesses."

Goldwater continued, suggesting that our foreign policy failures were the result of our failures at home, including the corruption of our leaders. "Tonight there is violence in our streets, corruption in our highest offices, aimlessness among our youth, anxiety among our elderly, and there's a virtual despair among the many who look beyond material success toward the inner meaning of their lives." The next lines took on added meaning to his 1964 audience, well aware that during his career of public service Lyndon Johnson had become a millionaire many times over, and that his close aide Bobby Baker and associate Billy Sol Estes had been involved in questionable dealings, which in Estes's case ultimately resulted in his imprisonment. "And where examples of morality should be set," argued Goldwater, "the opposite is seen. Small men seeking great wealth or power have too often and too long turned even the highest levels of public service into mere personal opportunity. Now certainly simple honesty is not too much to demand of men in government." At this point Goldwater turned his attention to

> the growing menace in our country tonight, to personal safety, to life, to limb and property, in homes, in churches, on the playgrounds and places of business, particularly in our great cities, [which] is the mounting concern, or should be, of every thoughtful citizen in the United States. Security from domestic violence, no less than from foreign aggression, is the most elementary and fundamental purpose of any government.

Having indicted the Democratic administration's conduct of foreign policy and having suggested corruption within the Johnson administration, Goldwater looked for a cause. "Now we Republicans see all this as more—much more—than the result of mere political differences, or mere political mistakes. We see this as the result of a fundamentally and absolutely wrong view of man, his nature and his destiny." Goldwater now launched into a long section in which he attempted to contrast the goals of liberal political philosophy, which he asserted was to "elevate the state and downgrade the citizen," with his conservative philosophy, which was just the reverse. He concluded this section by observing that "it is the cause of Republicanism to insure that power remains in the hands of the people—and so help us God, that is exactly what a Republican president will do with the help of a Republican congress."

Goldwater had sought a high-toned discussion of issues with Kennedy. His discussion of political philosophy suggests that he still had hopes for such a dialogue with Johnson. However, Goldwater was delivering an acceptance address, not a political science lecture. Hence, his explanation was framed in simplified and partisan terms.

Having, in effect, lamented a past full of foreign policy failures and domestic scandal, both caused by a fundamentally wrong political philosophy, Goldwater then turns to the future.

> I believe that the Communism which boasts it will bury us will instead give way to the forces of freedom. And I can see in the distant and yet recognizable future the outlines of a world worthy of our dedication, our every risk, our every effort, our every sacrifice along the way. Yes, a world that will redeem the suffering of those who will be liberated from tyranny.

At this point Goldwater claims that he seeks "an America proud of its past, proud of its ways, proud of its dreams and determined actively to proclaim them. But our examples to the world must, like charity, begin at home." Goldwater uses this passage to introduce his celebration of our domestic future. It includes a society where the needy are never abandoned, a thriving economy based on private property, a society that cherishes diversity, "diversity of thoughts, of motive, and accomplishments." Moreover, Goldwater saw a limited government, with "balance between the branches of government at every level."

Approaching his conclusion, Goldwater quoted Abraham Lincoln, who said in 1858 that the Republican party was composed of "strained, discordant and even hostile elements." Yet, Goldwater continued, "all of these elements agreed on one paramount objective: to arrest the progress of slavery, and place it in the course of ultimate extinction." Goldwater then made one of his few references to the crucial importance of this election. "Today, as then, but more urgently and more broadly than then, the task of preserving and enlarging freedom at home and of safeguarding it from the forces of tyranny abroad is great enough to challenge all our resources and to require all our strength."

Then, in the most controversial portion of the speech, Goldwater observed:

> Anyone who joins us in all sincerity we welcome. Those, those who do not care for our cause, we don't expect to enter our ranks in any case. And let our Republicanism so focused and so dedicated not be made fuzzy and futile by unthinking and stupid labels. I would remind you that extremism in the defense of liberty is not vice. And let me remind you also that moderation in the pursuit of justice is no virtue.

These lines triggered a tumultuous reaction from Goldwater's supporters. However, though Goldwater's adherents were pleased, elsewhere on the convention floor the reaction was far less positive. Television audiences saw members of the New York delegation, including Senator Kenneth Keating, leaving the hall in the midst of the Goldwater demonstration.

Perhaps anticipating some of the reaction his remarks about extremism were to generate, Goldwater quickly observed that "We must not see malice in honest differences of opinion, no matter how great, so long as they are not inconsistent with the pledges we have given to each other in and through our Constitution." Goldwater then reiterated that he accepted the nomination "with humbleness," thanked his audience, and was finished.

Lamenting the present and celebrating the future, and occasionally suggesting the urgency of the 1964 election, Goldwater had effectively assumed his role as the party leader and delivered a persuasive partisan message. However, he failed to generate as strong a positive response from his immediate audience as most candidates delivering their acceptance addresses do. That failure, in large part, was caused by his lack of any effort to unify his party, and indeed his speech seemed to sharpen divisions.

Liberal Republicans, perhaps waiting for some olive branch of accommodation to be extended to them, received nothing and reacted accordingly. Nelson Rockefeller called the speech "dangerous, irresponsible, and frightening."[57] Given an opportunity to reach out to new constituencies, Goldwater told them "Anyone who joins us in all sincerity we welcome. Those, those who do not care for our cause, we don't expect to enter our ranks in any case."

Goldwater's organization reacted sharply as well. Shadegg observed that in the command trailer these passages were perceived as a disaster. "In the mind of every politician this was the time for a conciliatory statement, the moment when arms should have been thrown open to welcome all those who had opposed Goldwater's nomination." Shadegg goes on to observe that this was a time "when Romney, Rockefeller, Scranton, Javits, Keating, Hatfield, and Lindsay [all prominent Republican liberals] should have been invited to the platform. Such an invitation, couched in the proper language, would have been most difficult for a Republican to reject." Instead, claims Shadegg, "Goldwater emphasized the dissension which his critics had been saying all along he meant to achieve. The phrase about extremism which for any other candidate in any other context might have been greeted with loud approval, ripped open old wounds and erected barriers which were never broken."[58]

Goldwater was fully aware of how his remarks on extremism might be taken. His press secretary, Ed Nellor, claimed that that passage had been underlined on Goldwater's reading text of the speech and that Goldwater had observed "I like those lines."[59] The lines themselves had been added to the speech at the suggestion of historian Harry Jaffa, who patterned them after a passage written by Thomas Paine.[60] Goldwater's comments about extremism and moderation were, in the words of one journalist, "a handy summary of the tone and substance of the convention."[61] Indeed, they became for many Americans a handy summary of the tone and substance of Goldwater's entire candidacy.

The next morning, reacting to the negative press coverage of Goldwater's speech, President Eisenhower asked Goldwater to visit him in his hotel suite and to explain what he meant by the extremism passage of the speech. Goldwater later recalled that meeting. "When I arrived Ike said he had read all the uncomplimentary remarks in the press and was worried. I replied, 'Mr. President, when you landed your troops in Normandy, it was an exceedingly extreme action taken because you were committed to the defense of freedom.' Ike's face broke into the inimitable grin, 'I guess you're right, Goldwater. I never thought of it that way.' "

Goldwater long believed that the press focused on his extremism statement to the exclusion of the rest of the speech.[62] In retrospect, Goldwater's speech looks better than it may have looked at the time. For example, history has largely vindicated Goldwater's comments about foreign policy. Virtually all his major comments on the topic have proven accurate.

First, Goldwater indicted the Johnson administration for lying about Vietnam. Though Goldwater's comments were criticized and denied by the Johnson administration, today few would deny their essential accuracy, though one might question the hyperbole with which Goldwater makes his points. For example,

> It has been during Democratic years that we have weakly stumbled into conflict—timidly refusing to draw our own lines against aggression—deceitfully refusing to tell even our own people of our full participation—and tragically letting our finest men die on battlefields unmarked by purpose, pride or prospect of victory. Yesterday it was Korea. Tonight it is Vietnam. Make no bones of this. Don't try to sweep this under the rug. We are at war in Vietnam. And yet the president, who is the Commander in Chief of our forces, refuses to say—refuses to say, mind you—whether or not the objective over there is victory, and his Secretary of Defense continues to mislead and misinform the American people.

Fifty thousand American deaths, an untold number of Vietnamese deaths, and a quarter of a century later, the secretary of defense to which Goldwater referred, Robert McNamara, acknowledged the accuracy of Goldwater's statement, long after many others had also thoroughly exposed the deceptive behavior of the president and many of his top aides, including McNamara.[63]

Second, Goldwater addressed world communism. Again, his comments have proven to be remarkably predictive, though they were virtually ignored at the time:

> I believe that we must look beyond the defense of freedom today to its extension tomorrow. I believe that the Communism which boasts it will bury us will instead give way to the forces of freedom. . . . I can see, and I suggest that all thoughtful men must contemplate, the flowering of an Atlantic civilization, the whole world of Europe reunified and free, trading openly across its borders, communicating openly across the world.

In light of the demise of Communist governments throughout Eastern Europe and the former Union of Soviet Socialist Republics, and with the massive expansion of NATO and the growth of the European Union, Goldwater's remarks seem unusually prophetic.

In light of the emphasis on free trade and globalism evident in American foreign policy of the late 1980s and 1990s, as well as such specific legislation as the North America Free Trade Association, Goldwater's third major observation about our relationships with other areas of the world again seems unusually prophetic.

> I can see a day when all the Americas—North and South—will be linked in a mighty system—a system in which the errors and misunderstandings of the past will be submerged one by one in a rising tide of prosperity and interdependence.

The accuracy of Goldwater's prophetic message did not prevent his address from being reduced to the lines about extremism and moderation.

It would not be unreasonable for Goldwater and his advisers to have anticipated that his remarks about extremism and moderation would be singled out and used to epitomize the entire speech. White, Shadegg, and other Goldwater advisers had dreaded the possibility that an ugly convention clash between the conservative and liberal wings of the party would be nationally televised. Mere hours earlier such incidents had taken place with the heckling of Rockefeller and the removal of NBC reporters from the convention floor. Certainly these events, which were being characterized as evidence of conservative extremism, might have alerted Goldwater and his advisors to the likelihood that his comments about extremism and moderation would generate a widespread negative reaction.

So, the questions must be asked: Why did Goldwater use his remarks on extremism and moderation? Why were they not eliminated from the speech?

The simplest, and perhaps most accurate, explanation is that Goldwater wanted to say them. For seven months the senator had been accused of extremism. For seven months he had seen his remarks often taken out of context or exaggerated. His suggestion that Social Security was financially unsound, and that it should be made voluntary, a viewpoint which has become more widely accepted with each passing decade, was characterized as a desire to end Social Security and ruin the lives of elderly Americans. His statement that in a battlefield situation the NATO commander should have a low-yield nuclear option, an option that the NATO commander did in fact have, was twisted into evidence that he was a nuclear madman prone to use nuclear weapons casually and without any understanding of their consequences. A principled vote, explained on constitutional grounds, suddenly overshadowed a lifetime of action on behalf of integration, as well as prior votes in favor of civil-rights legislation. That one vote was used to portray him as a racist of the worst kind. The press stories coming out of the convention did not focus on the triumph of the conservative movement that, after decades of unsuccessful efforts, had finally nominated a conservative Republican presidential candidate. Rather, they focused on the divisions within the party. In these contexts, Goldwater's comments about extremism and moderation appear to be his sincere reaction to the frustration he and his supporters had endured.

That frustration may have been overlooked because the intense focus on Goldwater's extremism and moderation comments ignores the context in which they were made. Immediately preceding those lines Goldwater had seemingly expressed his frustration when he hoped that "our Republicanism so focused and so dedicated not be made fuzzy and futile by unthinking and stupid labels." If "unthinking and stupid labels," such as *extremist*, were going to be used to characterize his views, Goldwater was telling his audience, such extremism was not vice. If "unthinking and stupid labels," such as *moderate* or *liberal* were going to be used to characterize his opponents, Goldwater was telling his audience, such moderation was no virtue. In effect, as it was written, Goldwater seemed to be using his statements about extremism and moderation as secondary support material. They were examples of "unthinking and stupid labels" used by others to make his brand of Republicanism "fuzzy and futile."[64]

EFFECTS

The Republican convention revealed a sharply divided party, and perhaps even worse, suggested to the television viewing public that the conservative element of that party had forced its views on the remainder of the party. The apparent intolerance of conservatives for other views, evidenced in the treatment of the liberals' attempts to change the platform and the harsh treatment shown to Nelson Rockefeller and the press, seemed only to be reinforced by Goldwater's acceptance address. As with many such addresses, the vast majority of the substance of the address was quickly forgotten. Rather, what remained in the voters' memory, subsequently to be reinforced repeatedly throughout the campaign, was Goldwater's defense of extremism. Unfortunately for the Arizonan, Americans don't vote for extremists. With the exceptions of five southern states and Arizona, Lyndon Johnson carried every state in the union.

But, it is unlikely that this speech was a major cause of Goldwater's defeat. Virtually every commentator concurs with Goldwater strategist F. Clifton White, who claimed that the principal reason Goldwater lost was the assassination of President Kennedy. White argues that history illustrates that the assassination of a president "molds an emotional climate which has always bequeathed a deep residue of sympathy to his party."[65] White offers three additional reasons for Goldwater's defeat. In order of importance, he claims that Goldwater lost because of the Republican attacks on him during the primaries and the convention, the "ill-concealed prejudice of large segments of the mass media," and what White calls "the candidate himself—or more accurately, the candidate created by the first three stated reasons."[66]

For reasons such as these, it is unlikely that Goldwater could have given a speech in the convention that would have reversed the eventual outcome of the campaign. But it is possible that Goldwater could have given a speech that would not have struck viewers as exemplifying many of the criticisms being leveled at him. He could have given a speech that did not seem to reinforce the attacks of other Republicans. He could have given a speech that would not have been as easy as this one for the press to characterize as "extreme."

This speech was a clear appeal to Goldwater's prior audiences. Conservatives, those who favored liberty over equality and were not prone to dramatically change the present system, as well as ardent anti-Communists, were the heart of Goldwater's audiences as he rose to prominence between 1959 and 1964.[67] While this speech offered much to them, it offered little to those who were not already committed to Goldwater. As we have seen, many of Goldwater's staff hoped this speech might launch a general election campaign in which Goldwater would expand his constituency. Such a speech would not have to deny his conservative beliefs, but it would have sought common ground with moderates and liberals. Moreover, in light of prior events in the convention and the primaries, it might have taken a conciliatory attitude toward moderates and liberals. But Goldwater, as we have seen, was in no mood to be conciliatory. Hence, when evaluated from the short-term perspective as the opening address of a general election campaign, this speech seems to have fallen short. It did not begin the process of expanding Goldwater's appeal beyond his conservative core.

However, when evaluated from the long-term perspective of solidifying the conservative grasp on the Republican party, this speech, and Goldwater's candidacy, is likely to be perceived more favorably. It is easy to underestimate the importance of that perspective for the conservative faction of the party in 1964. For twenty years Republicans had been nominating what conservatives in the party called "me-too Democrats": Wendell Wilkie, Thomas Dewey, Dwight Eisenhower, Richard Nixon. In 1964 Goldwater led a conservative revolution within the party. His campaign would attract many of those who in the decades to follow would help elect

Ronald Reagan and a series of far more conservative congresses. Their ardor and enthusiasm might well have been lost if Goldwater had compromised his positions in this speech and throughout the campaign.

Importantly, polls suggested that Goldwater's general election debacle did not diminish enthusiasm for his conservative ideas. Opinion Research Corporation polls found that after the election, 65 percent of all Republicans still considered themselves conservatives.[68] Lou Harris polls reported slightly different figures but found a consistent pattern from 1964 to 1967. Throughout that period, 48 to 55 percent of Republicans identified themselves as conservatives, in contrast to the 8 to 15 percent who identified themselves as liberals.[69]

Goldwater's campaign energized the conservative movement in a variety of ways. Previously reliant primarily on large contributors and identified as the party of wealth, in 1964 more than 1,500,000 Americans made financial contributions to Goldwater's campaign. The breadth of his fundraising effort was startling in contrast to prior Republican campaigns.[70] Similarly, the Goldwater campaign benefited from the volunteer effort of more than 500,000 Americans.[71] Political scientist Nelson Polsby observed that Goldwater likely changed "the composition of the activist core of the Republican party."[72]

Moreover, Goldwater's "Southern Strategy" became the strategy of the national Republican campaigns in the decades that followed. Within twenty-five years, the Republican party would become the dominant party in the once solid Democratic South. That dominance was not without cost. It no doubt contributed appreciably to Democrats solidifying their popularity among the nation's black voters. Nevertheless, the Goldwater nomination signaled a shift in Republican power. The party was shifting philosophically from the moderate liberalism of "me-too Democrats" to the conservatism of Goldwater and Reagan. Within the party, power was clearly shifting from the East and Northeast to the South and West. No doubt these shifts were in the making and would likely have occurred even without Goldwater or his 1964 candidacy. However, as one student of the Republican party has observed, Goldwater's candidacy and organization "hastened them."[73]

Goldwater faced long odds in the general election. Though his acceptance address might have better initiated the campaign, it is unlikely that anything Goldwater said or did, from the moment of his nomination to voting day, would have won the election. Political scientist Stanley Kelley accurately claims that in the spring of 1964 virtually every factor known to be related in an important way to the outcome of elections favored a landslide victory for Lyndon Johnson. Voters who considered themselves Democrats far outnumbered those who considered themselves Republicans. Dr. George Gallup put the ratio at over 2–1; the University of Michigan's Survey Research Center reported it to be about 5–3. Moreover, while some 24 percent of the nation's voters felt themselves to be strong Democrats, only 11 percent felt themselves to be strong Republicans. The federal government was in Democratic hands . . . Congress . . . the executive branch. Because Lyndon Johnson was the incumbent President, he had the heightened ability to command respect, attract attention, and order events that accrues to any chief executive. Democrats held about two-thirds of the governorships, controlled the majority of state legislatures, and held the office of mayor in considerably more than half of the nation's large cities. The Democratic Party almost certainly, therefore had patronage resources and resources in disposable favors superior to those available to the Republican party. President Johnson stood very high in public favor, far higher than his opponent. His handling of his job was approved by 74 percent of the voters and disapproved by only 13 percent. He was, much more than Senator Barry Goldwater a known quantity to voters. In the period between President John F. Kennedy's assassination and Goldwater's nomination, no Republican leader won the support of more than 30 percent of the voters in Gallup poll trial heats against Johnson. . . . Mass opinion on issues of public policy favored Johnson and the Democrats.[74]

To secure a nearly foregone conclusion, Johnson waged an effective, though often questionable, campaign. Theodore White claimed that "never in any campaign had I seen a candidate so heckled, so provoked by opposition demonstrations within his own demonstrations, so cruelly billboarded and tagged" as was Goldwater by the Johnson campaign.[75] Others have also remarked on the exceptionally negative campaign waged by Johnson.[76]

In sum, clearly this speech was not successful from the short-term vantage point of launching the campaign. It was not conciliatory. It did not reach out to broaden Goldwater's appeal. However, from the long-term vantage point of maintaining and increasing a movement, the speech may have contributed positively to the resurgence of conservatism both within the Republican party and within the nation in the decades that followed. No doubt it was for these long-term effects, rather than any short-term effects, that communication scholars recently evaluated this speech as the most outstanding acceptance address delivered by a presidential candidate in the twentieth century.[77] Clearly it is impossible to ascertain the precise effects of one speech given in the midst of a campaign by a speaker who delivered hundreds of speeches. However, in contrast to the acceptance addresses of other defeated presidential candidates, it seems likely that Goldwater's uncompromising speech sustained the "already converted," at a time when their party, their beliefs, and their leader were being labeled radicals who were outside the mainstream of American politics. In sustaining the conservative core of his followers, whose numbers would grow to a national majority in such elections as the presidential campaigns of 1980, 1984, 1988, and hundreds of congressional races in the 1990s, Senator Barry Goldwater's acceptance address to the Republican National Convention in 1964 has likely had a greater impact on the American political arena than any other single address by a contemporary losing presidential candidate.

NOTES

1. Kevin Phillips, *The Emerging Republican Majority* (New Rochelle, NY: Arlington House, 1969), and James L. Sundquist, *Dynamics of the Party System: Alignment and Realignment of Political Parties in the United States* (Washington, DC: Brookings Institution, 1973).

2. Indeed, prior to Goldwater, southern support of the Democratic party was so strong that the expression "solid South" was used to characterize its support of Democratic candidates. But Goldwater received the electoral votes of five of the thirteen states of the old Confederacy and from 1964 forward the South has been an important component of the Republican base. In 1960 Richard Nixon received 32 percent of the black vote nationally, and Eisenhower before him had run well among blacks. Goldwater received 6 percent of the black vote, and even Ronald Reagan could not approach one-third of the black vote. Most recently, in 2000, George W. Bush received only 8 percent of the black vote.

3. Karl A. Lamb and Paul A. Smith, *Campaign Decision-Making: The Presidential Election of 1964* (Belmont, CA: Wadsworth, 1968), p. 46.

4. Barry M. Goldwater, *With No Apologies* (New York: Berkley Books, 1980), p. 93.

5. Ibid., p. 95.

6. Ibid.

7. See Lamb and Smith, *Campaign Decision-Making*, pp. 49–50, and Goldwater, *With No Apologies*, p. 95, for accounts of the writing of *Conscience of a Conservative*.

8. Theodore H. White, *The Making of the President 1960* (New York: Pocket Books, 1961), p. 239.

9. Accounts of this speech can be found in Goldwater, *With No Apologies*, pp. 113–14, and Lamb and Smith, *Campaign Decision-Making*, p. 51.

10. The *Time* poll is cited by David W. Reinhard, *The Republican Right since 1945* (Lexington: University of Kentucky Press, 1983), p. 159.

11. The best account of this meeting is in F. Clifton White, *Suite 3505: The Story of the Draft Goldwater Movement* (Ashland, OH: Ashbrook Press, 1992), pp. 36–37.

12. Reinhard, *Republican Right*, p. 179.

13. There is reason to believe Goldwater about his candidacy. At this time Nelson Rockefeller was working ardently to secure Goldwater's support. Goldwater had a natural affinity to Rockefeller's strong position on military preparedness. Moreover, as Goldwater later recalled, "the Nelson Rockefeller I saw in 1961 and 1962 appeared much more conservative than this public image." See Goldwater, *With No Apologies*, p. 159.

14. Quoted in White, *Suite 3505*, pp. 121.

15. During this period *New York Times* columnist James Reston observed that "Goldwater is not running the conservatives, the conservatives are running him." Reston is quoted in Reinhard, *Republican Right*, p. 181. Also see White, *Suite 3505*, pp. 114–22, and Stephen Shadegg, *What Happened to Goldwater? The Inside Story of the 1964 Republican Campaign* (New York: Holt, Rinehart and Winston, 1965), pp. 56–72, on the draft movement.

16. Goldwater, *With No Apologies*, p. 162.

17. Ibid.

18. Reinhard, *Republican Right*, p. 169.

19. Goldwater voted against the Civil Rights Act of 1964 for philosophical reasons, as will be discussed later. However, at this point he had consistently been supportive of civil-rights legislation and in Arizona his stores were among the first major businesses to be totally desegregated.

20. Reinhard, *Republican Right*, p. 177.

21. Kennedy defeated Nixon by only 120,000 out of 68 million votes cast in 1960. See Todd Lindberg, "It's the Dukakis Campaign, Stupid," *Weekly Standard* 14 June 1999, p. 22.

22. Goldwater's remark was first reported in *U.S. News and World Report*, 21 Dec. 1964. See Reinhard, *Republican Right*, p. 181.

23. Goldwater, *With No Apologies*, p. 156.

24. Shadegg, *What Happened*, p. 82. Shadegg also claims that the changes in Goldwater were evident to other Goldwater advisers, including Dean Burch, John Grenier, Richard Kleindienst, and Clif White, as well as many Arizonians who had been with him since the early 1950s.

25. See Goldwater, *With No Apologies*, pp. 156–58, for Goldwater's perceptions of what a Kennedy-Goldwater campaign might have been. Also see Shadegg, *What Happened*, p. 81.

26. Shadegg, *What Happened*, p. 81.

27. Ibid.

28. See Reinhard, *Republican Right*, p. 181, for an account of the 8 December meeting.

29. See the report of Goldwater's announcement in *U.S. News and World Report*, 13 Jan. 1964, p. 19.

30. The best brief account of how the Goldwater organization operated can be found in Nicol C. Rae, *The Decline and Fall of the Liberal Republicans from 1952 to the Present* (New York: Oxford University Press, 1989), pp. 54–77. Also see White, *Suite 3505*, pp. 277–331, and Shadegg, *What Happened*, pp. 85–128.

31. Perhaps the best account of the New Hampshire primary is that found in White, *Suite 3505*, pp. 257–74. White, who of course headed the early draft-Goldwater movement, attempts to illustrate the press misrepresentations of Goldwater. Also see Reinhard, *Republican Right*, p. 184–85, and Goldwater, *With No Apologies* p. 167–69.

32. White, *Suite 3505*, p. 294.

33. Both White, *Suite 3505*, and Shadegg, *What Happened*, provide thorough accounts of the California primary. Also see Theodore H. White, *The Making of the President 1964* (New York: Atheneum, 1965), pp. 146–59.

34. Quoted in White, *Suite 3505*, p. 337.

35. Ibid. On the Scranton campaign, especially his dealings with Eisenhower, see White, *Making of the President 1964*, esp. pp. 174–90.

36. Quoted in Charles McDowell, *Campaign Fever: The National Folk Festival, from New Hampshire to November, 1964* (New York: William Morrow, 1965), p. 70.

37. White, *Making of the President 1964*, p. 191.

38. See McDowell, *Campaign Fever*, p. 97. McDowell also notes that the Goldwater campaign had purchased five minutes of time for each of three programs a day on a local TV station. However, the use of portable radios caused the campaign to focus on the radio programs as a means of getting information quickly to delegates.

39. White, *Suite 3505*, p. 353.

40. Alvin S. Felzenberg, "Birth of the Right: The 1964 Goldwater Campaign and Its Consequences," *Weekly Standard*, 16 Apr. 2001, p. 39.

41. Goldwater, *With No Apologies*, p. 184.

42. This portion of the platform is quoted in McDowell, *Campaign Fever*, p. 106.

43. John Margolis, *The Last Innocent Year: America in 1964* (New York: William Morrow, 1999), p. 259.

44. The full text of this letter can be found in McDowell, *Campaign Fever*, pp. 108–10.

45. This quotation from Goldwater and all others relevant to the Scranton letter that are used in the next few paragraphs can be found in White, *Suite 3505*, pp. 187–90.

46. On the Goldwater-Scranton relationship, see White, *Suite 3505*, p. 356. Goldwater also claims that Scranton had urged him to run for the presidency. Also see Goldwater, *With No Apologies*, pp. 183; 190–91.

47. The brief cover letter is reproduced in McDowell, *Campaign Fever*, p. 111.

48. See McDowell, *Campaign Fever*, p. 112. Raymond Moley, writing in *Newsweek*, observed that "Their immoderate language belies their claims to be moderate." He is quoted in White, *Suite 3505*, p. 353.

49. Quoted in White, *Suite 3505*, p. 370.

50. McDowell, *Campaign Fever*, p. 122.

51. Ibid. McDowell claimed that before the convention opened NBC News General Manager Robert Northshield had told him that NBC had put a great deal of expensive and sophisticated communications equipment in the San Francisco Cow Palace to facilitate its coverage. However, Northshield continued, "I have the feeling that this is the lull before the lull. But if it gets deadly, we are prepared to make our own show." McDowell felt that "this strange talk about making his own show demonstrated how deep was the fear in the television community that the Republicans would settle everything in advance and then come out to the Cow Palace to listen to a few dull peacemaking speeches and play with their telephones." Clearly, conflict made for better television.

52. White, *Making of the President 1964*, pp. 243–45.

53. White, *Suite 3505*, pp. 370–71.

54. Judith S. Trent and Robert V. Friedenberg, *Political Campaign Communication: Principles and Practices* (Westport, CT: Praeger, 2000), pp. 217–18.

55. For a fuller explanation of each of these acceptance address strategies that were operative in 1964, and a discussion of additional strategies that have been utilized since that time, see Trent and Friedenberg, *Political Campaign Communication*, pp. 218–25.

56. This and all subsequent references to Goldwater's acceptance address are drawn from the text as found on the National Center for Historical Documents home page at http://www.nationalcenter.org. This speech has been widely anthologized and reprinted. See, for example, Richard J. Jensen, William H. Lyon, and Philip Reed Rulon, *Great Speeches in American History* (Edina, MN: Burgess, 1990), pp. 203–6; White, *Suite 3505*, pp. 409–15.

57. Rockefeller is quoted in Reinhard, *Republican Right*, p. 196.

58. Shadegg, *What Happened*, p. 165.

59. McDowell, *Campaign Fever*, p. 137.

60. Margolis, *Last Innocent Year*, pp. 272–73. Paine's line was "Moderation in temper is always a virtue, but moderation in principle is always a vice."

61. McDowell, *Campaign Fever*, p. 137.

62. Goldwater, *With No Apologies*, p. 193.

63. See Robert McNamara, *In Retrospect* (New York: Times Books, 1995). Also see Robert McNamara, "We Were Wrong, Terribly Wrong," *Newsweek*, 17 Apr. 1995, pp. 45–54. McNamara indicates that the Johnson administration consistently withheld information from the public. With the war going badly in late 1964, Johnson dramatically increased American involvement in early 1965. Planning was underway for this increase during the campaign. McNamara observed that "during this fateful period, Johnson initiated bombing of North Vietnam and committed U.S. ground forces, raising the total U.S. troop strength from 23,000 to 175,000—with the likelihood of another 100,000 in 1966 and perhaps even more later. All of this occurred without adequate public disclosure or debate, planting the seeds of an eventually debilitating credibility gap." McNamara pictures a president "who refused to take the American people in his confidence,"

which, with the wisdom of hindsight, McNamara called "an unwise and ultimately self defeating course." McNamara, "We Were Wrong," pp. 50–51.

64. I am indebted to Kathleen Hall Jamieson, *Packaging the Presidency: A History and Criticism of Presidential Campaign Advertising* (New York: Oxford University Press, 1984), pp. 182–83, for this analysis. Jamieson goes on to make the point that in his oral presentation of the speech Goldwater paused between the sentence in which he speaks about "unthinking and stupid labels," and those in which he speaks about extremism and moderation. Jamieson suggests that this pause "untethered subordinate material from its contexts," hence, allowing the focus on the extremism and moderation passages as the dominant idea, rather than as examples.

65. White, *Suite 3505*, p. 382.

66. Ibid.

67. See John C. Hammerback, "Barry Goldwater's Rhetoric of Rugged Individualism," *Quarterly Journal of Speech* (Apr. 1972): 176–178, for an analysis of Goldwater's audiences.

68. White, *Suite 3505*, p. 389.

69. M. Stanton Evans, *The Future of Conservatism: From Taft to Reagan and Beyond* (New York: Holt, Rinehart and Winston, 1968), p. 73.

70. Shadegg, *What Happened*, p. 4.

71. Ibid.

72. Nelson W. Polsby, "Strategic Considerations," in Milton C. Cummings, Jr., ed., *The National Election of 1964* (Washington: Brookings Institution, 1966), p. 101.

73. Reinhard, *The Republican Right*, p. 197.

74. Stanley Kelley, Jr., "The Presidential Campaign," in Milton C. Cummings, Jr., ed., *The National Election of 1964* (Washington: Brookings Institution, 1966), pp. 43–44.

75. White, *Making of the President 1964*, pp. 390–91.

76. Exemplifying this negative effort was what is perhaps the classic example of negative advertising, the famous "Daisy" television advertisement that implied, without actually naming him, that Goldwater would destroy the world. The advertisement featured a young girl sitting in a field of daisies disappearing into a nuclear mushroom. It generated enormous protest and was withdrawn after but one showing. However, its very withdrawal generated great publicity and it was used on a variety of news programs, giving it considerable exposure. See Jamieson, *Packaging the Presidency*, pp. 198–200.

77. Martin Medhurst and Stephen Lucas, "Top 100 Speeches of the Twentieth Century" (Paper presented at the annual meeting of the National Communication Association, November 2000, Seattle, WA). The full list can be found at http://www.news.wisc.edu/mis/speeches/. Goldwater's address is ranked sixty-fourth on the list, and no other nomination acceptance address is included on the list.

Chapter Three

1968—Richard M. Nixon

> When the strongest nation in the world can be tied down for four years in a war in Vietnam with no end in sight, when the richest nation in the world can't manage its own economy, when the nation with the greatest tradition of the rule of law is plagued by unprecedented lawlessness, when a nation [that] has been known for a century for equality of opportunity is torn by unprecedented racial violence, and when the President of the United States cannot travel abroad or to any major city at home without fear of a hostile demonstration—then it's time for new leadership for the United States of America.

Richard Nixon described 22 December 1967 as "one of the longest" days of his life.[1] It was the day he decided not to run for the presidency. Had Nixon remained true to that decision, contemporary American history would have been dramatically different. But within three days, largely at the urging of his daughters, his determination not to run was wavering.

Always the political realist, Nixon well recognized that having lost his last two elections, the presidency in 1960 and the governorship of California in 1962, he would have to win in many of the Republican primaries in 1968. Only by doing so could he establish that he was still capable of winning elections, a prerequisite if he was to again secure the Republican nomination for president. With the early New Hampshire primary scant months away, by December 1967 it was time for Nixon to decide whether he would be a candidate in 1968.

On 22 December, after he and his wife Pat had hosted their annual Christmas party, Nixon went to his den. On a yellow legal tablet, while the rest of the family slept, Nixon wrote, "I have decided personally against becoming a candidate." He went on to itemize the reasons. First, he did not need the presidency "in order to be someone." Driven to succeed since childhood, evidently Nixon had arrived at a position in life where he was pleased with himself. Second, he claimed that if he ran and lost "it could be an emotional disaster for the family." Finally, he wrote that while he had four of the personal qualities needed to be an effective campaigner: brains, judgment, guts, and experience, he was no longer sure that he had the fifth, "the heart." For these reasons, on 22 December 1967, Nixon decided not to run for the presidency.[2] Nixon shared his decision with each member of his immediate family individually.

On Christmas Day, the Nixon family gathered to discuss his decision. It was clear that Pat did not want to go through the rigors of yet another campaign. However, she told her husband that if he felt he had to enter the race she would help. Daughters Tricia and Julie agreed that he should run. However, they offered different reasons. Julie told her father, "You have to do it for the country." Tricia suggested that he had to do it for himself. She claimed, "If you don't run, Daddy, you really have nothing to live for." Three days later Richard Nixon left for his winter retreat in Key Biscayne, Florida, telling his family that he wanted to debate with himself "the most important decision of my life."[3]

THE SPEAKER

Richard Nixon was born in Yorba Linda, California, on 9 January 1913, in a house that his father built. When he was eight years old, the family moved to Whittier, California. Nixon has been the subject of a host of biographies, and so the details of his life are readily available and do not need to be dwelt upon at length here.[4] However, what is significant for our purposes is to note that Nixon was, from an early age, concerned with speaking well. Nixon notes that his father served as both model and coach. "Whatever talent I have as a debater," wrote Nixon, "must have been acquired from my father, from his love of argument and disputation."[5]

In high school, Nixon excelled as a student and orator. He graduated third in his class and won the major oratorical contests in both his junior and his senior years.[6] Family finances dictated that Nixon's college education be inexpensive, and hence he attended nearby Whittier College. Nixon was active in student government, drama, sports, and most important, as a debater. Rhetorician Hal W. Bochin observes that Nixon's debate experience provided him with several lessons. First, claims Bochin, was the importance of immediate feedback.[7] Nixon derived his feedback from debating society judges and from his father, who occasionally observed his debates. In his early political races, his wife Pat provided him immediate feedback. Bochin finds that Nixon also learned the importance of emotion. As a debater at Whittier College, he learned to control his emotions while speaking, but he learned too that the appropriate display of emotion would enhance his presentations. In high school, Nixon had met with success as an impromptu speaker but he also had come to value the importance of research and preparation. As a debater at Whittier, Nixon prepared diligently and often attempted to win debates by treating aspects of the topic on which he and his partner were well prepared, but upon which their opponents were unlikely to be prepared.

In an interview Nixon granted while he was vice president, he observed that "preparing a speech is about the hardest work I know. Even when a speech is 'off the cuff' I have to devote a great amount of time to outlining in detail the thoughts I want to express."[8] Nixon went on to add that his speech preparation involved five steps. First, he did a great deal of reading and research about his topic. Second, he would write down the thoughts he felt were worth developing. Third, he would make a rough outline "in which I try to develop one central theme." Fourth, he would "make usually three or four more outlines, the final one is almost a complete copy of the speech." Finally, he would dictate a draft into the Dictaphone.[9]

Nixon's skills as a speaker served him well. Upon graduating second in his class from Whittier, he won a scholarship to Duke Law School. He ranked third in his graduating class at Duke, and in his senior year, though the depression was in full swing, he considered several employment options, including joining a major New York law firm and joining the FBI. However, FBI budget cuts and Nixon's distaste for New York City caused him to return to Whittier, where in 1937, at the age of twenty-four, he passed the California bar exams and joined the oldest law firm in the city, Wingert and Bewley. Approximately a year later he was made a partner. During the next few years he built his law practice, in part by joining a variety of Whittier organizations, including the Kiwanis, and the Whittier College Alumni Association. Nixon was also active in amateur theater, and in 1938 while trying out for a part, he met Pat Ryan, who had come to Whittier to teach at the local high school. Nixon claimed that "for me it was a case of love at first sight." After a two-year courtship, they were married on 21 June 1940.

Returning from their honeymoon in Mexico, the Nixons resumed their lives in Whittier. Nixon, by now well known in the community, was mentioned as a possible candidate for the state legislature. However, in late 1941 one of Nixon's former professors at Duke, David Cavers, recommended him for a position with the Office of Price Administration in Washington. Though the job involved a pay cut, the Nixons decided to accept it. Nixon claimed that he wanted the opportunity to "observe the working of the government firsthand."[10] The Nixons arrived in Washington a month after Pearl Harbor. Nixon worked for eight months on the rationing of rubber and automobile tires. Though it is possible that Nixon's government position, and his Quaker faith, might have secured him a deferment, in 1942 he applied for a commission in the U.S. Navy. Nixon served in the South Pacific through 1944. During the last months of the war and the first months of peace, Nixon finished his naval service by utilizing his legal training to help the Navy to terminate wartime contracts.

Nixon's postwar political career is well known. What is not so widely known is the critical role that his debating skills played in his advancement. In 1946 Whittier Republicans recruited the young naval officer to run against incumbent Democratic congressman Jerry Voorhis. Nixon was aggressive in his campaign against Voorhis. In a series of five debates he pounded Voorhis on two issues. In both instances, Nixon illustrated that he had mastered the lessons of his youthful debating. He was far better prepared than Voorhis on both issues and he used emotion effectively.

Consistent with the national Republican party attempt to portray the Democratic party as a party that unwittingly gave political respectability to many communist sympathizers, Nixon claimed that Voorhis had received support from many leftist labor leaders. In their first debate, Nixon confronted Voorhis with newspaper clippings reporting that Voorhis received the endorsement of left-leaning political action committees. These were committees that many believed had been infiltrated by communists. Voorhis at first denied the endorsements, claiming that Nixon was confusing his endorsement by the CIO PAC with the less reputable National Citizens Political Action Committee. Nixon responded by walking across the stage while "reading aloud the names of the board members of each organization, many of which were the same."[11] Voorhis subsequently legitimized Nixon's claim by repudiating the NCPAC endorsement and asking them to withdraw it.

Throughout his public life, Nixon has frequently been condemned for being a "red baiter" because of this, his first campaign. While he certainly attempted to paint Voorhis as soft on communism, his critics are in error when they suggest that he pioneered this tactic. Indeed, as *New York Times* Washington Bureau chief and columnist Tom Wicker has pointed out, Nixon was "following the general lead of many national and state Republican leaders. And his use of it [the tactic of depicting Democrats as soft on communism] was relatively tame stuff compared to others' inflammatory rhetoric."[12] Voorhis, as Wicker points out, was a target for such an attack for a variety of reasons besides his endorsement by the NCPAC: his endorsement by the controversial Henry Wallace and his refusal to serve on, and his often-voiced criticism of, the House Un-American Activities Committee.

Second, Nixon hammered at Voorhis for being an ineffective congressman. Nixon had thoroughly researched Voorhis's congressional record. He illustrated that in his last two terms, Voorhis had introduced more than one hundred bills, and only one of them had been enacted into law. That bill transferred jurisdiction over rabbit breeders from the Department of the Interior to the Department of Agriculture. Using humor, Nixon suggested that Voorhis better represented rabbits than voters.[13] Though Nixon treated the rabbit bill humorously, he relentlessly challenged Voorhis in the debates as well as in newspaper ads to illustrate even one significant accomplishment in his last four years in Congress. Nixon had done his research. The incumbent had no response.

Nixon's 1946 congressional victory was a consequence of many factors, including the national trend away from Truman and toward the Republicans, who won the Senate in 1946 and gained fifty-five seats in the House. Moreover, Voorhis ran a very poor campaign. Evidently confident, the five-term incumbent ignored the fact that Nixon, facing primary competition for the Republican nomination, began to campaign ten months in advance of the general election and five months prior to the primaries. Voorhis really only began to campaign after the June primary. Moreover, Voorhis ignored the fact that between 1944 and 1946 his district had registered 5,594 new Republicans and only 2,831 new Democrats.[14]

Nixon's first election victory in 1946 evidenced many of the characteristics that were to help him win reelection in 1948, win election to the Senate in 1950, win the vice presidency in 1952 and 1956, and come within 118,000 votes of winning the presidency in 1960. Nixon consistently attacked his opponents, attempting to pick the battleground, define the issues, and put his opponents on the defensive. He excelled in debate. He prepared thoroughly for his speeches, and for the most part his campaigns were also thoroughly prepared to respond to his opponents. In 1946 he used the dominant medium, the newspaper, effectively. By the late 1950s the dominant medium in national races had become television. On two occasions, his 1952 Checkers Speech (a nationally televised address made in response to charges that wealthy supporters had set up a secret fund to buy his favor) and his extemporaneous 1959 debate with Soviet premier Nikita Khrushchev at the American National Exhibition in Moscow, Nixon displayed his adeptness at handling this new medium.

In 1960 Nixon met his match in a candidate who, in many respects, was similar to him. As Christopher Matthews has illustrated, Nixon and John F. Kennedy, also a former naval officer, also first elected to congress in 1946, also an ardent anti-communist, were good friends during their early years together in Congress.[15] The 1960 election contest between these two one-time friends resulted in Nixon's first electoral loss. After losing the closest presidential election in American history, Nixon was emotionally drained after the 1960 campaign. The emotional impact was made all the worse by the fact that Nixon was likely the victim of vote fraud in both Illinois and Texas. Indeed, many of Nixon's staff and the Republican National Committee had urged him to contest the election in the courts.[16] In an ill-conceived attempt to remain a viable national figure, in 1962 Nixon ran for the governorship of California. His loss in this race seemed to end Nixon's political career. As subsequent events illustrated, Nixon's political career was not over by 1962. But it would take a "new" Nixon to resurrect it.

THE NEW NIXON: NOVEMBER 1962–DECEMBER 1967

After his 1962 loss, Nixon felt that his political career was over for good. On the day after the election Nixon presided over one of the strangest press conferences ever held by a contemporary political figure. He concluded the conference by telling the press that "as I leave you I want you to know—just think how much you're going to be missing. You won't have Nixon to kick around anymore, because gentlemen, this is my last press conference."[17] Like Nixon himself, his family, his party, the press, and the public all presumed that Richard Nixon's political career was over.

Seeking a new start, in 1963 Nixon moved to New York and joined an already highly successful firm as a partner; the firm soon became known as Nixon, Mudge, Rose, Guthrie and Alexander. Nixon's exemplary ability as a lawyer and the many contacts he had made through his years of public service soon made him able to provide his family with the financial security they had not had while he had served in public office. Moreover, his family enjoyed living in New York, finally out of the public spotlight.

In 1964 Nixon, ever the party loyalist, delivered a series of speeches on behalf of Barry Goldwater. Although many moderate and liberal Republicans disassociated themselves from the party's conservative nominee, Nixon campaigned on his behalf. Goldwater's massive defeat raised questions about the political viability of any conservative Republican. Hence, by early 1965, Republican eyes began to turn to Nixon. He was perceived as a unifying force within the party, for he seemed to be a moderate. At the same time, his loyalty to the Goldwater ticket made him acceptable to the party's conservative wing. Moreover, events were conspiring to thrust Nixon into renewed prominence.

By 1965 the war in Vietnam was becoming the most important issue confronting the nation. Nixon began to attack President Lyndon Johnson for failing to commit whatever forces were necessary to win. As 1965 progressed into 1966 and inflation began to increase, Nixon sensed that the Democratic congress would also be vulnerable in the November congressional elections. By January of 1966, in a room next to his law office, three full-time employees and "Miss Ryan," as Patricia Nixon was euphemistically called when she would occasionally pitch in, were working to keep Nixon's name before the public.[18] His three aides and Pat scheduled his speaking engagements, made travel arrangements, and helped him to write a steady flow of speeches and newspaper and magazine pieces.

During the 1966 congressional elections, Nixon soon became the principal spokesman for his party. Speaking on behalf of fifty Republican candidates for the House of Representatives and scores of candidates for other offices, Nixon built up a reservoir of political debts. In 1966 the Republicans won big, picking up forty-seven seats in the House, three Senate seats, eight governorships, and more than 500 seats in state legislatures.[19] By December 1966, as Republicans looked to 1968, Nixon was no longer dismissed. Rather, he was once more becoming a force within his party.

However, though Nixon may have been pleased by his growing political stature, his pleasure was not fully shared by his family. Pat, in particular, was happy in New York. She had never been fond of political campaigning and the demands it made on her husband and family. Sensing what might be on her husband's mind, after the congressional elections she told her daughters that "she could not face another presidential race." At the same time, Nixon's close friend Bebe Rebozo told Nixon that he should stay out of presidential politics. Rebozo recalled that "to me it was a personal thing. I didn't want him or the family to get hurt again. I'd seen what had happened in 1960 and especially in 1962. It just wasn't worth it."[20]

As the Vietnam War continued to baffle the administration and Americans grew more and more disenchanted with Johnson throughout 1967, Nixon continued to attack the president's handling of both the war and the inflationary economy. Finally, by December 1967 it was clear that Nixon had to signal his intentions. Whatever hopes he may have privately harbored, he had continually dismissed talk of another presidential campaign. Like Kennedy in 1960, Nixon recognized that in 1968 he would have to win in his party's primaries. Only with a string of primary wins could Nixon dispel the fears of Republican party leaders that he could not win the general election. After discussing his decision with his family, this most introspective of men left for his winter retreat in Key Biscayne, Florida, to make his decision. Nixon returned from Florida ready to run.

THE NEW NIXON: 1968, FROM LOSER TO WINNER

Nixon's announcement of his candidacy suggested that the nation might see a new Nixon. His announcement suggested a thoughtful, statesmanlike, regal, dignified approach to the campaign. It stood in marked contrast to Nixon's hectic 1960 campaign, which saw him visiting all fifty states in a frantic effort. Nixon's announcement event, for it was an event, had three parts. First, on 31 January, the Nixon organization mailed a letter to every registered voter in New Hampshire observing that America needed new leadership. His letter seemed to take aim at Michigan governor George Romney, who had little experience with national issues or foreign policy, but who was already campaigning in New Hampshire. The Nixon campaign warned New Hampshire voters, "you can't handshake yourself out of the kind of problems we've got today. You've got to think them through and that takes a lifetime of getting ready." The letter was mailed on the 31st so that it would be received by New Hampshire voters as they were reading of Nixon's formal announcement. That came the next day, 1 February, when Nixon invited the press to his apartment. Here he presented the press with the letter that had been mailed to New Hampshire's voters.

> Peace and freedom in the world, and peace and progress here at home, will depend on the decisions of the next President of the United States. For these critical years, America needs new leadership. During fourteen years in Washington, I learned the awesome nature of the great decisions a president faces. During the past eight years, I have had a chance to reflect on the lessons of public office, to measure the nation's tasks and its problems from a fresh perspective. I have sought to apply those lessons to the needs of the present and to the entire sweep of this final third of the 20th century. And I believe I have found some answers.[21]

From the very outset the "new" Nixon was serious, yet quietly confident. That confidence was evident the next day, when the third act of the Nixon announcement drama unfolded. Nixon held a press conference in the Manchester, New Hampshire, Holiday Inn. "Gentlemen, this is *not* my last press conference," he began. Nixon went on to claim that the question he had to answer was whether he could win and announced that he would use the primaries, starting in New Hampshire, to prove that he could.[22]

Nixon faced the three R's in his quest for the nomination; Romney, Rockefeller, and Reagan. Michigan governor George Romney was the first contender with whom Nixon had to deal. He was the only other Republican contesting New Hampshire. But Romney's campaign was in shambles. The popular three-term Michigan governor had effectively doomed his campaign before it ever started. In September 1967 he announced that he could no longer support the president's Vietnam policy. Romney was by no means the only political figure to reevaluate his or her position on the war. But in explaining his newly found antiwar position, Romney claimed that his initial endorsement of the president's position was based on visiting Vietnam, where he had been "brainwashed" by the generals and diplomats who hosted him in Saigon. Romney would never live down the remark. American presidents should be able to see through military briefings and diplomatic doubletalk. The fact that Romney felt he had been "brainwashed" suggested a gullibility and weakness that undermined everything he said. Indeed, in New Hampshire he was frequently asked how he would recognize the truth when it was being told to him. Within three weeks of Nixon's entering the campaign, Romney's own polls indicated that Nixon would defeat the Michigan governor by a margin of 70 percent to 10 percent in New Hampshire and that the situation was equally bad in other states. Romney could not question the poll, which was done by Market Opinion Research, a Detroit firm that he owned![23] By the end of January, Romney had withdrawn, leaving Nixon unopposed in New Hampshire.

Though Romney's withdrawal diminished the luster on Nixon's first election victory in a dozen years, the New Hampshire primary gave the Nixon organization an opportunity to perfect its techniques. Nixon was taking an entirely new approach to campaigning. It was consistent with his desire to appear statesmanlike. Nixon's New Hampshire campaign, like his campaign through the rest of the primaries and the general election, would be dignified and reserved. Unlike 1960, he would not shake hands at factory gates and rush to give ten or more speeches a day, often in high school gyms or senior citizens' homes. Rather, Nixon made only twenty appearances in New Hampshire during the approximately two-month-long primary campaign.

Following the instructions of his new campaign team, among whom were Herb Klein, Len Garment, Bob Haldeman, Roger Ailes, Frank Shakespeare, John Ehrlichman, and John Mitchell, Nixon would campaign primarily through television. He accepted the advice of Haldeman, who, when preparing Nixon for the primaries, had critiqued his 1960 campaign and concluded that "giving speeches all day was no way to run for president." Haldeman believed that a candidate "would become punchy, mauled by his admirers, jeered and deflated by his opponent's supporters, misled by the super stimulation of one frenzied rally after another."[24] Nixon had determined, virtually simultaneously with his decision to run, that he would not run as he had in 1960 but would follow the advice of Haldeman and others. He would be rested and ready for each of his speeches. He would utilize television, but he would utilize it in formats that he and his staff controlled. Believing that events were conspiring against Johnson, and that if he could run a largely error-free campaign he would win, Nixon's campaign team scheduled him for one major event a day and the networks were forced to use film of that event, for there was nothing else to use.[25]

On 12 March Nixon ran up the largest vote total ever received by a Republican in the New Hampshire primary, sweeping 80 percent of the GOP vote. Though he was effectively unopposed, a situation that might be expected to diminish turnout, Nixon's victory was nevertheless impressive. Only two other obstacles remained between Nixon and the GOP nomination. With thirteen primaries left and a party consensus gradually growing around Nixon, only New York governor Nelson Rockefeller or California governor Ronald Reagan appeared to have any chance of defeating Nixon.

Meanwhile, Lyndon Johnson had been strongly challenged in the Democratic primaries. Building his campaign around his opposition to Johnson's Vietnam war and mobilizing students from throughout the country on his behalf, Minnesota senator Eugene McCarthy had received 42 percent of the 12 March New Hampshire Democratic primary vote against a sitting president of his own party. Four days later, Senator Robert Kennedy, brother of the slain president, jumped into the Democratic race.

By mid-March, New York Governor Rockefeller seemed on the verge of announcing his candidacy. The bitter three-way fight shaping up in the Democratic party made the incumbent Johnson's position uncertain. Hence, the Republican nomination was growing more valuable. If Rockefeller was going to run, he had to make his decision by 22 March, for on that date, if he had not announced to the contrary, the law in Oregon required that he would be on its ballot. Every indication was that Rockefeller would run. Maryland governor Spiro Agnew had organized a "draft Rockefeller" movement. If the New York governor did not run, Nixon would likely win the nomination and with the party behind him might well win the general election against a divided Democratic party. As an incumbent, he would likely be the candidate again in 1972. Thus, if the 64-year-old Rockefeller ever expected to be his party's nominee, he had to step forward. But on 21 March, much to the chagrin of Agnew and many other supporters, Rockefeller announced that he perceived that "a considerable majority" of the Republican leadership wanted to nominate Richard Nixon. "It appears equally clear that they are keenly concerned and anxious to avoid any such divisive challenge within the party as marked the 1964 campaign."[26]

Ten days later, on 31 March, the country received another stunning political announcement. President Johnson concluded an address to the nation by announcing that he would not be a candidate for reelection. His vice president, Hubert Humphrey, now contemplated candidacy. But even before Humphrey could act, the nation was staggered again. This time, it was the assassination of Martin Luther King, Jr. The death of the civil rights leader was the impetus for rioting in scores of cities throughout the nation and moved race relations, along with the war, to the forefront of the nation's agenda. Moreover, the backlash that was created by King's assassination and the subsequent rioting fueled speculation that Alabama governor George Wallace and his American Independent Party movement might prove to be a factor in the general election.

With the nation still trying to fully recover from the shocking events of the preceding month, on 27 April, in the ballroom of Washington's Shoreham Hotel, Vice President Hubert Horatio Humphrey announced his candidacy for the presidency. Making his announcement less than a month after his own president had in effect been driven from office, delivered three weeks after the assassination of the nation's foremost civil rights leader, delivered as the nation was at war overseas and seemingly at war in its own cities, Humphrey proclaimed

> Here we are, just as we ought to be, the people, here we are, in a spirit of dedication, here we are, the way politics ought to be in America, the politics of happiness, the politics of purpose, and the politics of joy. And that's the way it's going to be, all the way, from here on in![27]

One journalist responded to Humphrey's speech by calling him Hubert the Happy who "Goes yackety, yackety, yackety, yackety, yack."[28] Certainly Humphrey's announcement seemed out of tune with the national mood and the concerns of his principal rivals for the Democratic nomination, McCarthy and Kennedy.

Perhaps sensing that with Johnson's withdrawal 1968 was truly going to be a Republican year, on 1 May Nelson Rockefeller reversed his prior decision and announced that he would challenge Nixon. The New Yorker's campaign was once more, as it had been in 1964, late out of the starting gate. Moreover, his earlier analysis, that his candidacy would be taken as petty and divisive, was more likely true in May than it had been when first made in March. By May it was too late for Rockefeller to get on any of the primary state ballots. Nixon had energized much of the Republican party, who saw him as a winner in the general election and was giving him large vote totals in the primaries. Moreover, with the Democratic party in the midst of a divisive primary season and the nation seemingly daily growing more dissatisfied with the policies of the Democratic administration, most Republicans felt that if they united behind the moderate Nixon, they could win the White House in November. Hence, Rockefeller would be forced to persuade delegates to the convention, one by one, to support him.

Rockefeller's only viable argument, as in 1964, was that he would be more likely to win the general election than his opponent for the nomination. Yet, as Nixon proved popular in the primaries, and the Democrats faced a bitter three-way split in their party, with a fourth Democratic faction already having left to follow third-party candidate George Wallace, even this argument lacked credibility for Republicans. The final nail in Rockefeller's coffin was hammered a week before the convention opened. On Monday, 29 June, the final preconvention polls were in. They showed Rockefeller running even with Humphrey, each with 36 percent of the vote, with 21 percent going to Wallace and the remainder undecided. But they showed Nixon with 40 percent of the vote in a three-way race, Humphrey trailing with 38 percent and Wallace at 16 percent. The polls crushed any remaining hope that Rockefeller had of arguing that he could win in November and that Nixon could not.[29]

Nixon continued his march through the Republican primaries, winning all eleven primaries that he entered. He chose not to contest California, where Governor Ronald Reagan was a favorite son. Nixon and the nation awaited the results of the bitterly contested California Democratic primary, the last in the nation. The results might well indicate the Democratic nominee whom Nixon would face. Once more the nation was shocked. As millions of Americans watched on their televisions, mere minutes after winning the California primary, Senator Robert Kennedy was assassinated.

Hubert Humphrey had always controlled the machinery of the Democratic party. Though Eugene McCarthy had exposed the vulnerability of Lyndon Johnson in the New Hampshire primary, it was Robert Kennedy who was truly the choice of most of the antiwar wing of the Democratic party. Moreover, it was Robert Kennedy who the antiwar wing of the party felt could win in November. With Kennedy's death, the opportunity for the rank and file of the party to reject their leadership's support of Humphrey was dramatically diminished. McCarthy was not the inspirational leader that many Democrats found in Kennedy. The net result was that, as the primary season drew to a close, the two major parties had evidently settled on Richard Nixon and Hubert Humphrey as their candidates for the fall.

The Republican convention, held in Miami, promised little in the way of excitement. It lived up to that promise. On 5 August Ronald Reagan arrived in Miami, and announced that he was dropping his favorite-son status and declaring his candidacy. With California as his base, Reagan hoped to deny Nixon the nomination by securing votes from the growing conservative southern delegations. Though many of those delegates were sympathetic to the conservative California governor, they remained committed to Nixon.

Nixon had lined up the support of key southern Republicans, including South Carolina senator Strom Thurmond, Texas senator John Tower, Mississippi Republican state chairman Clarke Reed, and most important, the man that many southern conservatives still revered, Barry Goldwater. Thurmond introduced Nixon when the candidate spoke to Southern delegations. When he spoke to them in private, Nixon told them what they wanted to hear. It did not differ in any way from what he had said in public. He pledged that he would not pick as a running mate "anyone who would divide this party." Clearly he would not pick a liberal who might prove unacceptable to the South. Thurmond also made this point with numerous southern delegates, observing that he, Thurmond, would be at the table when Nixon discussed potential vice presidents with the party leaders. Nixon told southerners that he did not favor busing for the sole purpose of integration. Another point he made also fell on welcoming ears: "it is the job of the courts to interpret the law, not make the law."[30] Hence, Reagan was unable to crack Nixon's delegate strength in the South and the last challenge to Nixon disappeared.

Nixon's selection of Maryland governor Spiro Agnew as his running mate came as a surprise. It was a modestly controversial choice, as would have been virtually any choice meant to satisfy all elements of the party. Agnew had won election in the Democratic state of Maryland as a moderate Republican. He had headed the original draft-Rockefeller movement. These credentials, while not satisfying to the liberal wing of the party, were not totally unacceptable. On the other hand, after Martin Luther King's death and the subsequent rioting in Baltimore, Agnew had called together many of the city's black leaders. In his widely publicized address, he chastised them for not actively working to quell the riots and reduce the tensions in his state's largest city. This contributed to a strong law-and-order image that hurt him with liberals but made him acceptable to the South.

Shortly after Rockefeller had embarrassed Agnew as head of the national draft-Rockefeller movement by initially dropping out of the race, Maryland congressman Rogers Morton, a Nixon ally, had arranged for Agnew to meet Nixon. The two men found that they had similar views and seemed compatible. They met several additional times after that initial meeting and Nixon seemed impressed on each occasion.[31]

If Reagan's last-minute candidacy and the selection of Agnew provided a bit of drama to the Republican convention, it was tame indeed compared to the drama of the Democratic convention. The details of that convention have been frequently recounted and to do so here would not serve our purpose.[32] Rather, what is important to note is that from the moment of his announcement through the convention, Hubert Humphrey was the choice of the party professionals who controlled the convention. Since Humphrey did not run in the primaries, it is impossible to determine whether he was the choice of the rank-and-file registered Democrats. Moreover, the death of Robert Kennedy and the third-party candidacy of Alabama's Democratic governor George Wallace complicates any such speculation. Nevertheless, as Richard Nixon prepared to deliver his acceptance address, he knew full well that he would be running against Vice President Hubert Humphrey. McCarthy and Kennedy had both attacked Humphrey in the primaries. They had portrayed him as the heir to the unpopular policies of Lyndon Johnson. Nixon had been speaking in opposition to Johnson since 1964. Though the target of Nixon's remarks had changed with Johnson's withdrawal from candidacy, the thrust of his remarks had not. It remained to be seen how the new Nixon, the cool, reserved, dignified, statesmanlike Nixon, would introduce himself to the public in his acceptance address.

NIXON'S ACCEPTANCE ADDRESS

By 1968 few Americans were as recognizable as Richard Nixon. He had been on the national political scene for sixteen years. For most of those sixteen years, certainly those prior to 1960, he was often thought of as an aggressive, highly partisan, often divisive figure. His early rise to political prominence had been achieved, in part, by attacking his opponents as soft on communism. In his two vice-presidential campaigns he had, in the tradition of vice-presidential candidates, often taken the low road, attacking his opponents, while allowing Dwight David Eisenhower to take the high road and appear presidential. In 1960, when he had the chance to appear presidential himself, he lost. Two years later, in his home state of California, he lost again. It was these two images, that of the partisan attacker and that of the loser, that Nixon hoped to dispel in 1968.

The primaries had helped him with the second. The nation had watched as he ran off a string of eleven straight victories in the Republican primaries. He had done so, in large part, by presenting himself as a "new Nixon." But he had presented himself in only eleven states. On 8 August 1968, he would have the opportunity to introduce the entire nation to the new Nixon. Nixon hoped to move from the partisan attacker, who had lost the biggest race of his life, to the matured and thoughtful statesman, able to lead the nation in these perilous times. His success or failure in shifting his image, in leaving the old Nixon behind and establishing the new Nixon in the public's mind, would likely play a critical role in the election. With an expected audience of 75 million or more, Nixon's acceptance address loomed as critical to his success.[33] Nixon believed that "no other campaign speech would be as important."[34]

As we have seen, Richard Nixon claimed that writing speeches was difficult work. Nevertheless, he was actively involved in writing his major addresses. Typically, Nixon had writers provide him with drafts of major addresses and reworked the efforts of his writers until he was satisfied.[35] This speech was no exception. In the weeks preceding the convention, Nixon had asked speechwriter Ray Price to draft his acceptance address. Price had worked from the stock speech that Nixon had been delivering throughout the campaign. In the days preceding the speech, Nixon isolated himself in a five-room cottage at Montauk Point, on the eastern tip of Long Island, to rework the materials that Price and his staff had provided him.[36]

Most of the first half of the speech reflects the work of Price, William Safire, and other staff members. Reporters who had heard Nixon throughout the campaign readily recognized passages in the first half of the speech as ones that Nixon had used before.[37] The concluding sections of the speech were meant to get beyond Nixon's stock speech. They were meant to offer Nixon's view of the future and to relate it to his view of America's past and its role in the world. These were the passages that would best illustrate to his audience that they were listening to the new Nixon. At the very end of the speech, Nixon became very personal. He subsequently observed that "I had written the conclusion of the speech as a personal testimony to the political and social opportunity we have in the United States. It was intentionally dramatic, and it was completely true."[38]

Nixon was very conscious of how to enter a room or, in this case, a hall. "You have to walk right in and take charge. A lot of politicians," he claimed, "never learn that, they just mosey in or kind of poke their heads in first—that's all wrong. You have to make sure the door is open, that they're ready for you, and you start striding out a few steps before you get to the doorway—then you sweep in like a leader, and they know you're there."[39] They knew Nixon was there when he strode to the podium, for he did so amidst a thunderous ovation.

Typically, as we have seen in an earlier chapter, acceptance addresses serve four purposes. First, the candidate uses them to formally accept the nomination, thereby assuming his role as party leader. Normally this is done in a few sentences in which candidates humble themselves before the convention and thank the delegates for their nomination. From the very outset, even in so simple a task as accepting the nomination of his party, Nixon was suggesting that the public was hearing the new Nixon.

Sixteen years ago I stood before this convention to accept your nomination as the running mate of one of the greatest Americans of our time or of any time—Dwight D. Eisenhower. Eight years ago I had the highest honor of accepting your nomination for President of the United States. Tonight I again proudly accept that nomination for President of the United States. But I have news for you. This time there's a difference—this time we're going to win!

From his first words, Nixon was suggesting his image as a partisan loser was no longer an accurate one. Linking himself with the most popular American in postwar America, Nixon claimed to be a winner.

He continued his opening remarks hammering home his contention that he was and would be a winner. Observing that Eisenhower "lies critically ill in the Walter Reed Hospital tonight," he told the delegates that Mrs. Eisenhower says "that there is nothing that he lives more for, and there is nothing that would lift him more than for us to win in November. And I say, let's win this one for Ike." Sounding almost like a cheerleader for himself, Nixon enumerated some of the reasons he would win. He would win because the party was united behind him, because his party had given him a sound platform upon which to run, because his running mate is " a statesman of the first rank who will be a great campaigner," and "most important we're going to win because our cause is right."

The second function often served by acceptance addresses is to generate a strong positive response from the immediate audience. By doing so, acceptance addresses can help inspire this core of dedicated campaign activists. Nixon's speech did just that. From his initial call "to win this one for Ike" to his conclusion, reminiscent of Martin Luther King, that "the time has come for us to leave the valley of despair and to climb the mountain so that we may see the glory of the dawn, a new day for America, a new dawn for peace and freedom to the world," Nixon provided his audience with repeated applause lines. Indeed, many of the applause lines out of his stock speech had been incorporated in this speech for that very purpose.[40]

Third, the acceptance address provides the candidate with an opportunity to unify the party and rally support from those elements of the party that previously favored other candidates. By the time of the convention, the party had already unified around Nixon and he had no need to spend time unifying his party, though he did acknowledge Governors Reagan, Rockefeller, and Romney for their good campaigns.

Finally, acceptance addresses present candidates with an opportunity to deliver a highly partisan persuasive message. As we will see, Nixon did deliver a highly partisan message, but he was careful at the same time to choose a message that contributed to creating the image of the new Nixon, a dignified statesman and leader rather than a bitter partisan.

Traditionally, political candidates have used a variety of rhetorical strategies to fulfill these four purposes. Nixon's 1968 acceptance address evidences his use of the four major strategies commonly used by candidates of his era, when political parties were still reasonably strong. In addition, as we will see shortly, it foreshadows a rhetorical strategy that has become more common with the weakening of political parties since the 1960s. In common with his contemporaries, first Nixon made use of simplified partisan statements, but he makes less use of such statements than was usual in such addresses. Second, Nixon laments the present and celebrates the future. His indictment of the current state of the nation under a Democratic administration is strong, but he frequently builds on specific examples, which made it seem less partisan than similar indictments had sounded. Third, Nixon stresses the crucial nature of this election. Typically, candidates indicate that this election is taking place at a critical moment in history. Nixon finds that this is a critical moment in American history and that the consequences of the 1968 election will be far-reaching. Finally, candidates of Nixon's era commonly utilized acceptance addresses to unify their party and appeal to other constituent groups whose support will be necessary to win the general election. With relatively little opposition in the primaries, Nixon makes a considerable effort in this speech to reach out beyond the Republican party to the public at large.

As election campaigns have become more candidate-centered and less party-centered in recent years, so too have acceptance addresses become more candidate-centered. Communications scholar Kurt Ritter has pointed out that contemporary candidates "face a voting public who will judge them not so much on the basis of their political party as on their personal appeal on television." He finds that as a consequence contemporary candidates are increasingly utilizing their biographies as important material in their acceptance addresses.[41] The trend Ritter saw in the 1996 acceptance addresses were foreshadowed in 1968, for Richard Nixon also drew heavily on his biography for what were arguably the most dramatic and compelling moments of his acceptance address.

Like his contemporaries, Nixon utilized simplified partisan rhetoric in his acceptance address, but, no doubt sensitive to his past reputation, he uses it relatively infrequently for this type of address. Nixon is almost a quarter of the way through this speech before his first overtly partisan statements.

We've had enough of big promises and little action. The time has come for an honest government in the United States. And so tonight I do not promise the millennium in the morning. I don't promise that we can eradicate poverty and end discrimination and eliminate all dangers of wars in the space of four or even eight years.[42]

The implication that the Democrats have lied and have exaggerated to the point of dishonesty is clearly a partisan statement. Yet Nixon makes the charge covertly, by implication, not directly. The partisan pit bull of his early campaigns is disappearing, to be replaced by the new Nixon.

Similarly, Nixon's discussion of Vietnam is partisan. But audience members likely did not perceive it to be so. Nixon began by observing

if the war is not ended when the people choose in November, the choice will be clear. For four years this Administration has had at its disposal the greatest military and economic advantage that one nation has ever had over another in a war in history. For four years America's fighting men have set a record for courage and sacrifice unsurpassed in our history. For four years this Administration has had the support of the loyal opposition for the objective of seeking an honorable end to the struggle. Never has so much military and economic and diplomatic power been used so ineffectively. And if after all of this time, and all of this sacrifice, and all of this support, there is still no end in sight, then I say the time has come for the American people to turn to new leadership not tied to the mistakes and policies of the past.

Nixon clearly lays blame for Vietnam on the Democratic administration. But in doing so he seems to be making accurate claims. Clearly, the military disparity between the United States and Vietnam is enormous, as he claims. Clearly, American troops have fought to the best of their abilities. Clearly, the Republicans have, with few exceptions and none so conspicuous as the many vocal exceptions in the Democratic party, been loyal in supporting the administration's war effort. All this makes Nixon's characterization of the administration's failure to honorably end the war in Vietnam seem almost factual.

In this case Nixon's partisanship is one of omission, not commission, which makes it harder to identify. Nixon omits the fact that we cannot utilize our military superiority to the utmost. We cannot use nuclear weapons, for fear of starting a world war. We cannot use our infantry effectively in a jungle war against the guerrilla tactics of the Vietnamese. Hence, our military advantage is not as great as it might appear. Nixon omits the facts that military morale was exceedingly low in Vietnam, that the fragging of officers was likely more common than in any prior American war, as was the widespread use of drugs. All these factors served to reduce the efficiency of our fighting men. Upon a few moments of thought, omissions such as these may be obvious. Nixon is still a partisan. However, these errors of omission serve to diminish the appearance of partisanship. On the surface, Nixon's criticism of the Democratic administration seems to be little more than the thoughtful common sense of a leader who like all Americans is frustrated by the inability of the Democratic administration to resolve this conflict.

Nixon's second strategy was to bemoan the past and rejoice at what the future will bring. From almost the very outset of his speech, Nixon lamented the past eight years of Democratic rule. After accepting the nomination, Nixon immediately turned to the past.

> As we look at America we find cities enveloped in smoke and flame. We hear sirens in the night. We see Americans dying on distant battlefields abroad. We see Americans hating each other; fighting each other; killing each other at home. And as we see and hear these things, millions of Americans cry out in anguish: Did we come all the way for this? Did American boys die in Normandy and Korea and in Valley Forge for this?

Nixon answers his own question by continuing to illustrate the failures of the incumbent Democratic administration.

> When the strongest nation in the world can be tied down for four years in a war in Vietnam with no end in sight, when the richest nation in the world can't manage its own economy, when the nation with the greatest tradition of the rule of law is plagued by unprecedented lawlessness, when a nation [that] has been known for a century for equality of opportunity is torn by unprecedented racial violence, and when the President of the United States cannot travel abroad or to any major city at home without fear of a hostile demonstration—then it's time for new leadership for the United States of America.

Nixon concludes this section by praising America's people and finding that the nation is in trouble "not because her people have failed, but because her leaders have failed. What America needs are leaders to match the greatness of her people."

Throughout the speech, Nixon laments the past policies of the Democratic administration but rejoices at the policies that his administration will effect. Perhaps this is most evident in his remarks about foreign policy:

> Look at our problems abroad. Do you realize that we face the stark truth that we are worse off in every area of the world tonight than we were when President Eisenhower left office eight years ago? That's the record. . . . All of America's peace-keeping institutions and all of America's foreign commitments must be reappraised. . . . What I call for is not a new isolationism. It is a new internationalism

in which America enlists its allies and its friends around the world in those struggles in which their interest is as great as ours. And now to the leaders of the Communist world we say, after an era of confrontations the time has come for an era of negotiations. Where the world superpowers are concerned there is no acceptable alternative to peaceful negotiation. Because this will be a period of negotiations we shall restore the strength of America so that we shall always negotiate from strength and never from weakness.

Americans were hearing the new Nixon. Essentially what Nixon was articulating, without using the term, was what later became known as his policy of détente, a relaxation of the tension between the superpowers. This was not the Nixon who challenged communists wherever he found them. This was not the young congressman, senator, or even vice president whose reputation was based in large part on his harsh and confrontational tactics in dealing with communism. This was the new Nixon, a Nixon who was mature and thoughtful, a Nixon who was ready to be a major actor on the world stage.

We shall never be belligerent. But we shall be as firm in defending our system as they are in expanding theirs. We believe this should be an era of peaceful competition not only in the productivity of our factories but in the quality of our ideas. We extend the hand of friendship to all people. To the Russian people. To the Chinese people. To all people in the world. And we shall work toward the goal of an open world, open sky, open cities, open heart, open minds. The next eight years my friends, this period in which we're entering—I think we will have the greatest opportunity for world peace, but also face the greatest danger of world war of anytime in our history.

Thomas Paine believed that he had lived "in the times that try men's souls"; the Revolutionary era. Richard Nixon was suggesting that the next decade would also be a time that would try people's souls. What was called for was a leader who was strong, but flexible; who hewed to basic American principles but recognized the need to accommodate those principles with the rest of the world. As Nixon lamented the past with the American people, he could simultaneously celebrate the future that was offered by fresh American leadership, the leadership of the new Nixon.

Implicit in Nixon's examination of Vietnam and foreign affairs, as well as his discussion of domestic policy, was the notion that this was a critical election. Efforts to stress the critical nature of the election are so common in acceptance addresses that they constitute a third rhetorical strategy. The critical nature of the 1968 election was implicit in all that Nixon said. However, he also made explicit efforts to stress the vital nature of the election.

He did so twice during the address. First, in transition from his introduction to the body of his address, Nixon told his audience, "We make history tonight, not for ourselves but for the ages. The choice we make in 1968 will determine not only the future of America but the future of peace and freedom in the world for the last third of the twentieth century." Similarly, Nixon stressed the urgency of the 1968 election when he shifted from the body of his speech to the conclusion.

> My fellow Americans, I believe that historians will recall that 1968 marked the beginning of the American generation in world history. Just to be alive in America, just to be alive at this time is an experience unparalleled in history. Here's where the action is. Think: Thirty-two years from now most of Americans living today will celebrate a New Year that comes once in a thousand years. Eight years from now, in the second term of the next President, we will celebrate the 200th anniversary of the American revolution. And by our decision in this we—all of us here, all of you listening on television and radio—we will determine what kind of nation America will be on its 200th birthday. We will determine what kind of a world America will live in in the year 2000.

Not only was this an important election because of the impact it would have on the future, but Nixon also found it to be important because of the daunting challenges that would face the next president. In his conclusion, Nixon observed that

> The next President of the United States will face challenges which in some ways will be greater than those of Washington or Lincoln, because for the first time in our nation's history an American President will face not only the problem of restoring peace abroad, but of restoring peace at home.

Thus, this was an urgently important election, claimed Nixon. Not only would the next president's actions affect the nature of both America and the world for decades to come, but that president would face almost unprecedented challenges.

The fourth rhetorical strategy frequently used in acceptance addresses is based on the fact that most candidates view their acceptance addresses as opportunities to broaden one's constituency. As the first address of the general election, candidates utilize acceptance addresses to both secure the base of voters that they used to win the nomination and to broaden that base by appealing to other members of the constituency. For Nixon, who had won the nomination by appealing to the traditional Republican constituency—middle- and upper-class business leaders and conservative midwesterners and southerners—this meant trying to attract blue-collar industrial, often ethnic, working-class Americans and black Americans. Nixon made overt appeals to these groups and others in an effort to broaden his support.

After indicting the Johnson administration for creating and bogging us down in an unwinnable war abroad and domestic violence at home, Nixon attempted to identify himself with much of the nation; those who also questioned the current Johnson-Humphrey policies.

> Listen to the answers to these questions. It is another voice, it is a quiet voice in the tumult of the shouting. It is the voice of the great majority of Americans, the forgotten Americans, the non-shouters, the non-demonstrators. They're not racists or sick; they're not guilty of the crime that plagues the land; they are black, they are white; they are native born and foreign born; they're young and they're old. They work in American factories, they run American businesses. They serve in government; they provide most of the soldiers who die to keep it free. They drive the spirit of America. They give lift to the American dream. They give steel to the backbone of America.

Like these Americans, the forgotten Americans, Nixon also has serious questions about the policies and leadership of the administration that the Democratic candidate, Vice President Hubert Humphrey, represents.

Some foreign journalists covering the campaign found that perhaps Nixon's most thoughtful remarks during the early primaries had been those in which he discussed his perception of the role government should play in handling the problems of black America.[43] In his acceptance address, Nixon utilized the same arguments, though in abbreviated form without detail, in attempting to reach out to blacks.

> And let us build bridges, my friends, build bridges to human dignity across the gulf that separates black America from white America. Black Americans—no more than white Americans—do not want more Government programs which perpetuate dependency. They don't want to be a colony in a nation. They want the pride and the self-respect and the dignity that can only come if they have an equal chance to own their own homes, to own their own businesses, to be managers and executives as well as workers, to have a piece of the action in the exciting ventures of private enterprise. I pledge to you tonight that we shall have new programs which will provide that equal chance.

Thus, Nixon attempted to reach out, to broaden his constituency, by appeals to blue-collar America. Though these Americans had often been supportive of Democratic candidates, Nixon was suggesting that the current Democratic administration had essentially "forgotten" them. Similarly, Nixon attempted to reach out to black America. He did so by reiterating his oft-stated belief that rather than welfare programs the government should work to facilitate more and more blacks becoming capitalists and sharing in the American dream.

Nixon's fifth and final rhetorical strategy in this address foreshadowed a practice that has become considerably more widespread since his time. As campaigns have become more candidate centered, so too have the acceptance addresses of candidates drawn more heavily on their own personal lives. Perhaps the most moving moments in Nixon's speech reflect his attempt to indicate how his life molded his vision of America and what it should be. Nixon introduces his conclusion by observing that he sees the face of a child. "He lives in a great city, he's black or he's white, he's Mexican, Italian, Polish, none of that matters. What matters is he's an American child." But Nixon fears for that child, for

> he sleeps the sleep of a child, and he dreams the dreams of a child. And yet, when he awakens he awakens to a living nightmare of poverty, neglect and despair. He fails in school. He ends up on welfare. For him the American system is one that feeds his stomach and starves his soul. It breaks his heart. And in the end it may take his life on some distant battlefield.

But, Nixon continued, "I see another child tonight." At this point Nixon, referring to himself in the third person, goes into an autobiographical passage. This other child was "helped on his journey through life." That help came from "a father who had to go to work before he finished the sixth grade and sacrificed everything he had so that his sons could go to college." This other child was helped by "a gentle Quaker mother with a passionate concern for peace, who wept when he went to war, but she understood why he had to do so." Nixon continues, mentioning others who have helped him throughout his life. Nixon concludes this autobiographical passage by observing of this child that "tonight he stands before you, nominated for President of the United States of America. You can see why I believe so deeply in the American dream."

In sum, this acceptance address presented Nixon with an enormous audience at the outset of the general election. Consequently, it was an exceptional opportunity for him to introduce the "new Nixon" to the American public. However, this opportunity had to be balanced with an awareness of the rhetorical situation in which candidates find themselves when delivering acceptance addresses. Richard Nixon fulfilled the principal functions of acceptance addresses, utilizing the principal strategies followed by candidates of his era, and foreshadowing one strategy that is more commonly and extensively used today.

What was most significant was that he was able to meet the demands inherent in an acceptance address while simultaneously introducing the new Nixon. From the very outset he portrayed himself as a winner, linking himself to former president Eisenhower. From the very outset he stressed the unity of his party, by implication contrasting it to the fractionalized Democratic party to heighten the impression that he was a winner. This was not the old Nixon who had lost to John F. Kennedy and subsequently could not even win the governorship of his home state. This was the new Nixon who had won eleven straight Republican primaries, besting a field that consisted of the three most popular Republican governors in the nation. This was not the old Nixon who had received a tepid endorsement from Eisenhower in 1960 and kept his distance from Eisenhower throughout the campaign.[44] This was the new Nixon who had the unequivocal support of former president Dwight David Eisenhower and readily linked himself to Eisenhower at the first opportunity.

The new Nixon was not only a winner, but he was an experienced and seasoned leader. This was not the harsh, confrontational anticommunist. Yes, he was still an anticommunist. But his anticommunism was tempered with an awareness of the realities of the world. This was a thoughtful world leader who sought peaceful competition and recognized that much as he might wish to eliminate communism, realistically America would have to coexist with it. This was not an impetuous youth who had all the answers. This was an experienced leader who recognized that the most important answers often came from the lessons of history, and from the common citizenry, including those who are not always among his natural constituency. This was not the old Nixon, with whom many Americans had difficulty identifying. This was a Nixon whose biography was one with which many Americans could identify.

EFFECTS

In 1968 Richard Nixon became the only 20th-century president to win the nation's highest office after having suffered defeat in a previous national presidential campaign.[45] Nixon won thirty-two states with 301 electoral votes. He received 43.4 percent of the popular vote. He carried most of the south with the exception of Texas and most of the west, including California. He also carried such large states as Ohio and Illinois. Humphrey carried fourteen states with 191 electoral votes. He came exceedingly close in the popular vote, carrying 42.7 percent of it and losing to Nixon by only 517,000 votes out of a total of over 73 million. Third-party candidate

George Wallace won five states with 46 electoral votes and 13.5 percent of the popular vote.[46]

In contrast to the smooth Republican convention, the chaos of the Democratic primaries carried over into the convention. Thousands of student protesters descended on Chicago for the Democratic convention. Thwarted by the death of Bobby Kennedy and the party leadership's decision to nominate Vice President Hubert Humphrey rather than Senator Eugene McCarthy or any other antiwar Democrat, their demonstrations turned violent. Sleeping in the parks, the demonstrators shouted obscenities and threw rocks and bags of urine and feces at the authorities, who attempted to keep them from the convention hall and the delegates. Democratic mayor Richard Daley instructed his police force to do what was necessary to prevent the disruption of the convention, and the result was what later was widely called a "police riot" as the Chicago police responded to the demonstrators with mace, nightsticks, and brute force. It was difficult to tell whether the biggest story coming out of the Democratic convention was in the convention—where Humphrey, who had never entered any primary, won the nomination and named Maine senator Edmund Muskie as his running mate—or outside, where the antiwar protesters and police battled for control of the streets.

The Nixon team delayed the outset of their campaign until the Democratic convention was over, giving themselves time to organize and conceding that the Democrats would be the focus of media attention during the days between the two conventions. However, Nixon's first campaigning in the general election was scheduled for Chicago. He received an exceptional reception. More than 500,000 people turned out to line the streets of Chicago and cheer him. The contrast between Nixon's visit and the Democratic convention days earlier was stark. Nixon went into the general election ahead of Humphrey by 10 percent of the vote in most polls, with Wallace trailing Humphrey by 10 percent.[47]

As the election progressed, the Wallace vote shrunk, most of it going to Humphrey.

It is impossible to know the precise effects of one speech in a political campaign. One might argue that Humphrey's speech delivered in Salt Lake City on 30 September was as critical as was Nixon's acceptance. Humphrey used his speech to announce that if he was elected "he would stop the bombing of North Vietnam as an acceptable risk for peace."[48] This speech signaled Humphrey's break from Johnson and began to identify him as an antiwar candidate. From this point forward the race tightened. However, even with the president declaring a bombing halt, as he did days before the election, Humphrey lost.

Nixon's acceptance address introduced the new Nixon to millions of voters. Many of his campaign staff felt that the speech was an enormous success. Bob Haldeman believed that "it probably had a greater effect in shifting votes than any acceptance speech in the last 25 years."[49]

Nixon himself was equally happy. At 1:30 in the morning, hours after leaving the convention hall, with a glass of scotch in hand, Nixon reflected about the speech with speechwriter William Safire. Safire reports that Nixon felt that his suggestion that the convention "win one for Ike," would be criticized by the press, but that he liked the line, for he felt that common Americans could identify with it. He was very pleased with the applause lines. But he did regret that now that those lines had been heard by a national audience he could not use them again on the stump. He was especially happy with the last moments of the speech. The very last lines of the speech; "the time has come for us to leave the valley of despair and climb the mountain so that we may see the glory of the dawn—a new day for America and a new dawn for peace and freedom in the world," reminded many listeners, including this author, of Martin Luther King, Jr. However, Nixon claimed, it was really based on a statement made by Benjamin Franklin to George Washington.[50]

Nixon's support did not diminish significantly as the campaign progressed. His campaign utilized the speech in advertisements.[51] Though the election grew tighter after Humphrey's 30 September address, Humphrey was not able to tighten the race at Nixon's expense. Rather, during the last month of the campaign many of Wallace's supporters abandoned him. Humphrey was able to persuade many northern Wallace supporters that a vote for Wallace was in effect a vote for Nixon. Humphrey was successful in convincing many of them to return to the Democratic party and thus the race tightened. Significantly, however, though Humphrey was able to attract Wallace voters, he was not able to attract a significant number of Nixon voters.

Certainly, Richard Nixon's 1968 acceptance address to the Republican National Convention contributed to his eventual election. He delivered an address that fulfilled audience expectations for such an address. Recognizing the constraints inherent in acceptance addresses, he was able to fulfill the principal functions of such addresses, utilizing strategies that had frequently proven themselves effective in acceptance addresses. He had utilized a strategy that has become more common today. Perhaps most important, while satisfying audience expectations for an acceptance address, he was able to effectively introduce the nation to the new Nixon. The Nixon that the nation observed accepting his party's nomination on 8 August 1968 sounded like a thoughtful, seasoned leader who had matured. Yes, he had lost, but the Nixon the audience observed that evening seemed to have learned from those losses and become a better leader for them. Because it was not only a sound acceptance address, but also an acceptance address that contributed significantly to remaking the image of the speaker, Nixon's 1968 acceptance address may well have been the most significant speech of the entire campaign.

NOTES

1. According to the recollections of his daughter Julie. See Julie Nixon Eisenhower, *Pat Nixon: The Untold Story* (New York: Simon and Schuster, 1986), p. 233.

2. Nixon's memo to himself is discussed in Eisenhower, *Pat Nixon,* p. 233.

3. The best account of the family discussion is in Eisenhower, *Pat Nixon,* p. 234.

4. Among the better studies is Steven E. Ambrose's multivolume biography. On Nixon's early life see Ambrose's *Nixon: The Education of a Politician, 1913–1962* (New York: Simon and Schuster, 1987). Also see Ambrose, *Nixon: The Triumph of a Politician, 1962–1972* (New York: Simon and Schuster, 1989); Tom Wicker, *One of Us: Richard Nixon and the American Dream* (New York: Random House, 1991). Perhaps the best account of the 1968 election is that of Lewis Chester et al., *An American Melodrama: The Presidential Campaign of 1968* (New York: Viking Press, 1969). Nixon has also left a large body of autobiographical writing, of which the first thirty pages of *Memoirs of Richard Nixon* (New York: Grosset and Dunlap, 1978) provide insight into his early life.

5. Nixon, *Memoirs,* p. 6.

6. Ibid., p. 15.

7. The lessons Nixon learned from his early speaking that are discussed in this paragraph are drawn from Hal W. Bochin, *Richard Nixon: Rhetorical Strategist* (Westport, CT: Greenwood Press, 1990), pp. 4–7.

8. Ben Padrow and Bruce Richards, "Richard Nixon: His Speech Preparation," *Today's Speech*, Nov. 1959, p. 11.

9. Ibid., p. 12.

10. Nixon, *Memoirs*, p. 25.

11. Nixon, *Memoirs*, pp. 38–40.

12. Wicker, *One of Us*, p. 39.

13. Nixon, *Memoirs*, p. 40.

14. Wicker, *One of Us*, p. 42.

15. Christopher Matthews, *Kennedy and Nixon: The Rivalry That Shaped Postwar America* (New York: Simon and Schuster, 1996). On the similarities and early friendship between Kennedy and Nixon, see the introduction and Chapters 1 and 2.

16. See Lawrence Sabato, *Dirty Little Secrets: The Persistence of Corruption in American Politics* (New York: Random House, 1966), pp. 277–78, and Matthews, *Kennedy and Nixon*, pp. 181–83.

17. The best readily available account of this press conference is in Jules Witcover, *The Resurrection of Richard Nixon* (New York: G. P. Putnam's Sons, 1970), pp. 17–22.

18. Nixon's political staff at this time consisted of Shelly Scarney, who had helped Nixon during the 1960 campaign, Pat Buchanan, then twenty-seven years old and hired off the editorial staff of the *St. Louis Globe Democrat*, and Nixon's long-time secretary, Rose Mary Woods.

19. David English, *Divided They Stand* (Englewoods Cliffs, NJ: Prentice-Hall, 1969), p. 79.

20. Rebezo is quoted in Eisenhower, *Pat Nixon*, p. 231.

21. On the text of Nixon's announcement letter to the voters of New Hampshire see Ralph De Tolendao, *One Man Alone: Richard Nixon* (New York: Funk and Wagnall's, 1969), p. 344. Also see English, *Divided*, pp. 79–80.

22. Nixon's remarks are quoted in Ambrose, *Nixon*, p. 135.

23. See English, *Divided*, pp. 62–63, 80–81, for details of the ill-fated Romney campaign.

24. Haldeman's memo is quoted in Matthews, p. 257.

25. The best account of Nixon's new approach to campaigning is Joe McGinniss, *The Selling of the President 1968* (New York: Pocket Books, 1970). For a concise description of the Nixon approach, see Matthews, *Kennedy and Nixon*, pp. 257–65.

26. For the text of the key portion of Rockefeller's announcement, see Wicker, *One of Us*, p. 311.

27. For excerpts from Humphrey's speech, see Chester et al., *An American Melodrama*, p. 162.

28. See Chester et al., *An American Melodrama*, pp. 162–63, for press reaction to Humphrey's speech. The quote used here is from Maryann Mannes.

29. See Wicker, *One of Us*, p. 342, for a discussion of the polls.

30. The *Miami Herald* had planted a tape recorder in one of the caucus rooms where Nixon met in private with southern delegations. The transcripts of those meetings were subsequently widely distributed. Nixon never said anything that he had not said in public. But his very willingness to respond to southern questions, and the ever-present endorsement of Strom Thurmond, no doubt helped to reassure any delegates who might have been considering a bolt to Reagan. For excerpts from the transcripts, see Ambrose, *Nixon*, pp. 169–70, and Wicker, *One of Us*, pp. 343–44.

31. On the Agnew selection and the relationship between Nixon and Agnew, see Nixon, *Memoirs*, pp. 310–16, and Chester, *An American Melodrama*, pp. 244–46.

32. See Chester, *An American Melodrama*, pp. 561–668, for a particularly good account. Also see English, *Divided They Stand*, pp. 260–302, and James T. Patterson, *Grand Expectations: The United States 1945–1974* (New York: Oxford University Press, 1996), pp. 690–98. For an insightful account by one of the

key participants, see Eugene McCarthy, *The Year of the People* (New York: Doubleday, Inc., 1969), pp. 197–226.

33. William Safire, *Before the Fall: An Inside View of the Pre-Watergate White House* (Garden City, NY: Doubleday, 1975), p. 55, quotes Nixon as estimating his audience to be 75 million.

34. Nixon, *Memoirs*, p. 313.

35. Safire reports that Nixon was aware of what his writers had done and did not hesitate to give them credit for passages of his speeches that he had accepted with little change. See Safire, *Before the Fall*, pp. 55–56. This is consistent with the fact that Nixon was the first president to openly acknowledge that he had speechwriters on his White House staff.

36. Ambrose, *Nixon*, pp. 166–67.

37. See Witcover, *Resurrection of Richard Nixon*, pp. 357–59, on Nixon's use of his stock speech.

38. Nixon, *Memoirs*, p. 315.

39. Nixon is quoted by Safire, *Before the Fall*, p. 53.

40. Safire, *Before the Fall*, pp. 54–55.

41. Kurt Ritter, "The 1996 Presidential Nomination Acceptance Addresses: What Do the Speeches by Dole and Clinton Tell Us about the Genre of Acceptance Speeches?" (Paper presented at the annual meeting of the Speech Communication Association, San Diego, Nov. 1996), pp. 1–3.

42. This and all subsequent quotations from Nixon's acceptance address are in Aaron Singer, *Campaign Speeches of American Presidential Candidates: 1928–1972* (New York: Frederick Unger, 1976), pp. 356–66.

43. *London Daily Express* writers covering the campaign were especially impressed by Nixon's approach to this issue. See English, *Divided They Stand*, pp. 180–81, for both excerpts from Nixon's primary speaking on government and black America and the reaction of these members of the British press.

44. The relationship between Eisenhower and Nixon had often seemed cool. Eisenhower had been wary of the very characteristics that Nixon was trying to dispel with his new image, his partisanship and his lack of stature. Those concerns surfaced on 24 August 1960, when Eisenhower was asked to comment on Nixon's influence during his years as vice president. Charles Mohr of *Time* asked a series of questions about Nixon's responsibilities as vice president, which Eisenhower answered by stating that Nixon participated fully in meetings and his opinion was valued, but the ultimate decisions had to be made by the president. Perhaps uncomfortable with the line of questioning, or anxious for the press conference to end, Eisenhower was clearly irritated by Mohr's persistent questioning. Finally, when Mohr asked whether Eisenhower could give an example of a major idea of Nixon's that Eisenhower had utilized, Eisenhower responded. "If you give me a week I might think of one. I don't remember." Unfortunately for Nixon, this was the last question of the press conference and Eisenhower had no opportunity to clarify. Eisenhower subsequently apologized to Nixon, and when Eisen-

hower's grandson married Nixon's daughter, the two men became much closer. By 1968 Eisenhower clearly favored Nixon. See Wicker, *One of Us*, pp. 224–25.

45. Ellen Shields-West, *The World Almanac of Presidential Campaigns* (New York: World Almanac, 1992), p. 215.

46. Ibid. Also see Paul E. Boller, *Presidential Campaigns* (New York: Oxford University Press, 1985), p. 327.

47. English, *Divided They Stand*, p. 363, and Shields-West, *Almanac*, pp. 314–15.

48. Hubert Humphrey, "Campaign Speech, Salt Lake City, September 30, 1968," in Singer, *Campaign Speeches*, p. 382.

49. This statement was written by Bob Haldeman in a memo to William Safire, 5 Sept. 1968, in Safire, *Before the Fall*, pp. 63–65.

50. Safire, *Before the Fall*, pp. 54–56.

51. Kathleen Hall Jamieson, *Packaging the Presidency: A History and Criticism of Presidential Campaign Advertising* (New York: Oxford University Press, 1984), pp. 253–54.

Chapter Four

1980—Ronald Reagan

> At this very moment some young American coming up along the Virginia or Maryland shores of the Potomac is seeing for the first time the lights that glow in the great halls of our government and the monuments to the memory of our great men. Let us resolve tonight that young Americans forever more will see those Potomac lights, that they will always find there a city of hope in a country that is free. And let us resolve that they will say of our day and of our generation that we did keep faith with our God, that we did keep faith with ourselves, that we did protect and pass on lovingly that shining city on a hill.

In late October 1964 Barry Goldwater's presidential campaign staff was engaged in a heated discussion. A half-hour of prime time television had been purchased for the Arizona senator's campaign. A group of wealthy California supporters had purchased the time to air a speech on Goldwater's behalf, delivered by Ronald Reagan. Having heard Ronald Reagan speak, they were impressed with his persuasive ability. They felt that if he were to deliver a speech he had been delivering throughout California on behalf of conservative ideas, it would resonate well nationally for Goldwater. Moreover, it would give exposure to Reagan, whom they were beginning to groom as a prospective candidate for high office in California.

But now, days before the speech was to air, the Goldwater staff was concerned that Reagan's speech was excessive. They feared that it would drive voters from Goldwater, rather than toward him. They were especially sensitive to passages in Reagan's speech in which he claimed that Social Security was presented to America during the Roosevelt administration as an insurance program but had evolved into a welfare program that had been administered with rampant fiscal irresponsibility that threatened its future. Goldwater had been dogged throughout the campaign by the accusation that he would abolish Social Security. His staff felt Reagan's speech might resurrect that issue in the final days of the campaign, just as they were putting it behind them.[1]

Moreover, Reagan had made a host of other potentially controversial statements, many of which were similar to remarks that Goldwater had been making throughout the campaign. Claiming that "government does nothing as well or as economically as the private sector," Reagan had indicted the Tennessee Valley Authority, federal agricultural subsidies, urban renewal programs, and welfare programs. Some on Goldwater's staff feared that Reagan's attacks on a confiscatory tax system that claimed 37 cents of every dollar earned by Americans would alienate moderates. Moreover, Goldwater staff members were concerned that Reagan's attacks on "the architects of accommodation" would alarm those who were concerned about Goldwater's foreign policies. In sum, Goldwater's advisers feared that Reagan's speech seemed to look to the past for inspiration and would resurrect many of the charges that Goldwater was a reactionary.[2]

Hence, in late October, Goldwater's staff considered using the time to present a rebroadcast of an earlier commercial, "Brunch with Barry," in which Goldwater discussed his ideas with a group of housewives, or a similar program in which Goldwater discussed his ideas with former president Eisenhower, still perhaps the most admired person in America. Goldwater's advisers felt that both programs would be less controversial than what they perceived to be the potentially inflammatory rhetoric of Reagan. Moreover, some argued, linking Goldwater to Eisenhower made more sense than linking him to a potentially reactionary stage personality who had never held public office.

With division in his staff, Goldwater called Reagan. It was no doubt an awkward conversation for both men. The airtime had been purchased by the Californians, specifically for the speech by Reagan. Goldwater reviewed the concerns of his staff about Reagan, evidently suggesting that the Goldwater-Eisenhower program be substituted for the Reagan speech. Reagan responded:

> Barry, I've been making the speech all over the state for quite a while and I have to tell you, it's been very well received, including whatever remarks I've made about Social Security. I just can't cancel the speech and give away the airtime; it's not up to me. These gentlemen raised the money and bought the airtime. They're the only ones who could cancel or switch it.[3]

Goldwater replied, "I haven't heard or seen the speech yet; they've got a tape here, so I'll run it and call you back." Goldwater, accompanied by several staff members—including Reagan's brother, who was a vice president of the advertising agency handling the Goldwater campaign and traveling with Goldwater during that portion of the campaign—then viewed the speech. When the viewing was finished, Goldwater looked at his staff and said, "What the hell's wrong with that?"[4]

The decision was made. On 27 October 1964, Ronald Reagan's "A Time for Choosing" was broadcast to the entire nation. When the speech was finished, John Kilroy, national chairman of TV for Goldwater-Miller, asked the audience to contribute to the Goldwater campaign. Within days, Goldwater would suffer one of the most one-sided defeats in presidential campaign history. But Ronald Reagan's "A Time for Choosing" would have a dramatic effect on the course of history.

Replayed frequently on local stations during the last week of the campaign and used as the centerpiece at scores of Goldwater fundraising events during the closing days of the campaign, "A Time for Choosing" almost immediately brought in $1 million for the Goldwater campaign and was ultimately credited with raising $8 million. Reagan's address raised more money than any political speech in history.[5] It may help to understand the enormity of this figure in 1964 by recognizing that $8 million was more than either the Goldwater campaign or the Johnson campaign spent on television airtime, the dominant carrier of political advertising, in their 1964 campaigns.[6] Political observer David Broder of the *Washington Post* called Reagan's speech "the most successful political debut since William Jennings Bryan electrified the 1896 Democratic convention with his 'Cross of Gold' speech."[7]

"A Time for Choosing," which almost was never broadcast, introduced Ronald Reagan as a political advocate to the nation. Thanks to the success of "A Time for Choosing," within weeks of its initial showing and after the massive defeat of Goldwater, Ronald Reagan had almost overnight become the foremost conservative political figure in the nation. "A Time for Choosing" launched the political career that two years later carried Reagan to the governorship of California and by the evening of 3 November 1980 would bring him to the threshold of the presidency. On that evening, Reagan concluded his 1980 presidential campaign by delivering a nationally televised election eve address. Remarkably, in his election eve 1980 address to the nation, Ronald Reagan gave voice to the same basic themes that had first brought him to national attention in 1964. For sixteen years his message had remained consistent. Once more, in 1980, it was a time for choosing.

THE SPEAKER

Ronald Reagan was born on 6 February 1911 to Jack and Nelle Reagan. Reagan has frequently claimed that "we were poor, but we didn't know we were poor."[8] Though Reagan and his older brother Neil may not have known they were poor, certainly his parents recognized their financial problems. As his sons were growing up, Jack was forced to move his family to a series of small Illinois towns, including Galesburg, Monmouth, and Tampico, as well as a brief stay in Chicago, as he attempted to support them as a shoe salesman. In 1920 the Reagans settled permanently in Dixon, Illinois.[9]

Reagan claims that he was always somewhat introverted and from an early age was a "a bookworm of sorts." Indeed, he recalled that by the age of five, without formal instruction, he had learned to read.

> I suspect I'd learned how to read through a kind of osmosis: My mother always came into our room at bedtime and wedged herself between my brother and me to read us a story. As she read, she followed each line on the page with her finger and we watched. I think I just picked it up that way.[10]

Reagan's early reading was all the more remarkable for the fact that he had a vision problem that was undetected until he was thirteen.[11]

Though Reagan was close to his brother while the two were growing up and had many friends, he nevertheless tended to withdraw into himself, finding pleasure as a child in reading, cartooning, and exploring the local wildlife. He attributed much of his early introspection and insecurity to his vision problem that made him a poor athlete until it was corrected. Nancy Reagan acknowledges that Reagan "often seems remote and doesn't let anybody get too close." But she attributes it to a different cause. Recalling her husband's childhood, she claims, "it's hard to make close friends or to put down roots when you're always moving, and I think this—plus the fact that everybody knew his father was an alcoholic—explains why Ronnie became a loner."[12]

The Reagan boys had always known that there was something different about their father. Reagan recalls that "when Nelle thought Neil and I were old enough to know, she sat us down and explained why my father sometimes disappeared and told us the reason for those sudden unexpected trips from home." His mother described his father's alcoholism as a "sickness." But Reagan's father was not abusive and was often able to go for extended periods of times without drinking.[13]

Moreover, Reagan's father Jack, a Catholic in the Protestant Midwest, set an enduring example of tolerance for Reagan, by both speaking and acting against religious and racial intolerance. He refused to let his sons see a revival of *Birth of a Nation* because of the way the movie glorified the white southern treatment of blacks. "The Klan is the Klan and a sheet's a sheet, and any man who wears one over his head is a bum," Jack told his sons.[14] On another occasion, while on a sales trip, he was told by the desk clerk of the only hotel in a small town that he would like the hotel because it wouldn't accept Jews. Jack Reagan stormed out of the hotel, telling the clerk that soon they would probably reject Catholics, and spent the evening sleeping in his car.[15] Moreover, his father was an accomplished storyteller and raconteur, a skill that he passed on to his son and that helped him to prosper in Dixon to a greater extent than he had elsewhere.

It was his mother, Nelle, who first got Ronald Reagan in front of an audience. Dixon had a group of citizens who were interested in the oral interpretation of literature. She was a frequent and able performer within the group. Though he was shy, Reagan recalls that after seeing his brother applauded for his first performances with the group, "I guess there was something competitive enough in me that made me want to try to do as well as my brother and I finally agreed." Reagan could not recall what he performed,

> but I'll never forget the response: people laughed and applauded. That was a new experience for me and I liked it. I liked that approval. For a kid suffering childhood pangs of insecurity, the applause was music. I didn't know it then, but, in a way, when I walked off the stage that night, my life had changed.[16]

Encouraged by his high school English teacher, Reagan soon became active in student theatrical productions. Reagan recalled that his teacher, B. J. Frazer, constantly forced him to try to understand the motivations of the characters he played. "After a while, whenever I read a new script, I'd automatically try first to understand what made that particular human being tick by trying to put myself in his place. The process, called empathy, is not bad training for someone who goes into politics."[17]

After high school, Reagan followed his high school sweetheart to Eureka College. Eureka was not far from Dixon and had offered Reagan a football scholarship, without which he could never have afforded college. His scholarship and a series of campus jobs enabled him to attend. During the 1980 campaign, Reagan was asked to name the single most important influence on his life. Without hesitation, Reagan answered, "the depression."[18] Shortly before the onset of the depression, Jack Reagan had fulfilled his longstanding ambition and opened his own shoe store. But the depression cost him his store, sent him back out on the road as a traveling salesman, forced Nelle to work for $14 a week in a dress shop, and made the Reagan boys enormously cost-conscious as they worked their way through Eureka

College.[19] At Eureka, Reagan became a big man on campus. In addition to playing football and swimming for Eureka, he worked on the yearbook and was active in student government and in dramatic productions. In his senior year, Reagan was elected student body president.

It was his activity in student government that resulted in Reagan's first speaking experience. Eureka was experiencing a serious budget crunch, and the president decided to lay off part of the faculty and impose other cuts. He planned on doing this during the Thanksgiving break of Reagan's freshman year, while students were home on vacation. But his plan became public knowledge, and both the students and faculty were angered. The plan would have made it difficult for many juniors and seniors to graduate because some of the classes that many of them needed to graduate could not be taught after the faculty layoffs. Moreover, the entire campus community resented the way the president had never consulted with either students or faculty to discuss alternative ways of cutting expenses.

As a consequence, a week before the Thanksgiving break, a student committee was elected to consider a student strike. Reagan was a freshman representative. When the trustees ratified the president's proposals, the strike committee called a meeting of students and faculty in the campus chapel. Because he was a freshman and so not as directly affected by the layoffs as the upperclassmen, Reagan was asked to present the committee's proposal for a student strike.

> Giving that speech—my first—was as exciting as any I ever gave. For the first time in my life, I felt my words reach out and grab an audience, and it was exhilarating. When I'd say something, they'd roar after every sentence, sometimes every word, and after a while it was as if the audience and I were one. When I called for a vote on the strike, everybody rose to their feet with a thunderous clapping of hands and approved the proposal for a strike by acclamation.[20]

The strike began immediately after the Thanksgiving break. Students refused to attend classes. Within a week, the president had resigned and Eureka returned to normal. Thus, Reagan's first speaking experience left a lasting impression on him.

It was not until his senior year that Reagan began to think about acting as a career. He performed a major role in a Eureka production that was entered in a national competition held at Northwestern University near Chicago. Reagan recalls that after his performance, the head of the Northwestern speech department called Reagan to his office and suggested that he seriously consider acting as a career.[21]

But Eureka College and Dixon, Illinois, were a long way from Hollywood. Moreover, Reagan was graduating at the outset of the depression. He wanted a job quickly and could not afford to travel to Hollywood and apprentice at a series of low-paying jobs in the hopes of eventually hitting it big. But if Hollywood was distant, Chicago was nearby. Chicago was a major center of the rapidly growing radio industry. Reagan knew precisely what he wanted to do in radio. He would combine his love of speaking and acting with his love of athletics to become a sports announcer.

Reagan's melodious voice and flair for the dramatic soon helped him find work and success in radio. He learned to read, in what sounded like a spontaneous manner, from a script. He recognized the importance of practice. His success in radio made Reagan a regional personality. But he still aspired to stardom.

In 1937 Reagan took a vacation in Hollywood. A friend he had met through his radio work introduced him to Bill Meiklejohn, a successful agent who at that time was representing Robert Taylor and Betty Grable. Meiklejohn landed Reagan a contract with Warner Brothers. For the next twenty years, from 1937 to 1957, Reagan made fifty-two full-length feature films.[22] Throughout his film career, Reagan made hundreds of speeches on behalf of his movies.[23]

During World War II, Reagan served in a military unit that made training films. After the war, Reagan increased his activities in the Screen Actors Guild, eventually serving seven terms as that union's president. In this capacity, Reagan made hundreds of speeches, many on behalf of ridding Hollywood of communist influence. All these activities helped Reagan improve his considerable public-speaking skills.

As Reagan's film career declined, he turned to television. He appeared in more than fifty television dramas as well as serving as the host for "General Electric Theater." He eventually also served as that company's principal spokesman. In this capacity he gave thousands of speeches as he toured General Electric plants around the country. Reagan found this latter responsibility particularly revealing. It provided him a sense of what was on the mind's of middle America. Reagan felt that in Hollywood he had lost touch with the country.[24] Later he hosted *Death Valley Days*, another long-running television show. Thus, throughout the 1950s and early 1960s, Reagan's professional activities were providing him with opportunities to enhance his effectiveness as a speaker.[25]

By the early 1960s Reagan was blending his popularity and name recognition as an actor with his quasi-political activities in the union and as a speaker. He had been raised in a Democratic household, his father even having worked during the depression as a local official of Franklin Roosevelt's

Works Progress Administration. Nevertheless, though he never lost his affinity for FDR, he gradually lost his enthusiasm for the Democratic party. By the 1960s, Reagan believed that the Democratic extensions of the original Roosevelt depression programs, particularly Lyndon Johnson's Great Society programs, were not warranted by the times. Moreover, Reagan believed that these programs of the Democratic party did little more than confiscate the property of some Americans to subsidize others. Reagan felt that programs of this sort could never solve the problems of America's underclasses. In1952 Reagan had been a "Democrat for Eisenhower." By 1960 he was ready to change parties outright, but Nixon's advisers urged Reagan to campaign for Nixon as a Democrat, claiming he would be most effective in that capacity. Reagan agreed, but two years later he formally switched parties.[26] Reagan subsequently defended switching parties by claiming that he had not changed, but that the Democratic party had changed, growing far more liberal. By 1964 Reagan felt comfortable in the Republican party. Speaking about Republican presidential candidate Barry Goldwater, Reagan said that he "admired him greatly. Goldwater's book, *Conscience of a Conservative*, contained a lot of the same points I'd been making in my speeches and I believed the country needed him."[27] As a result, Reagan readily accepted when he was offered the opportunity to chair the Goldwater California campaign and speak throughout the Golden State on Goldwater's behalf.

Reagan's speaking on behalf of Goldwater in California resulted in the speech discussed in the introduction to this chapter. Ronald Reagan's performance in 1964 was one of the few bright spots Republicans had that year. He immediately filled the vacuum left by the defeat of Goldwater as the preeminent spokesperson for the conservative faction of the Republican party.[28] Within months of Goldwater's defeat, the group of wealthy Californians who had financed the national broadcast of "A Time for Choosing" approached Reagan about running for the governorship. In Reagan they perceived a candidate who reflected their own conservative beliefs and who could win, even against an incumbent Democratic governor.[29] His daughter Maureen, his brother Neil, and most important, his wife Nancy, all urged him to do the same. At least one close associate of Reagan's claims that

> Reagan, usually the reactive man, would never have sought elective office except for the insistence of those who came to him and the absence of any other untarnished Republican candidate available to run against Governor Brown. Certainly, he would not have taken the initiative in seeking office.[30]

Thus, in 1966, at the age of fifty-five, Ronald Reagan, for the first time, became a candidate for public office.

REAGAN THE CAMPAIGNER: 1966–1976

In 1966 Ronald Reagan solidified his position as the leader of the conservative element of the Republican party. He had, almost by default, inherited that mantle from the defeated Senator Goldwater in 1964. But he held it without benefit of ever having won a public office. In 1966 he won election as governor of California. From the mid-1960s through his election as president in 1980, Reagan was the "beau ideal" of America's conservatives.

Throughout the decade and a half that preceded his election to the presidency, Reagan was constantly involved in political campaigns. In 1966 and again in 1970, he was elected governor of the nation's largest state. In 1972, during his second term as governor, and with an incumbent Republican, Richard Nixon, as president, Reagan simply lent his support to the Republican ticket. In 1976 he made a serious challenge to the unelected Republican incumbent, President Gerald Ford. Though Ford ultimately won the nomination, Reagan's challenge resulted in the most hotly contested Republican nomination fight since the 1952 Eisenhower-Taft struggle. With Ford's defeat by Jimmy Carter in 1976, Reagan stood, as he had in 1964, as the preeminent spokesperson of the conservative faction of the Republican party. But, unlike twelve years earlier, he was now an experienced political campaigner who had twice won elections in the nation's largest state, had a largely successful eight-year record as governor of California, and had almost wrested the Republican presidential nomination from a sitting president.

Although Reagan had little political experience in 1966 and was challenging an incumbent governor in Edmund "Pat" Brown who four years earlier had defeated Richard Nixon, he was running in a state whose history had minimized the importance of parties and maximized the importance of a candidate's name recognition and personal qualities.

In the early twentieth century, California's progressive reformer, Hiram Johnson, had little use for political parties, believing that in his state they were little more than tools of the Southern Pacific Railroad. Winning election as governor in 1910 by promising to diminish the power of the railroads, Johnson did so by spearheading a host of government reforms. Those reforms included laws that made it illegal for party organizations to endorse candidates. Moreover, Johnson spearheaded the movement that established a novel open primary, which allowed a candidate to seek the nomination of both parties.[31] Since parties could not endorse and candidates often ran in more than one primary, California developed a strong tradition of nonpartisanship, and the functions served by parties in most states were often served by political consultants in California.[32] Though Johnson's unique cross-filing primary system had been abolished by 1966, the legacy of nonpartisanship and the stress on a candidate's personal qualities lingered. Such a state was made for the candidacy of Ronald Reagan.

Preparing for his first race, Reagan drew on his strong conservative philosophy and a group of issues-oriented consultants. Reagan's antitax philosophy was well suited to California in 1966. Governor Brown had instituted massive new programs, including an exceptionally expensive construction project designed to facilitate moving water from the north to the drier south of the state. Reagan's concern for law and order also resonated well with many Californians, who were concerned by the Watts riots of 1965 and the student demonstrations that were starting on many state campuses.

In the primary, Reagan had little trouble beating back the challenge of former San Francisco mayor George Christopher, who had already lost two statewide races. In contrast, Brown had considerable trouble beating back the challenge of former Los Angeles Mayor Sam Yorty. Yorty attacked Brown for his lack of leadership, dramatized by the fact that Brown was in Europe during the Watts riots.

In the general election, Reagan stuck to basic themes. Invariably, any specific issue that Reagan utilized was always used to support his overarching theme that Governor Brown's leadership had failed. Brown's failure of leadership had, claimed Reagan, manifested itself in the growing cost of welfare to California taxpayers, the inability of educators to prevent lawlessness on the state's campuses, and a host of lesser issues. Brown focused his attack on Reagan as an actor and an extremist. But, as others would find in subsequent elections, neither issue took with California's voters.

Reagan was an exceptionally effective candidate. Observers had anticipated that Reagan would be effective in delivering prepared speeches. Indeed, early in the campaign, Brown claimed that Reagan was simply an actor reading speeches that someone else wrote, as he had read scripts that had been written by others. Reagan responded by changing his presentations. He gave exceedingly brief opening remarks, and then spent virtually all his time answering questions.[33] Reagan proved unusually adept at answering questions and in so doing, negated Brown's implication that he did not have a mind of his own. Reagan's ability was a function of the fact that he had a coherent political philosophy that he could fall back on whenever he had difficulty with a question, and that he worked hard to master the art of responding to questions. Early in the campaign, fearing the very charge that Brown would subsequently make, Reagan improved his ability to answer questions by working in long practice sessions with press secretary Lyn Nofziger.[34] Reagan's affability soon won over many members of the California press corps as well.

Meanwhile, Brown continued to flail at Reagan as a mere actor. He stressed his own accomplishments as governor. Typically, he would rattle off a series of his own accomplishments and then conclude that he was doing all this while Ronald Reagan was making *Bedtime for Bonzo.* In one of his more infamous attacks on Reagan the actor, Brown ran a commercial that depicted him talking to a group of young children. "I'm running against an actor," Brown told the children. "And you known who killed Abe Lincoln, don't you?" Reagan recalls that when he saw that advertisement, "I knew he knew he was in trouble."[35]

Brown was not successful in responding to Reagan's indictment of his leadership. Neither did Brown's scorn for Reagan's acting career likely sit well in a state where the entertainment industry was a major contributor to the economy, besides the fact that it ignored Reagan's many years of activities in quasi-political leadership positions such as his union work.

Reagan won by almost a million votes, taking 58 percent of the votes cast. He carried virtually the entire Republican ticket with him. According to Fred Dutton, one of Governor Brown's closest advisers, the incumbent simply underestimated Reagan. Having defeated Nixon four years earlier, Brown anticipated that much like Goldwater, Reagan would be perceived as a harsh and divisive figure by voters. However, as Dutton subsequently observed,

> Reagan has no harsh edge to him. Part of what happened is that we took him on as an actor, putting down one of the great industries of the state, but the roots of the mistake go deeper. Reagan is terribly pleasant, highly articulate and has a serious approach about politics. People like him, and we didn't understand that. We missed the human dimension of Ronald Reagan.[36]

In 1970 Reagan ran for a second term. Reagan's principal accomplishment during his first term was a popular reform of California's welfare program. Compromising with the Democratic legislature, Reagan's reforms significantly narrowed the number of Californians eligible for welfare. However, his program provided greater benefits, including automatic cost-of-living increases to those who did qualify.[37] Running with a record of accomplishment, hence largely nullifying the "actor" issue, Reagan had no trouble winning reelection in 1970. He readily defeated former Assembly speaker Jesse Unruh.

In 1976 Reagan mounted a serious challenge to President Gerald Ford for the Republican presidential nomination. Though unelected, having succeeded to the presidency after Nixon resigned, Ford still controlled the machinery of the Republican party. It looked initially as if the Republican organization and the goodwill that many Republicans were willing to extend Ford (who had inherited the White House from the disgraced Richard Nixon) would secure Ford the nomination with little trouble. The president defeated Reagan in a close first primary in New Hampshire. Then Ford beat Reagan in Florida. He followed those victories with victories in two states that Reagan had chosen not to contest, Vermont and Massachusetts. In Reagan's home state of Illinois, Ford won big. Reagan's candidacy seemed all but over.

However, when the primaries moved south, Reagan began to find his footing. With a big helping hand from North Carolina's conservative Republican organization, Reagan scored his first victory in the Tarheel State. Seeking to knock out Reagan for good, Ford made a major push in the Texas primary. But Reagan's conservative western appeal was made for Texas. The Californian swept the Texas primary, winning all 100 of the state's delegates. With that victory, it was clear that Ford and Reagan would both contest the nomination up to the convention. Ultimately, Ford was able to beat back the challenge from Reagan. Reagan won 1,070 of the delegate votes to Ford's 1,187.[38]

But the legacy of Richard Nixon and the Watergate scandal was too much for Ford to overcome in the general election. Ford was defeated by Jimmy Carter. Thus, by early 1977, Ronald Reagan had become the leader of his party. The 1980 nomination was his, if he did not stumble on his way to getting it.

REAGAN THE CAMPAIGNER: 1980 PRIMARIES

Accompanying Ronald Reagan as he campaigned during the early primaries, journalist Elizabeth Drew described the typical Reagan rally. Reagan's advance team would arrange for a local high school band to strike up "Stars and Stripes Forever" as the candidate entered the auditorium. Reagan would speak with a backdrop decorated in red, white, and blue, often with an American flag prominently displayed behind him. Throughout the crowd, supporters would be wearing straw boaters with red, white, and blue hatbands into which were tucked pictures of a smiling Reagan. Prominently displayed throughout the room on banners, leaflets, buttons, and other campaign paraphernalia was the Reagan campaign slogan, "Let's Make America Great Again." Drew observed that "over the years, the Reagan campaigns have done better than any other at appropriating the patriotic symbols."[39]

In the same manner as he did in his California campaigns, Reagan opened with brief remarks and then took questions from the audience. Because of the lengthy question-and-answer sessions, Reagan referred to his appearances as "dialogues" with his audiences, rather than speeches.[40] This format made Reagan seem both knowledgeable and accessible to his audience. The consistency of his positions for more than a decade contributed to his mastery of the materials he needed to answer virtually every question. Though he held four-by-six index cards with notes on a variety of issues, Drew claimed that he rarely used them.[41]

With the country facing daily reminders of such problems as high unemployment, high inflation, and diminished respect overseas, Reagan's message was well received not only by conservative Republicans, but by voters of all political stripes. Reagan was also a far more appealing messenger than prior conservative leaders. Though he struck some of the same notes as Goldwater, or even Nixon, Reagan was not a harsh and divisive figure. Using examples and stories to humanize his points, delivering his message smoothly, mixing in just a bit of humor, and frequently reminding his audiences of his competency as governor, Reagan came across in 1980 as a highly plausible candidate for the presidency. Reagan's message, and indeed his own image and persona, invoked a day when America was a more prosperous and stronger nation. No doubt for many Americans, he was the person who could indeed "Make America Great Again."

During the years after he left the governorship, Reagan had written a newspaper column and taped radio editorials. These ventures provided him an audience in hundreds of communities around the country. During the campaign, these efforts were discontinued, since the media outlets that carried them would face equal-time problems. However, when Reagan was making a campaign appearance during the primaries, his staff frequently arranged interviews with the papers and stations that had carried his show.[42]

Reagan's message was well received by New Hampshire Republicans, who gave him an overwhelming victory in the nation's first primary. Reagan defeated former congressman, ambassador to the United Nations, director of the CIA, and ambassador to China, George Bush. Bush had scored a victory in the Iowa straw polls and seemed to be the most formidable challenger to Reagan. Meanwhile, former President Ford was angling to be drafted by the party. Ford claimed that a conservative Republican simply could not win a national election.[43]

Though signaling his availability, Ford was not ready to actively campaign. Meanwhile, Reagan was making quick work of those who were actively contesting the nomination. Within three weeks, Reagan won seven of the nine primaries after New Hampshire. In so doing, he eliminated former

Texas governor and secretary of the treasury John Connally, who threw his support to Reagan. Moreover, by beating Bush with almost a 2–1 margin in several states, he began to dry up the enthusiasm and donations that his principal challenger had once generated. Moreover, Reagan's strong showing in the early primaries had deflated much of Ford's argument, and on 15 March Ford announced that he would not be a candidate and "would support the nominee of my party with all the energy I have. America," he continued, "is in deep deep trouble and needs the help of all of us."[44] By the 18 March Illinois primary, two more challengers, Senators Robert Dole and Howard Baker, had dropped out of the race. Besides Bush, the only challengers left were two Illinois congressmen.

Congressman Phil Crane was never a serious threat to Reagan. Indeed, there was no candidate in the field whose conservative political beliefs were as close to Reagan's as Crane. His candidacy had never generated strong enthusiasm at the national level and was perceived as a means of advancing his political standing within his home state. But Congressman John Anderson was not a conservative. Though more liberal than Bush, he had not been able to displace Bush as the principal alternative to Reagan in the early primaries. However, Anderson hoped that in his home state of Illinois he might do just that.

Thus, the 18 March Illinois primary became the critical primary for Reagan's foes. If Reagan could not be stopped in a major midwestern state, it was likely he could not be denied the nomination. Having lost New Hampshire, Bush had fought Reagan to a draw in liberal Massachusetts and Vermont. Reagan had prevailed throughout the South. Bush needed a win in Illinois to rejuvenate his own campaign and legitimize the claim that Reagan was too conservative to win a national election. As in many of the earlier primary states, the candidates agreed to debate in the Illinois primary.

During the debate, Anderson claimed that he would rather have Senator Edward Kennedy, then challenging President Carter for the Democratic nomination, as president than Ronald Reagan. Reagan, with a big smile, responded: "John, would you really find Teddy Kennedy preferable to me?" As the audience laughed, Congressman Crane jumped in, showing the audience a fundraising mailer Anderson had signed for four of the most liberal Democratic members of the Senate, Frank Church, George McGovern, John Culver, and Birch Bayh. In effect, Crane was illustrating that Anderson had become so liberal that he no longer had much in common with many Republicans. Anderson, clearly hoping to succeed Bush as the liberal alternative to Reagan, focused most of his remarks and campaigning on Bush. On election day Reagan carried the Illinois Republican primary with 48 percent of the vote. Anderson had succeeded in defeating Bush. Anderson carried 37 percent of the vote, and Bush but 11 percent.[45] However, neither candidate could hope to defeat Reagan for the Republican nomination.

Anderson made it official a month later, when he ended his candidacy for the Republican nomination and announced he would run as an independent.[46] Bush continued to campaign, winning in Pennsylvania and Michigan, with the help of the liberal Republican state organizations in those two states. But Reagan won everywhere else. By 20 May Reagan had won 29 of the 35 primaries and had won almost 400 of the 478 delegates picked by state caucuses.[47] The nomination was his.

The GOP convention, held in Detroit, was an opportunity for Reagan to unify the party. Though Reagan left the convention with the party unified behind him, it was not without a bit of drama. The major question to be decided at the convention was whom Reagan would select for the vice presidency. Representatives of former president Ford let it be known that the former president would consider the second spot on a ticket headed by Reagan. On the surface, this so-called "dream ticket" had much to recommend it. Ford was still an enormously popular figure within the party. Moreover, President Carter's many problems might well have made many Americans regret that they had not voted for Ford in 1976. But as soon as serious negotiations between Ford's representatives and those of Reagan began, it was obvious that the "dream ticket" was just that, a dream. From the standpoint of one of Reagan's representatives, Ed Meese, the problem was that if the Reagan-Ford ticket was elected

> it appeared a kind of "co-presidency" might be sought—Ford having certain areas of responsibility, and power, beyond those customary for a vice president. I had no doubt that, from Kissinger's [former Secretary of State Henry Kissinger represented Ford during these discussions] standpoint, this meant control over important facets of foreign policy and arms control. . . . From my perspective as a negotiator, this was a complete nonstarter. . . . I didn't think that Ronald Reagan had campaigned for president in 1976 and again in 1980 to wind up with others calling the shots on foreign policy—or to barter away other aspects of the executive authority conferred on the president by the Constitution.[48]

Reagan determined not to make the offer to Ford, at just about the same time that Ford was himself evidently determining that such an arrangement was not practical.[49]

In the end, Reagan turned to George Bush, who had run second to him in the primaries. Bush offered many of the characteristics that Ford offered. He was a moderate and—unlike Goldwater's selection of Representative William Miller, another conservative—Reagan's selection of Bush was perceived as an attempt to broaden support of the ticket and unify the party. Between them, Reagan and Bush had won 85 percent of the votes in the Republican primaries.[50] Moreover, Bush had a wealth of government experience. Much of Bush's experience was in foreign affairs, an area where some questioned Reagan's knowledge. He brought geographic balance to the ticket in addition and was universally perceived as well prepared to step into the presidency should something happen to Reagan.[51]

In 1976 the Reagan forces had contested the Republican party platform at the convention. In 1980 the platform was adopted with little controversy. It was largely a traditional Republican document, but it offered something to almost every faction of the party. For example, though the platform was strongly pro-life as conservatives wished, it took no position on the Equal Rights Amendment, claiming that that was an issue for each state to decide. This neutral position helped quell moderate dissatisfaction.[52] Rather than divide Republicans, the platform unified them in repudiating the Carter administration.

Reagan's acceptance address to the Republican National Convention was also calculated to unify the party and broaden his support during the general election. Reagan's effort to broaden the base of his party and reach out beyond conservatives is evident throughout the address.

- I'm very proud of our party tonight. This convention has shown to all America a party united with positive programs for solving the nation's problems; a party ready to build a new consensus with all those across the land who share our community of values embodied in these words: family, work, neighborhood, peace, and freedom.
- More than anything else, I want my candidacy to unify our country, to renew the American spirit and sense of purpose. I want to carry our message to every American, regardless of party affiliation, who is a member of this community of shared values.
- Everywhere [Nancy and I have traveled] we've meet thousands of Democrats, independents, and Republicans from all economic conditions, walks of life, bound together in that community of shared values of family, work, neighborhood, peace, and freedom. . . . They are the kind of men and women Tom Paine had in mind when he wrote, during the darkest days of the American Revolution, "We have it in our power to begin the world over again."
- I ask you to trust that American spirit which knows no ethnic, religious, social, political, regional, or economic boundaries; the spirit that burned with zeal in the hearts of millions of immigrants from every corner of the earth who came here in search of freedom.

Hence, as the general election opened, Ronald Reagan headed the ticket of a unified Republican party that was seeking to broaden its support.

RONALD REAGAN THE CAMPAIGNER: 1980 GENERAL ELECTION

President Carter and Governor Reagan started the general election with what both felt were reasonably secure regional bases. Carter anticipated holding most of the South that he had won four years earlier. Moreover, he anticipated that the Democratic Northeast could be counted on for support. Reagan anticipated running strongly in the West, including his home state of California. Though Carter had done well in his native South in 1976, Reagan's conservative philosophy, and the continued growth of the Republican party throughout the South, caused him to focus on two large southern states, Texas and Florida. Nevertheless, it was clear that the critical states for both candidates would likely be the industrial states of Pennsylvania, Ohio, Michigan, and Illinois. Some reports had Reagan devoting 40 percent of his campaign time to these states, Texas, and Florida.[53]

Consistent with the themes he developed in "A Time for Choosing" and much of his early political speaking, Ronald Reagan had one overarching theme that was the hallmark of his campaign. He consistently argued that he had faith in America and that he was optimistic about the future. His optimism was based on his firm belief that if the country followed the policies he was advocating, America would be restored to its former greatness. Rhetorical critics Kurt Ritter and David Henry have characterized Reagan's 1980 campaign speaking as "A Restoration Jeremiad."[54] It is an apt characterization. Reagan's speeches were secular sermons.

Ritter and Henry argue that a secular jeremiad involves three parts. First, "the promise, which stresses America's special destiny as the promised land—literally its covenant with God." Second, "the declension, which cites America's failure to live up to its obligations as the chosen people." Third, "the prophecy, which predicts that if Americans will repent and reform, the promise can still be fulfilled." Ritter and Henry argue that "much of the power of Reagan's political speeches derive from his skill at adapting this old Puritan sermon form to contemporary campaigning."[55]

Reagan focused the declension of his 1980 jeremiads primarily on Carter's economic policies and secondarily on his military and defense policies. Reagan argued that America under Carter had failed to live up to its obligations. Throughout the campaign Reagan indicted Carter on three counts. First, that Carter's energy policies and related economic policies amounted to giving up on future economic growth. Second, that Carter's economic policies had produced economic misery. Finally, Reagan argued that Carter's defense policies had weakened the American military position relative to the Soviet Union.[56] The lack of respect America commanded, most evident in Iran's seizing of hostages, underscored Reagan's foreign policy claims. Reagan and his campaign team felt that his message had to illustrate that the traditional Republican economic values and the traditional Republican support for a strong defense offered America an optimistic future. They felt that the contrast to Carter's defense of his largely failed economic policies would be striking and attract millions of new Republican voters, such as ethnic minorities, urban Catholics, and blue-collar workers who rarely voted Republican.

Reagan attacked Carter's economic polices for contributing to the growth of inflation. This attack was especially damaging. Inflation has traditionally been an issue where conservatives are perceived to have better answers than liberals, because government spending, waste, and inefficiency can often be portrayed as causing much of the problem. Reagan went out of his way to select settings that highlighted his economic message. He frequently spoke in depressed urban areas and at closed or underutilized factories.[57]

Nevertheless, the overall mood of Reagan's campaign was upbeat. If America had failed under Carter to live up to its obligations, it was not too late to reform. The prophecy of Reagan's jeremiads provided the optimistic view that permeated Reagan's campaign speaking. The promise of America's special destiny could be fulfilled if voters would turn to Reagan. For Reagan would return the nation to the old values and virtues it had lost during the Carter administration and in doing so, lead us to our special destiny. Reagan's use of the jeremiad form allowed him to focus on the shortcomings of the Carter administration while nevertheless remaining optimistic about the future.

Carter had serious problems throughout the campaign. During the primaries he had won renomination only after beating back a strong challenge from Massachusetts Senator Edward Kennedy. The senator and Democrats such as California governor Jerry Brown had been emboldened to challenge a sitting president from their own party because of his lack of accomplishment and the perception that he was not in the liberal tradition of his party.

As the general election opened, the nation was suffering from high unemployment and high inflation. Moreover, Carter's foreign policy record was also weak. For nine months, America had been unable to secure the release of fifty-two hostages from Iran or secure changes in the OPEC oil policies, which were contributing to inflation. Carter entered the general election in June 1980 with the lowest job-approval ratings of any incumbent president since the Gallup poll had begun taking such measurements in the 1940s. Only 31 percent of the public approved of the job Carter was doing. In July Carter's approval rating reached an all-time low of 21 percent. In contrast, four years earlier, in June 1976, 45 percent of the public approved of the job Ford was doing at the outset of an election campaign that he would soon lose.[58]

Having difficulty in defending his own record and convincing the public that he deserved another term, Carter was left with few alternatives to attacking Reagan. Essentially, Carter attempted to argue that Reagan could not be trusted with the presidency. In accepting the Democratic nomination, Carter set the tone for much of what would follow as he attempted to portray Reagan, much as Johnson had done with Goldwater, as a threatening and divisive figure. Imagining life under a Reagan administration, Carter claimed

> I see despair—the despair of millions who would struggle for equal opportunity and a better life—and struggle alone. And I see surrender—the surrender of our energy future to the merchants of oil, the surrender of our economic future to a bizarre program of massive tax cuts for the rich, service cuts for the poor and massive inflation for everyone. And I see risk—the risk of international confrontation: the risk of an uncontrollable, unaffordable, and unthinkable nuclear arms race.

Political candidates typically caricature their opponents. From his acceptance address forward, the major thrust of Carter's campaign was to caricature Reagan as a warmonger and a tool of the rich who had little sympathy for the middle class and poor.

In October Carter's attacks on Reagan began to backfire. Carter had repeatedly suggested that the Carter-versus-Reagan choice was a choice between peace and war. To claim that Reagan might not exert good foreign policy judgment, or lacked the background to conduct foreign policy skillfully, might have been legitimate claims. But suggesting that Reagan's election would result in war seemed intemperate to most observers. Moreover, Carter compounded his difficulty when, speaking in Chicago, he claimed that the 1980 election would "determine whether or not this America will be unified or, if I lose the election, whether Americans might be separated, black from white, Jew from Christian, North from South, rural from urban."[59] Journalists quickly jumped on Carter for running a "mean" campaign. With the war charge already out on the table, his October claims that Reagan would divide the country by race, by religion, and by geography reinforced the image that Carter was a "mean" campaigner. Carter's "meanness" was surfacing at the same time that he was refusing to debate Reagan and independent candidate John Anderson. This led the public to perceive the president as relying on exaggerated attacks on his opponent because he was both unwilling and unable to defend his own policies.

Carter attempted to remedy both problems. First, his staff arranged an opportunity for Carter to apologize in an interview with TV journalist Barbara Walters. But his apology made him appear weak and indecisive.[60] This played into the image that many people were developing of Carter based in part on his refusal to participate in the 21 September debate between John Anderson and Reagan.

Finally, the Carter campaign determined that he would have to debate. Fortunately for him, Anderson's standing in the polls dropped below the 15 percent level that the League of Women Voters had used to justify inviting him to the first debate. Consequently, they did not invite him to the second, and Carter was able to debate Reagan without Anderson. Carter had consistently refused a three-person debate, claiming he would be debating two Republicans who would both attack him. The negotiations about the debate had extended throughout much of the general election period. It was not until 28 October, one week before the election, that the two men would debate.

While neither candidate seemed to have a decisive edge on the issues discussed in the debate, Reagan seemed "presidential," and his stage presence and gentle humor helped to dispel the charges that he was a harsh and divisive figure who would lead us into war. Reagan's closing statement during the debate focused the audience's attention on Carter's shortcomings. Reagan suggested that voters ask themselves, "Are you better off than you were four years ago? Is it easier for you to go and buy things in the stores than it was four years ago? Is there more or less unemployment in the country than there was four years ago? Is America respected throughout the world as it was? Do you feel that our security is as safe, that we're as strong as we were four years ago?"[61]

Carter used the debate to continue his attacks on Reagan. Far more than Reagan, the president attacked. As he had throughout the campaign, he attempted to illustrate that there were sharp differences between the two candidates. Moreover, he continually reminded the audience that he was the president. In effect, he was telling the audience that he was a proven quantity compared to the risky Reagan. In addition, he attempted to reinforce his support among voter blocs that he had targeted as critical to his reelection.[62]

As the final weekend of the election approached, the public had largely concluded that Carter's presidency had been a failure. Even the president's election eve address virtually acknowledged that he had done a poor job.[63] By the same token, as the election approached, the public still had reservations about the Republican candidate. Carter's attacks, while perhaps exaggerated, nevertheless had identified the concerns that many voters had about Reagan's domestic economic policies and his approach to foreign policy. Hence, most observers were suggesting that it would be a close election.

The polls tended to confirm that view. Though survey research data suggest that in most elections two-thirds of the electorate has normally made up its mind before the political campaign ever begins, the 1976 election appears to have been an exception. When the conventions were over and the general election got under way, only 52 percent of the electorate had made up their minds. Moreover, 25 percent of the electorate did not make up their minds until the last two weeks of the campaign, and fully 8 percent did not decide how they would vote until election day.[64] The final Gallup poll, taken a few days before the election and published the day before, found 9 percent of the electorate undecided; when combined with those voters who were weakly committed to the candidate of their choice, Gallup reported that even at that late date about one-third of the electorate could still be moved.[65] John Anderson, who ultimately finished with 7 percent of the vote, claimed that one polling expert with whom he dealt reported that "never in his entire experience had he seen voters agonize as much over their final choice, their final selection, as they did in this election." Anderson claimed that fully 20 percent of the voters made up their minds in the last week of the election.[66]

Making the election even more difficult to predict was the fact that the presidential election is really a set of fifty separate state races. Hence, national trends may not be overly meaningful, since they tend to obscure state differences and the impact of those differences on the electoral college vote. By mid-October, state-by-state surveys were showing that Reagan was in front, but that Carter was closing in many states and that the election was too close to call.[67] While the accuracy of any of these studies could be questioned, the cumulative evidence does suggest that as late as the last few days of the campaign, the election was still very close.

On election eve, both candidates made their final appeals to the nation. Carter's appeal included pictures of statues of prior Democratic presidents, visuals of politicians praising Carter, and footage of the signing of the Camp David Peace Accords, his signal foreign-policy achievement. After these visuals, the scene shifts to Carter, seated at his desk and wearing a sweater. Reagan's appeal shows the candidate and his running mate seated in what appears to be a study, dressed in suits, talking to one another. After a few words from his running mate George Bush, Reagan spoke.

RONALD REAGAN'S 1980 ELECTION EVE ADDRESS

Richard Wirthlin, deputy director of strategy and planning for the Reagan campaign, responding to questions one month after the campaign, claimed that Ronald Reagan won because "he had a sense of vision of

America that provided a frame of reference for the strategy that gave us a consistent and directed thrust to the campaign right from the beginning to the end."[68] Wirthlin suggested that there were seven "imperatives" that drove the Reagan campaign. These imperatives served as a commonplace or topic system that provided Reagan with the themes he utilized as he preached his secular jeremiads:

- We place trust in the values of American society.
- We treat American leaders, both public and private, as accountable stewards, responsible for living up to what we identified in the campaign as certain commonly shared values of family, work, peace, freedom, and so on.
- We recognize the inherent value of individual initiative and operate on the basic premise that in a representative democracy, government—whether it be federal, state, or local—should not perform functions that are better handled by the individual citizens on their own behalf.
- Government's size and costs have exceeded what's reasonable and result in government doing things that are unnecessary and too often missing the mark on what is needed.
- The two demons of economics that we're dealing with, the sluggish economy and inflation, are principally caused by excessive government spending, taxation, and regulation.
- A once proud and strong America should not acquiesce to a secondary role in the world.
- Leaders have an obligation to translate not only the voters' but the people's best hopes and aspirations into public policy that will provide a direction and hope to the collective enterprise that was absent previously.[69]

Reagan's election eve address was consistent with the entire campaign. It clearly reflected the seven imperatives that Wirthlin believed had driven the campaign and utilized the key elements of a secular jeremiad: the promise, the declension, and the prophecy. However, Reagan's election eve address did not utilize the jeremiad elements in the normal order. On 4 November 1979, exactly one year before election day 1980, Iran had seized fifty-two American hostages. With this disturbing anniversary in mind, Reagan opened his speech by skipping the promise and moving directly to the declension, the recitation of America's failure to meet its mission, to live up to its obligations.

The decisions we make tomorrow will determine our country's course through what promises to be one of the most perilous decades in our history. I know that tonight the fate of America's fifty-two hostages is very much on the minds of all of us.

Like you, there is nothing I want more than their safe return, that they will be reunited with their families after this long year of their imprisonment. When they return, all of us will be turning to the concerns that will determine the course of America these next four years.[70]

At this point Reagan spends several minutes detailing what "many of us are unhappy about." He concludes this indictment of the Carter administration by claiming that America suffers from "a lack of leadership" and a government "that is too large, too bureaucratic, too wasteful, too unresponsive, too uncaring about people and their problems." Reagan claims that it is time for "reform and renewal" and that it is time "to make government responsive to the people and revitalize the values of family, and work, and neighborhood and restore our private and independent social institutions."

Reagan's development of the declension, the indictment of the Carter administration for its economic and foreign-policy shortcomings, also includes an indication of how he would govern. Reagan promises that he will help remedy the problems he discusses by reducing tax rates, reducing government regulation, restoring the health and vitality of state and local governments, and bringing into government public servants of high standards and integrity. He specifically mentioned preserving a fiscally sound Social Security program and cited his accomplishments in California to illustrate his ability to get things done. In this section of the speech Reagan treats issues that clearly reflect the first six of the seven imperatives that Wirthlin felt drove the campaign. Thus, within the first ten minutes of his presentation, Reagan treated the majority of the imperatives that dominated his campaign and indicted the Carter administration for its failure to lead the nation. What Reagan presented in the opening ten minutes of his election eve address does not differ markedly from what many other political figures might have done. He attacked his opponent.

What Reagan does in the remaining twenty minutes of this speech is distinctively Ronald Reagan. "Beyond even these reforms," Reagan continues, making the transition to the remaining portion of his speech, "there is something more, much more, that needs to be said tonight. That's why I want to talk to you not about campaign issues, but about America."

At this point in his address, Reagan uses a few sentences to quickly review American history since World War II. He concludes by observing

then came the hard years, the 1960s and the 1970s and then came the drift of the last four years. For the first time in our memory many Americas are asking . . . does history still have a place for America, for her people, for her great ideals. There are some who answer no; that our energy is spent, our days of greatness are at an end, that a great national malaise is upon us. They say we must cut our expectations, conserve and withdraw, that we must tell our children not to dream as we once dreamed.

But Reagan disagrees. "Our country," he claims, "is not ready for the dustbin of history."

As he illustrates why the nation is not ready for the "dustbin of history," Reagan is in effect presenting the section of the speech that equates to the promise in the jeremiad form. He presents America as a special nation that has been blessed by God with liberty. He illustrates the special nature of the nation by discussing recent American heroes, the returning Vietnam prisoners of war. Reagan asks, "Where does America get heroes like these?" He answers, "These men were the products of our shops, our farms, our city streets. They are just the product of the freest society the world has ever known." He continues the promise section of this speech by claiming that "it is our spiritual commitment more than all the military might in the world that will win our struggle for peace. It is not bombs and rockets, but belief and resolve. It is humility before God that is ultimately the source of America's strength as a nation." At this point Reagan concludes the promise section of the speech by using his oft-repeated story about John Winthrop and his desire to build a "Shining City upon a Hill."

Having reaffirmed America's promise, Reagan turns to the prophecy. Here he predicts that America will ultimately fulfill its promise. By implication, Reagan makes it clear that to fulfill that promise America needs to elect him. Reagan quotes Dr. Joseph Warren to lead into his last appeal for votes. Before the battle of Bunker Hill, Warren implored the men with whom he would soon fight and die: "Our country is in danger, but not to be despaired of. On you depend the fortunes of America. You are to decide the important questions on which rests the happiness and liberty of millions yet unborn. Act worthy of yourselves." Reagan immediately continues, "tomorrow morning you will be making a choice between different visions of the future. Your decision is a uniquely personal one. It belongs to no one but you. It will be critical in determining the path we will follow in the years ahead." At this point, much as he did in his closing statement of the debate, Reagan asks his audience to consider whether they are satisfied with the nation's progress on unemployment, inflation, personal security, and national security.

After what might be considered this almost obligatory election eve appeal for votes, Reagan concludes his address by reinforcing his prophecy:

At this very moment some young American coming up along the Virginia or Maryland shores of the Potomac is seeing for the first time the lights that glow in the great halls of our government and the monuments to the memory of our great men. Let us resolve tonight that young Americans forever more will see those Potomac lights, that they will always find there a city of hope in a country that is free. And let us resolve that they will say of our day and of our generation that we did keep faith with our God, that we did keep faith with ourselves, that we did protect and pass on lovingly that shining city on a hill.

In developing this prophecy section of his address, Reagan incorporates the last of the seven imperatives that Wirthlin indicated drove the Reagan campaign. He is utilizing people's hopes and aspirations to provide direction and hope for the public policy he anticipates implementing.

In sum, Ronald Reagan's 1980 election eve address reflects much of his 1980 campaign speaking, although it organizes the three major sections somewhat differently, opening with the declension rather than the promise—perhaps in part to capitalize on the publicity and anxiety surrounding the one-year anniversary of the seizing of America's fifty-two hostages by Iran. Nevertheless, Reagan's address fulfills the three functions of a secular jeremiad. It stresses America's special God-given destiny, cites America's failure to live up to its obligations, placing that failure squarely in the lap of the Carter administration, and prophesies that under new leadership, in this instance obviously to be provided by Reagan, America will fulfill her destiny. In fulfilling these three functions, Reagan treats virtually every one of the seven imperatives that drove his campaign. Though most were treated in the declension, when Reagan indicted the Carter administration, the first, that American values must be trusted and followed, and the last, that leaders have an obligation to translate the people's best hopes and aspirations into public policy that provide direction and hope, were largely treated in Reagan's discussion of the promise and the prophecy.

EFFECTS

The 1980 presidential election is an election that is frequently cited to support the contention that campaigns make a difference. After examining a host of public opinion polls, political scientist David Everson points out that at the height of the Iranian crisis, in January 1980, Carter led Reagan by nearly two to one in a two-man race. However, by the end of the primaries and the beginning of summer, Reagan had caught up and was moving ahead. After the Democratic convention, Everson reports that the national polls claimed the two major candidates were in a virtual dead heat and that the Anderson candidacy was in a sharp decline. Everson found that "on the eve of the election, most polls were saying that the election was 'too close to call.'"[71]

Reagan clearly benefited from the debate, held one week before the election.[72] By the Friday before the Tuesday election, the effect of the debate seemed to have been factored into the polls. They showed Reagan with a slight lead in a very close election. Having apparently weathered the debate, by Friday Carter campaign chairman Robert Strauss was optimistic that Carter would win.

> Reagan got his plus out of the debate early—he got a bit of a bump in the polls. I think we'll get ours when the Democrats go to vote. Carter talked to our constituents in the debate. That's not the sort of thing you win a debate on, necessarily, but it's how we get our Democrats back. It's close; it's very, very, very close. I think over the weekend people have to contemplate a Reagan Presidency, and we have to get our vote out.[73]

As the weekend opened, Carter's polling was providing Democrats with reason to be optimistic. Patrick Caddell, Carter's principal polling consultant, subsequently observed of the campaign's last week, "we had seen a drop after the debate, by Thursday and Friday, and we had started to see it moving back Saturday afternoon and Saturday night."

But Caddell reported that by Sunday, "we saw it beginning to unravel again."[74] By Sunday evening, Caddell's poll was showing that Carter was behind Reagan by five points. By one o'clock on election day, his poll was showing that Carter could lose to Reagan by as much as ten points.[75] The volatile poll results, even in the last days of the campaign, highlight the indecision in the electorate. The subsequent election results suggest that in the one to three days immediately preceding the election most of the undecided voters, as well as many of those who were lightly committed to Carter, chose to vote for Reagan. Reagan won by almost 8 million votes. He carried 51 percent of the vote to 41 percent for Carter. John Anderson received 7 percent of the vote, with the remainder divided among several other minor candidates. Reagan swept forty-four states and carried 489 electoral votes, compared to Carter's six states and the District of Columbia, with a total of 49 electoral votes.[76]

It is impossible to pinpoint any one factor that caused the large last-moment shift to Reagan. However, to the extent that Reagan's election eve address was likely the most widely watched address of either candidate during the critical last days, it cannot be ignored.[77] That it was broadcast at a critical time, as many voters were making up their minds, and that it was an artistically noteworthy speech also suggests the importance of Reagan's election eve address. Ronald Reagan has often been called the Great Communicator. While his 1980 election eve address is rarely mentioned as one of his most outstanding efforts, it warrants our attention as a political campaign speech of consequence. Delivered at a critical moment in the campaign, it was an artistically excellent speech, witnessed by many. It may well have been the pivotal speech of the 1980 presidential campaign.

NOTES

1. For details on the debate among the Goldwater staff, see Ronald Reagan, *An American Life* (New York: Simon and Schuster, 1990), pp. 140–41, and Paul Erickson, *Reagan Speaks: The Making of an American Myth* (New York: New York University Press, 1985), pp. 12–13.
2. The quotations used in this paragraph are drawn from the videotape of the speech, made available by the Ronald Reagan Presidential Library. This speech is commonly called "A Time for Choosing," or "The Speech." Speech texts can also be found in most anthologies of Reagan's speeches, including Ronald Reagan, *A Time for Choosing* (Chicago: Regnery Gateway, 1983), pp. 39–57.
3. Reagan, *An American Life*, pp. 140–41.
4. Ibid.
5. In his autobiography, Reagan discusses the repeated showings of the speech and uses the $8 million figure, ibid., p. 143. Lou Cannon, *Reagan* (New York: G. P. Putnam's Sons, 1982), seems to be discussing the immediate impact of the first showing of the speech when he cites the $1 million figure and claims it "was more money than had been raised by any political speech up to that time."
6. See Kathleen Hall Jamieson, *Packaging the Presidency*: New York: Oxford University Press, 1984), pp. 174. Jamieson states that the Republicans spent $6.4 million on television airtime in 1964 and the Democrats spent $4.5 million on television airtime in 1964.
7. Broder is cited in Cannon, *Reagan*, p. 13.
8. Cannon, *Reagan,* p. 22.
9. The details of Reagan's youth found in this and the following paragraphs are drawn primarily from Reagan, *An American Life*, pp. 22–40, and Cannon, *Reagan*, pp. 23–32.
10. Reagan, *An American Life*, p. 24.
11. Ibid., p. 36.
12. Nancy Reagan, *My Turn* (New York: Random House, 1989), p. 106.
13. In this passage and throughout his autobiography, Reagan refers to his parents by their first names. He observes that his brother and he started to call them Nelle and Jack when they were young and their parents liked the idea that their children felt so comfortable with them that they could address them as they addressed their friends. Hence, it became a lifelong habit.
14. Quoted in Nancy Reagan, *My Turn*, p. 106.
15. On Jack Reagan's attitudes and beliefs, see Cannon, *Reagan*, pp. 26–27.

16. Reagan, *An American Life*, p. 35.

17. Ibid., p. 42.

18. Cannon, *Reagan*, p. 31.

19. Ibid. Though the older of the brothers, Neil did not start college after high school. He worked for three years at a cement plant. Finally recognizing that there was no future for him in manual labor, he followed his younger brother to Eureka. Ron helped Neil get a football scholarship and a campus job so that he could afford school.

20. Reagan, *An American Life*, p. 48.

21. Ibid., p. 59.

22. For details on Reagan's Hollywood career, particularly those that focus on how that career prepared him for a political career, see Dinesh D'Souza, *Ronald Reagan: How an Ordinary Man Became an Extraordinary Leader* (New York: Free Press, 1997), pp. 43–55. Also see Reagan, *An American Life*, pp. 84–104, and Cannon, *Reagan*, pp. 59–70.

23. Kurt Ritter and David Henry, *Ronald Reagan: The Great Communicator* (Westport, CT: Greenwood Press, 1992), p. 6.

24. On Reagan's speaking at General Electric plants, see Erickson, *Reagan Speaks*, p. 19.

25. The details presented in the preceding two paragraphs can be found in any standard biography of Reagan. Also see Ritter and Henry, *Ronald Reagan*, pp. 6–7, Cannon, *Reagan*, pp. 70–97.

26. For a discussion of Reagan's evolving political beliefs during the period 1945–1960, see D'Souza, *Ronald Reagan*, pp. 61–62.

27. Reagan, *An American Life*, pp. 138–39.

28. Cannon, *Reagan*, p. 101–2.

29. Reagan's original supporters included Holmes P. Tuttle, an entrepreneur whose businesses included one of the most successful Ford dealerships in the country, A. C. (Cy) Rubel, chairman of the board of Union Oil Company, and Henry Salvatori, founder of Western Geophysical Company.

30. Cannon, *Reagan*, p. 102.

31. On the Johnson legacy in California, see Cannon, *Reagan*, pp. 104–5.

32. It is not an accident that the first contemporary political consulting firm, Whitaker and Baxter, founded in 1934, was a California firm, which worked almost exclusively within that state. See Robert V. Friedenberg, *Communication Consultants in Political Campaigns: The Ballot Box Warriors* (Westport, CT: Praeger, 1997).

33. Reagan, *An American Life*, pp. 151–52.

34. See Cannon, *Reagan*, p. 114.

35. See Reagan, *An American Life*, p. 149.

36. Dutton is quoted in Cannon, *Reagan*, p. 118.

37. See Robert Lindsey, "Dress Rehearsal," in Hedrick Smith, Adam Clymer, Leonard Silk, Robert Lindsey, and Richard Burt, *Reagan the Man, the President* (New York: Macmillan, 1980), pp. 42–43.

38. Any good account of the 1976 campaign will provide details about the Ford-Reagan battle. One account that presents an unusual and perhaps prophetic perspective is Martin Schram, *Running for President: A Journal of the Carter Campaign* (New York: Pocket Books, 1977). Schram, Washington Bureau chief for *Newsday,* was granted access to the inner workings of the Carter campaign. In a particularly prophetic passage, after reviewing Reagan's political assets, Schram writes, "There was one more factor. Star Quality. Reagan had it. He would walk into an airport without fanfare late at night and heads would turn and the word would spread and soon he would be signing autographs. It was not like this for any of the other would-be presidents in the primary campaigns of 1976" (p. 255).

39. Elizabeth Drew, *Portrait of an Election* (New York: Simon and Schuster, 1981), p. 113.

40. Ibid., p. 113.

41. Ibid.

42. See Congressional Quarterly, *President Reagan* (Washington: Congressional Quarterly, 1981), p. 77. Also see Drew, *Portrait,* p. 112.

43. Ford granted an interview that was printed on the front page of the *New York Times* five days after the New Hampshire primary in which he virtually invited the Republican party to draft him. See F. Clifton White and William J. Gill, *Why Reagan Won* (Chicago: Regency Gateway, 1981), p. 215.

44. Ford is quoted in White and Gill, *Why Reagan Won,* p. 217.

45. Congressional Quarterly, *President Reagan,* p. 79.

46. Not only did the independent Anderson lose that fall, but much more surprising, each of the liberal Democratic senators he endorsed also lost.

47. Congressional Quarterly, *President Reagan,* p. 79.

48. Edwin Meese, *With Reagan: The Inside Story* (Washington, DC: Regency Press, 1992), p. 44.

49. Ibid. In his account of these negotiations, Ed Meese suggests that Kissinger was really behind them and that Ford was never enthusiastic about the prospect of serving as Reagan's vice president.

50. Congressional Quarterly, *President Reagan,* p. 79.

51. Bush's criticism of Reagan during the primaries still troubled many of Reagan's principal supporters. Nancy Reagan recalled that "at the time I didn't like George Bush. The bitter campaigns of Iowa and New Hampshire were still fresh in my memory and George's use of the phrase 'voodoo economics' to describe Ronnie's proposed tax cuts still rankled." Nancy Reagan claims that if political considerations could have been ignored, Nevada senator Paul Laxalt, a close friend of Reagan since their days as governors of their respective states, would have been selected. However, though she depicts Laxalt as both Reagan's first choice and her own, she is quick to acknowledge that Bush was a fine vice president and a politically wiser choice than Laxalt, who lacked Bush's experience and like Reagan was a western conservative. See Nancy Reagan, *My Turn,* pp. 212–13,

52. Congressional Quarterly, *President Reagan*, p. 82.

53. David H. Everson, "The Presidential Campaign of 1980," in *The Presidential Election and Transition 1980–81*, ed. Paul T. David and David H. Everson (Carbondale: Southern Illinois University Press, 1983), p. 86.

54. Ritter and Henry, *Ronald Reagan*, p. 49.

55. Ibid., p. 38. Ritter and Henry base part of their analysis on the work of American studies and literary scholar David Howard Pitney.

56. Everson, "Presidential Campaign," p. 83.

57. On Reagan's economic attacks, see Meese, *With Reagan*, pp. 45–46; Everson, "Presidential Campaign," pp. 82–83; and William Schneider, "The November 4 Vote for President: What Did It Mean?" in *The American Elections of 1980*, ed. Austin Ranney (Washington: American Enterprise Institute, 1981), pp. 230–32.

58. Schneider, "November 4 Vote," p. 241.

59. Carter is quoted in Drew, *Portrait*, p. 306.

60. Drew, *Portrait*, p. 307. Drew's judgment was widely shared. How much his repeated attempts to avoid debating at this same time might have reinforced and contributed to that impression is difficult to judge.

61. For the text of this debate, see the appendices of Richard Harwood, *The Pursuit of the Presidency 1980* (New York: Washington Post/Berkley Books, 1980), pp. 359–400.

62. On Carter's strategies, see Kurt Ritter and David Henry, "The 1980 Reagan-Carter Presidential Debate," in *Rhetorical Studies of National Political Debates, 1960–1992,*" ed. Robert V. Friedenberg (Westport, CT: Praeger, 1994), pp. 80–85.

63. Drew, *Portrait*, p. 335. In his presentation, Carter talked about having learned from his first term and hence being prepared to be a better president in his second. He speaks of having made mistakes, but being willing to refine and change policies if they don't work.

64. All the data reported in this paragraph is drawn from Everson, "Presidential Campaign," p. 93. Everson used data from the University of Michigan Center for Political Research.

65. Ibid.

66. For Anderson's take on the election, see Jonathan Moore, ed. *The Campaign for President 1980 in Retrospect* (Cambridge, MA: Ballinger, 1981), p. 259. Anderson made these remarks shortly after the election.

67. Everson, "Presidential Campaign," p. 94.

68. Wirthlin's remarks are in Moore, *Campaign for President*, pp. 251–52.

69. Ibid., pp. 252–53.

70. This and all subsequent quotes and references to this address are taken from the videotape of the address provided to the author by the Ronald Reagan Presidential Library. The author wishes to express his thanks to the Ronald Reagan Presidential Library for their cooperation in providing this tape.

71. Everson, "Presidential Campaign," p. 94.

72. See Ritter and Henry, "The 1980 Reagan-Carter Presidential Debate," pp. 85–88.

73. Strauss is quoted in Drew, *Portrait*, p. 327. Strauss's reference to Carter having "talked to our constituents in the debate" is fully explicated by Ritter and Henry in their analysis of Carter's debate strategies. See Ritter and Henry, "The 1980 Reagan-Carter Presidential Debate," pp. 80–85.

74. Caddell is quoted in Moore, *Campaign for President*, p. 251.

75. Caddell is quoted in Drew, *Portrait*, p. 337.

76. For a full breakdown of the final voting statistics, see Congressional Quarterly, *President Reagan*, p. 85.

77. This claim is based on the fact that the Reagan address was broadcast on each of the three major networks. Carter's election eve program ran only once. See Drew, *Portrait*, p. 335.

Chapter Five

1992—Bill And Hillary Clinton

> I have acknowledged wrongdoing. I have acknowledged causing pain in my marriage. I have said things to you and to the American people from the beginning that no American politician ever has. I think most Americans who are watching this tonight they know what we are saying. They'll get it.

As 1987 opened, Arkansas's first family was making plans. As Chairman of the National Governors Association, Arkansas governor William Jefferson Clinton had stepped up his travel and speaking schedule. During the first three months of the year he made eighteen trips out of state and, as one Arkansas paper expressed it, gave "a convincing impression of a barnstorming candidate."[1] At one time the nation's youngest governor, Clinton was widely viewed as one of the most promising political figures in the Democratic party. Within Arkansas, where Clinton had long been perceived as "too transparently ambitious," speculation about a Clinton race for the White House was rampant.[2] It was clear by 1987, if not long before, that Clinton and his wife Hillary aspired to a larger political stage than that provided by Arkansas. Many felt that his presidential ambitions had first been kindled when, as a schoolboy, he had had the opportunity to shake hands with President John F. Kennedy. Regardless of how long ago his ambitions had first been nurtured, by early 1987 Clinton seemed on the verge of becoming a presidential candidate.

Like her husband, Arkansas first lady Hillary Rodham Clinton had been a remarkably high achiever throughout her life. A graduate of Wellesley College and Yale Law School, she had worked on the staff of the House Judiciary Committee during the impeachment investigations of Richard Nixon and had taught law at the University of Arkansas. While her husband served as governor, Hillary Clinton had become a partner in the state's most prestigious law firm. Moreover, she had been visibly involved in well-publicized efforts to improve the public school system of Arkansas.

As the Clintons prepared for a presidential bid, in early 1988 three events took place that each seemed to enhance Clinton's chance at securing his party's presidential nomination. First, New York governor Mario Cuomo signaled that he would not be a candidate for the nomination. The preeminent orator in the party, the successful governor of the nation's second-largest state, well connected in Democratic activist circles and in financial circles, Cuomo would likely have been a favorite had he run. Second, on 20 March Arkansas senator Dale Bumpers, also frequently mentioned as a possible presidential candidate, announced that he would not be a candidate. With his withdrawal, Clinton would have a secure base in Arkansas should he go after the nomination. Finally, in May 1987, the campaign of Democratic front-runner Gary Hart imploded. Hart, long known in political and journalist circles for his womanizing, had been caught by reporters from the *Miami Herald* with Donna Rice, often described as a "Miami party girl," having a weekend rendezvous in his Washington townhouse.[3]

With the Hart campaign over before it really started, liberal black activist and former presidential candidate Jesse Jackson became the best-known Democratic candidate. The Democratic party was not ready to nominate an exceedingly liberal black for the presidency, as evidenced by the fact that when Hart was forced to withdraw the party's focus shifted immediately to a host of more moderate white candidates, rather than to Jackson. They included Senators Joseph Biden of Delaware, Albert Gore of Tennessee, and Paul Simon of Illinois. Missouri congressman Richard Gephardt, former Arizona governor Bruce Babbitt, and Massachusetts governor Michael Dukakis were also receiving attention.

No doubt as he surveyed this field, Arkansas governor Bill Clinton could appreciate why the press had nicknamed Jackson and the other contenders "the seven dwarfs." Jackson was the only major national figure in the group. The Clintons began to signal to their close friends and political associates that Bill would run for the presidency. Hillary Clinton bought a condo for her parents in Little Rock, so that they might babysit for daughter Chelsea when both Clintons took to the campaign trail. The ballroom of Little Rock's Excelsior Hotel was secured for what was expected to be Clinton's announcement speech at noon, on Wednesday, 15 July. Many of Bill Clinton's friends had perceived him as preparing for the presidency throughout his life. On 14 and 15 July 1987 many of those friends were arriving in Little Rock to cheer his announcement of candidacy. They came from throughout the state, and others, like Mickey Kantor and Sandy Berger, came from across the nation to watch the forty-two-year-old governor kick off his first national campaign.

But Bill Clinton, like Gary Hart, had a problem. In late June 1987, roughly three weeks before his scheduled announcement, two of his closest backers had a private meeting with Clinton. They brought with them a list of some of the women with whom Clinton was believed to have been intimate. Clinton claimed that he did not even recognize many of the names, reportedly got red in the face, waved his arms, and said "Get this goddamned paper out of here. Hillary doesn't know any of this. What good is this goddamned paper?"[4]

Rumors began to circulate in Little Rock that the *Arkansas Democrat* was preparing an exposé of Clinton's womanizing, to be published on the morning of his scheduled announcement. Rumors also claimed that the *New York Times* was preparing an exposé.[5] Though rumors were widespread, no such story was in the works.[6]

What happened in the days immediately preceding Clinton's scheduled announcement is not entirely clear, as the accounts of several who were involved differ. However, most accounts claim that Clinton had at least two critical meetings. The first was with Betsy Wright, for eight years his chief of staff. The second was with Carl Wagner, a longtime friend whom Clinton had first met when the two of them worked together in the antiwar movement in 1970, and with whom he had worked again in Texas in 1972, in George McGovern's presidential campaign.

Two evenings before his scheduled announcement, Betsy Wright confronted Clinton. "Here's the list," she started, and then began to read the names of women with whom she had good reason to believe Clinton had slept. Wright challenged him. Had he slept with this one? How often was he intimate with this one? Would this woman talk? How about this other one? Among the names Wright asked Clinton about was a former Little Rock television reporter and nightclub singer, Gennifer Flowers. Wright claimed that Clinton "didn't try to hide anything" and "appeared contrite." After they had discussed all the women on the list, Wright advised Clinton that he could not run.

Clinton, she reported, resisted. He seemed to feel that few people knew about his womanizing and that few of the women would talk. He was still inclined to run. Finally, Wright claims, she had to personalize the argument. "I don't care what comes out, this is going to be bad for Hillary and Chelsea!!" she reports having shouted at Clinton. Wright believed that when their meeting was over, Clinton gave her his word that he would not run.[7]

But evidently Clinton had second thoughts. The next night he discussed his options with his old friend Carl Wagner. Wagner was the first of several old out-of-town friends who had flown to Little Rock for Clinton's announcement. Both Bill and Hillary discussed the potential issues and candidates with Wagner for several hours that evening. Then, when Hillary had gone to bed, Clinton asked Wagner, "So, what's the bottom line?" Wagner recalls telling Clinton, "When you reach the top of the steps, walk into your daughter's bedroom, look at her, and understand that if you do this, your relationship with her will never be the same." Before he went to bed, Wagner called his friend Steve Cohen. Cohen was a longtime Democratic party activist whom Clinton had met at Yale Law School. He was planning to fly to Little Rock for the announcement. "Jesus Christ," Wagner told Cohen, "this guy doesn't know whether he wants to run."[8]

At a private lunch immediately before the scheduled announcement, Clinton disclosed to a few close friends, including Bruce Lindsey and Webb Hubbell, that "I'm not going." It is not clear whether Clinton shared this decision with Hillary. If so, it is not clear whether he also shared the likely reason behind it. At the luncheon, Hillary appeared shocked. Two hours later, Clinton made his decision public. Hillary, standing to his left, was pictured wiping tears from her eyes as he spoke. Clinton explained his apparent change of heart.

> Our daughter is the most important person in the world to us and our most important responsibility. In order to wage a winning campaign, both Hillary and I would have to leave her for long periods of time. That would not be good for her or for us. . . . I hope I will have another opportunity to seek the presidency when I can do it and be faithful to my family, my state, and my sense of what is right.[9]

Associates claim that Hillary Clinton was both devastated by his decision and furious at him for having made it.[10] Whether it was fear of exposure, or whether it was out of concern for his daughter and their relationship, Clinton had shocked many of his closest friends and associates. Four years later, the outcome would be different.

THE SPEAKER: WILLIAM JEFFERSON CLINTON

Bill Clinton was born on 19 August 1946, in Hope, Arkansas. His mother was widowed four months earlier when her husband, William Jefferson Blythe was killed in an auto accident. Clinton was initially raised by both his mother, Virginia Blythe, and his maternal grandparents, Edith and Eldridge Cassidy. His grandparents, particularly his grandmother, played a major role in his upbringing. They raised him from the age of two to four, while his mother left Hope to study nursing so that she could support her family. Clinton later recalled that his grandparents "had a lot to do with my early commitment to learning." By the age of three he was reading children's books and by the time he was in the first grade, Clinton was reading the newspaper. He attributed his early reading largely to the influence of his grandparents.[11]

When Clinton was four, his mother Virginia married Roger Clinton, a car salesman. Bill took his stepfather's name. In 1954, when Clinton was eight, the family moved from Hope to Hot Springs. By the age of nine, Clinton was interested in politics. His family first bought a television in 1956. That year he watched the conventions on television. Though he read about politics in the papers, Clinton recalls that television made politics meaningful to him.[12]

At the age of sixteen, in the summer of 1963, Clinton was selected to be a delegate to Boys State, a camp where high school students learned about the electoral process and government. At Boys State, Clinton was elected to Boys Nation and thus won a trip to Washington. While touring Washington with Boys Nation, Clinton visited the White House, was photographed shaking hands with President John F. Kennedy, and had lunch with Arkansas senator J. William Fulbright. According to his mother, Clinton came back from Washington determined to make a political career for himself.[13]

Throughout his childhood, Clinton's family life was difficult. His half-brother, Roger Clinton, Jr., characterized the family as "dysfunctional" because of the alcoholism of his father and Bill's stepfather, Roger Clinton. Bill and his stepfather were reconciled before Roger's 1967 death from cancer; nevertheless, Roger's alcoholism and abusive treatment of Virginia and his family made for constant conflict between Roger and Bill Clinton. On several occasions Bill witnessed Roger verbally and physically abusing Virginia. On at least one occasion, Bill had to get outside help to stop the fighting.[14]

As the eldest son in the house of an alcoholic, Bill Clinton became a prototype "Family Hero." It is not unusual in the homes of alcoholic parents for one of the children to take on the role of either the protector of the family from its alcoholic member, or its redeemer to the outside world.[15] By his teenage years, Bill Clinton was serving both functions. Roger Clinton, Jr., opens his autobiography by recounting the day when he thought his father was going to kill his mother with a pair of scissors and rushed to the house next door to get his big brother Bill. According to Roger's account, Bill "wrenched my mother from my father's grasp," and shouted at his father:

"You will never hurt either of them again. If you want them, you'll have to go through me." Bill then pushed his mother and brother into another room, "shutting the door in Daddy's face," and after comforting his mother and brother, went back to confront his father. "Within seconds," Roger Clinton recalled, "we could hear them shouting, but Daddy was no match for Bill anymore. This time, Daddy left the house. Bill was sixteen then, still a kid to many, but he was much more than that to Mother and me."[16] Within his home, Clinton had become the family protector.

Outside his home, Clinton was the family redeemer. He was the bright young man who would make a name for himself and in so doing redeem the family. Clinton was a high achiever throughout his school years. At Hot Springs High School, among the best schools in the state, he was an excellent student and active in a host of musical and service organizations.

During his high school years Clinton delivered a number of speeches. In his Latin class, Clinton played the role of defense attorney in a mock trial of Catiline. After the experience, he told his teacher that the exercise had made him realize that someday he would study law. John F. Kennedy was assassinated four months after Bill Clinton shook his hand. As virtually the last resident of Hot Springs to have contact with the assassinated president, in the weeks after the assassination he was asked to speak to several Hot Springs service organizations.[17]

Graduating fourth in his class, Clinton gave what biographer David Maraniss calls "his first political speech" at his high school commencement. In the form of the commencement benediction, Clinton asked for the Lord's help as he and his classmates "prepare to live only by the guide of our own faith and character. We pray to keep a high sense of values while wandering through the complex maze which is our society."[18]

During his junior year, Clinton began to think about attending college in Washington, D.C., where he perceived that he could learn about foreign affairs, domestic politics, and economics. Not knowing what school was best, Clinton remembers "I just started asking people, including staff members of our congressional delegation, what was the most appropriate place. The consensus was that Georgetown was the most appropriate and the most academically respected and rigorous."[19]

At Georgetown, Clinton continued to maintain excellent grades in the classroom. Much of his most important learning, though, took place outside the classroom. He campaigned ardently and eventually won his class presidency at Georgetown. He was active in other school organizations. While a student at Georgetown, he also worked on Capitol Hill for Arkansas senator J. William Fulbright.

In 1968 he applied for a Rhodes scholarship to Oxford. Clinton has always believed that the recommendation he received from Senator Fulbright, himself a former Rhodes scholar, was critical in his winning the award.[20] After two years in England, where he took part in antiwar protests against American involvement in Vietnam, he returned to the United States, enrolling in Yale Law School.

At Yale he continued to excel as a student while at the same time engaging in a range of other activities. Most important, it was during his first year at Yale, in the fall of 1970, that he met Hillary Rodham. Clinton and Rodham were first introduced when they were waiting to be served in a cafeteria line. A mutual friend, Robert Reich, introduced them, but they did not seem to hit it off and quickly went their separate ways. Nevertheless, they both seemed to be highly aware of one another. Rodham recalls that "he was good looking. And I thought—you know, I kind of filed that thought away." A few weeks later they were both in the law library. Clinton was talking to another student but kept glancing at Rodham seated at the other end of the large room. Finally, Rodham took the initiative, walked the length of the room to where Clinton and his friend, Jeff Glekel, were talking, and said, "Look, if you're going to keep staring at me and I'm going to keep staring back, we might as well introduce ourselves." Before meeting Clinton, Rodham had avoided serious relationships, focusing on her education. But she broke her rule for Clinton. Many feel that at least on Hillary's part, it was virtually love at first sight.[21]

Clinton had dated several women prior to Rodham. Rodham was one of the few who was more than a match for both his intellect and his ambition. Though the two began to date, Clinton was spending a considerable amount of time working on the campaign of the local Democratic candidate for Congress, Joe Duffy. In 1972 he spent part of the year in Texas, working on the presidential campaign of George McGovern.

In 1973 Clinton graduated from Yale Law School. Unlike most of his classmates, who were seeking positions with prominent legal firms in Boston, New York, Washington, or other major cities, or who were hoping to serve as law clerks to prominent justices, Clinton wanted to go home to Arkansas. Several months before finishing his degree, Clinton asked a friend from the McGovern campaign, Arkansas State Senator Stephen Smith, to mention him to an associate dean at the University of Arkansas Law School. At least one member of the interview team, David Newbern, felt that Clinton might be interested in a position with the University of Arkansas Law School primarily as a stepping-stone for a political career in the state.[22] The law faculty was enormously impressed with Clinton's intellect. Though some questions were raised about whether Clinton would strive to be a serious legal scholar, the law faculty felt he would be an outstanding teacher and was worth the gamble. The final vote to offer him a position was unanimous.[23]

Clinton was well liked by the University of Arkansas law students, but it soon became clear that he had a political career in mind. On 25 February 1974, approximately eighteen months after teaching his first classes at the university, Bill Clinton initiated his political career by announcing his candidacy for the congressional seat from Arkansas's third congressional district. The incumbent was Republican congressman John Paul Hammerschmidt. Hammerschmidt had won his prior two elections with over 70 percent of the vote and ran especially well in the district's largest city, Fort Smith. The city had a large military-related population, and Hammerschmidt was a power on the House Veterans Affairs Committee. Hence, Clinton and his aides determined that in order to win they would have to beat Hammerschmidt throughout the rest of the district.

As Clinton lived the life of a law professor and candidate in Arkansas, Hillary Rodham was one of thirty-nine lawyers working on the House Judiciary Committee's impeachment inquiry staff. She had been recruited by John Doar, chief counsel of the committee. Doar met her while she was studying at Yale. Though they were separated, Clinton and Rodham managed to keep up their relationship. When the impeachment of Richard Nixon was concluded, she was at a crossroads. She could no doubt move into a big-city law firm, perhaps in her native Chicago or in Washington. Or she could opt to be with Clinton in Arkansas. She chose the latter. She had visited Clinton in Fayetteville on several occasions and had met the dean and many faculty members of the law school. As they had with Clinton, when she applied for a position they asked her in for an interview and were immediately impressed. In August of 1974 she moved to Arkansas to start the school year on the faculty of the law school, just in time to help with the final months of Bill Clinton's congressional campaign. Clinton lost, but he gave Hammerschmidt a good race and was widely perceived as a promising figure within the Arkansas Democratic party.

On 11 October 1975, Bill and Hillary were married in Fayetteville. Hillary's mother had come to town a few days earlier to help with the last-minute preparations. The ceremony was a private affair, with only the immediate families and a few close friends present. It was followed by a wedding party for two hundred. Both were teaching, so there was no honeymoon, though later the newlyweds and Hillary's family vacationed in Acapulco for ten days.[24]

The newlyweds spent the rest of 1975 readying themselves for Clinton's first statewide race. In 1976 he was elected attorney general of Arkansas.

Two years later, he was elected governor. At the age of thirty-two, he had become the nation's youngest governor. At that time the governor served only a two-year term. Thus, 1980 was a year of mixed blessings for the Clintons. Their daughter Chelsea was born, but Clinton was defeated in his bid for reelection. The nation's youngest governor quickly became its youngest ex-governor. During his first term Clinton and his youthful administrators championed a host of tax increases, most controversially an increase in the motor vehicle registration fees and gasoline and tire taxes. His abolishment of the Arkansas Department of Economic Development was perceived by many as reflecting an insensitivity to the dire economic plight of the state. An additional host of controversial measures won him the animosity of the state's physicians, the timber industry, truckers, and the poultry industry. Though he was successful in initiating a variety of educational reforms, he was forced to withdraw his most ambitious educational reform, a consolidation of the state's nearly 400 school districts, when opposition to it in the legislature became too great.

President Carter contributed to Clinton's 1980 political problems. Carter had housed almost 20,000 Cubans who had been "boat-lifted" out of Cuba, at Fort Chaffee, near Fort Smith. On two occasions in 1980 hundreds of the Cubans escaped and began to roam the countryside. These Cubans had been characterized by both the national and Arkansas press as criminals and drug pushers and users, as well as mentally and physically handicapped. Fidel Castro had, it was widely reported, emptied his jails and allowed the worst elements of Cuba to join the boat-lift refugees. Though the escapees were quickly captured, residents who lived near Fort Chaffee as well as citizens throughout the state were understandably concerned by the presence of the Cubans. Clinton was roundly condemned for not standing up to Carter and demanding that the Cubans be resettled somewhere else.[25]

In 1982 the "Comeback Kid" staged his first comeback, winning his second term as governor. He would win reelection in 1984, 1986, and, when the term of office was lengthened to four years, 1990. During his years as governor, Clinton focused his efforts on both educational reform and economic development. Moreover, as Clinton worked in Arkansas, he was steadily building a national following, particularly within the Democratic party. In 1985 he was elected chairman of the Southern Growth Policies Board and vice chairman of the National Governors Association. In 1986 he became chairman of the National Governors Association. In 1989, no doubt in part as recognition for his efforts on behalf of education in Arkansas, President Bush named him the Democratic Co-Chair of the President's National Educational Summit. In 1990 Clinton was named chairman of the Democratic Leadership Council.[26] This influential group of Democratic party leaders was tired of seeing its party lose one election after another, including the last three presidential elections, by offering the public exceedingly liberal candidates. The DLC hoped to make the party more centrist.

Having been on the verge of a presidential candidacy in 1988, during the following years the presidency was never far from Clinton's mind. As the 1992 elections approached, Clinton was, once more, considering a presidential bid. Clinton's 1990 governor's race was, in several respects, a dry run for the presidency. Clinton had reinforced his campaign organization with several national consultants who viewed him as a likely presidential candidate. In addition to longtime consultant Dick Morris, they included media consultant Frank Greer and polling consultant Stanley Greenberg. However, during a campaign debate, Clinton was asked whether he would serve his full term. His reply was succinct: "You bet."[27]

Nevertheless, throughout 1991 Bill and Hillary Clinton were exploring a presidential bid with many of their associates. Concerned about the consequences of breaking his pledge to serve a full four-year term, Clinton engaged in a well-scripted charade. He made what became known as "The Secret Tour," traveling throughout Arkansas and telling supporters that he was disturbed about breaking his pledge to serve out his term. As expected, those he talked to repeatedly told him to run. This gambit put Clinton in a position to say that though he had pledged to serve his entire term, his Arkansas supporters were urging him to run for the presidency.[28] The stage was set for the Arkansas governor to move up to the national political arena.

THE SPEAKER: HILLARY RODHAM CLINTON

Born in 1947, Hillary Rodham grew up in the upper-middle-class Chicago suburb of Park Ridge, the oldest of Hugh and Dorothy Rodham's three children. Both parents stressed the importance of self-reliance to their children and set exceedingly high standards for them. Though her father is often portrayed as a stern authoritarian who was virtually impossible to satisfy, at least one biographer claims that it was Hillary's mother who encouraged her to speak out and made her realize that as a woman she could accomplish anything she wished.[29] Though her parents treated Hillary and her brothers similarly, and strongly encouraged her every endeavor, there were minor differences typical of the times. One childhood friend recalls that though Hillary could have a variety of jobs, such as babysitter, lifeguard, or camp counselor, she never worked in her father's drapery business, though her brothers did. Her mother later recalled that just because she was a girl didn't mean she should be limited.[30]

Much like her husband, Hillary Rodham became interested in politics at an early age. However, while the young Bill Clinton was enamored of Kennedy, by the eighth grade Hillary was reading Barry Goldwater's *Conscience of a Conservative* and becoming, like her father and most of her neighbors, a strong Republican. Current events were a standard topic of dinner conversation in the Rodham family. She favored Richard Nixon in 1960 and served as a local "Goldwater Girl" in 1964, cheering at local rallies for the senator.[31]

Childhood friends remember Hillary Rodham as much less concerned about makeup and fashions than most of her high school peers. She was a high achiever in high school and often dominated the meetings of groups with which she affiliated. Task-oriented, she was a National Merit Scholar, in the top 5 percent of her class, a member of the Honor Society, a class officer, and a member of the student council, the speech and debate club, the Girls Athletic Association, and the Pep Club.[32]

While in high school, Hillary Rodham began to sense the nation's social problems. As she did so, her political orientation began to shift. The Rodhams were members of the Park Ridge Methodist Church. The youth minister, Don Jones, who arrived when Hillary was a teenager, began to introduce her to facets of American life that she had never before experienced. Jones developed a series of Sunday and Thursday evening programs that he called the University of Life. He exposed his young congregants to inner-city blacks and to migrant farmworkers. He brought in an atheist speaker to discuss the existence of God. Saul Alinsky, the radical labor organizer, spoke to the youth group about corporate America. Alinsky so impressed Hillary Rodham that she wrote her undergraduate thesis on him. Jones led discussions about a wide variety of topics, including teenage pregnancy and youth violence. In April 1962, when Hillary was fifteen, Jones took his youth group to Chicago's Orchestra Hall, where they joined 2,500 other people to listen to a young black minister, Martin Luther King, Jr., speak about racial injustice. After King's address, Jones arranged for his group to briefly meet King. Like Clinton's meeting with Kennedy, Rodham's meeting with King left an indelible impression on her. For Hillary Rodham, and no doubt for many of her teenage friends, Jones was exposing them to poverty, social injustice, and ideas that they had rarely if ever encountered in Park Ridge.[33]

Rodham's political views moved even further away from those of her parents when she was at Wellesley. As a freshman, she was elected president of the Young Republicans. But the Wellesley Republicans were Rockefeller liberals, not Goldwater conservatives. More important, her social conscience soon found a variety of outlets at Wellesley.

During the summer between her sophomore and junior years Rodham worked as a researcher and babysitter for a Wellesley professor who was writing a book on Vietnam. The experience helped solidify her growing disenchantment with the war and her move away from the Republican party. During her junior year she worked with poor black children in Roxbury, Massachusetts, and became active in the antiwar movement, initially supporting Eugene McCarthy. Returning home to Chicago that summer, she and a friend, contrary to the wishes of their parents, drove downtown to witness the demonstrations at the 1968 Democratic Convention. They did not participate.[34]

Issues of race and war soon dominated much of campus life at Wellesley, as they were doing on campuses throughout the country. A fine student at Wellesley, Rodham was active in several campus organizations, ultimately being elected student government president for her senior year.[35] That position would soon open a variety of doors for her.

As Rodham's 1969 commencement approached, it was announced that the speaker would be Massachusetts senator Edward Brooke. Brooke, a liberal Republican and the only black in the U.S. Senate, was no longer in favor with liberals. His support of Richard Nixon and the Vietnam War caused many at Wellesley to discuss staging some type of protest. It was Rodham's position as student government president that caused Wellesley president Ruth Adams to offer her an opportunity to speak at the commencement. Adams hoped that the presence of a student among the speakers would discourage any protest. Adams secured a promise from Rodham that she would provide Adams with an advance copy of her remarks and stick to them. However, after Brooke's remarks, it appeared as though Rodham's pledge meant nothing to her. She delivered an extemporaneous response critical of Brooke for his defense of Nixon and the Vietnam War. She claimed that her generation believed that "our prevailing acquisitive and competitive corporate way of life, including tragically the universities, is not the way of life for us. We're searching for more immediate, ecstatic, and penetrating modes of living."[36]

After Wellesley, Rodham entered Yale Law School. She was one of 30 women in a freshman class of 140. At Yale she became active in several organizations while continuing to maintain good grades. But more important, at Yale she met two people who were to have a profound effect on her life. During the summer between Wellesley and Yale, Rodham's commencement address had resulted in her being invited to a League of Women Voters Summer Conference on future trends in politics. While there she had met Marian Wright Edelman and had been impressed with Edelman's presentation to the conference.

Their paths crossed again when Marian Wright Edelman spoke at Yale on the subject of children and the law. After the speech, Rodham introduced herself to Edelman and offered to work the following summer for the Washington Research Project, the forerunner of Edelman's Children's Defense Fund. Receiving a grant from the Yale Law Students Civil Rights Research Council to cover her expenses in Washington, Rodham spent the summer working with Edelman's group and with the staff of Minnesota senator Walter Mondale researching the living conditions of migrant farmworkers and their children.

Rodham returned to Yale and did work at the Yale Child Study Center as well as at the Law School. Though she had come to care greatly about children's issues and the law, she was already being recruited by Washington law firms. In many respects, Marion Wright Edelman was to serve as a mentor, role model, and friend for Rodham throughout much of the rest of her life.[37] That same fall she met Bill Clinton. Together, they were soon involved in law school projects and political projects.

By 1972 Rodham had totally completed her transformation from a Goldwater Republican to a liberal Democrat. That summer, as Clinton worked in Austin at the McGovern campaign's state headquarters, Rodham worked for the Democratic National Committee in San Antonio, registering voters. The two managed to get together most weekends and often socialized with journalist Taylor Branch and with another McGovern worker who would play a major role in their lives, Betsy Wright. Summer extended into fall, and Rodham and Clinton missed most of their classes at Yale to continue working on the McGovern campaign. With McGovern's loss, they returned to Yale and crammed for their final exams. The following year Rodham and Clinton began to live together. Though Rodham was a year ahead of Clinton in school, she stayed in New Haven, living with him until he finished in 1973. During that year she did further work at the Yale Child Study Center. During that year Marion Wright Edelman, herself a Yale Law graduate, helped Rodham prepare "Children under the Law." It was Rodham's first published scholarly article. At that time children had few legal rights. Rodham argued that children should not be considered minors, a classification that deprived them of all legal rights. Rather, she felt they should be considered "child citizens" by the legal system. This new classification, she argued, could then be used to provide children with the same procedural rights given to adults.[38] Though the article later become highly controversial, writing it helped Rodham determine that regardless of what she would do with her life, she hoped "to be a voice for America's children."[39]

Though Clinton returned to Arkansas after Yale Law, Rodham accepted a position with the House Judiciary Committee. However, it was clear that both of them were thinking of marriage. It was also clear that both of them were thinking of Bill Clinton's political career.[40] When the impeachment hearings were over, therefore, she accepted a position with the University of Arkansas Law School and soon after she and Clinton were married.

For eleven of the sixteen years between 1975 and 1991, Hillary Rodham Clinton was the first lady of Arkansas. While helping to advance his political career, she developed her own law practice. At the same time, she developed a reputation as a children's advocate. Governor Clinton placed her in charge of the principal educational reforms of the Clinton administration in Arkansas. Because the governorship of Arkansas did not pay well, $35,000 per year during most of Clinton's tenure, Hillary Clinton also became the primary breadwinner for the family.

Ambitious for her husband and for herself, Hillary Rodham Clinton was disappointed when Bill did not go after the presidency in 1988. By the time Bill did decide to run, it was clear that his wife was his closest adviser. A talented lawyer who had moved in political circles all her adult life, she seemed destined to play a greater role in her husband's campaign, and if successful, his presidency, than the wife of any other presidential candidate in history. Thus, when Clinton was forced to deliver the critical speech of his 1992 presidential campaign, it came as no surprise that his wife was an equal participant.

THE EARLY CAMPAIGN OF 1992

Since incumbent president George Bush had no significant opposition on the Republican side, most of the attention during the early 1992 primary season was on the Democrats.[41] The 1988 loss of Massachusetts governor Michael Dukakis to George Bush strongly reinforced the perception of many Democrats that they needed to nominate a moderate for the presidency. Bush had attacked Dukakis for a great many liberal positions he had taken while governor. Further evidence was that, even while Bush maintained his popularity through the first two years of his administration, largely as a consequence of his foreign-policy success, the brightest 1990 Democratic election successes were moderate southern Democrats, such as Ann Richards and Lawton Chiles, who won the governships of Texas and Florida. Typically, by 1991 presidential candidates would have been positioning themselves for the race. However, the diplomacy leading up to the Persian Gulf War, and then the war itself beginning in mid-January, created an undeclared moratorium on presidential politics throughout late 1990 and early 1991. The success of that war made President Bush a prohibitive favorite to win reelection throughout much of 1991.

In May 1991 Paul Tsongas, who had served two terms in the House of Representatives and one term in the Senate from Massachusetts before retiring because of cancer, declared his candidacy. Claiming to be cured of cancer, Tsongas, an intelligent and thoughtful senator, had little in the way of political credentials or organization to challenge a popular incumbent president. Moreover, after the Democrats' experience with Michael Dukakis four years earlier, the Democratic party had little desire to nominate another Massachussetts liberal.[42]

The leading candidates that the Democratic party could offer to the country were declining the opportunity to run. Dukakis's principal challengers in 1988 had been Jesse Jackson, Senator Albert Gore, Jr., of Tennessee, and House Majority Leader Richard Gephardt. After several unsuccessful attempts to secure the Democratic nomination, Jackson seemed more inclined to influence the party and the candidate by maintaining his prominence among black Democrats, rather than engage in yet another unsuccessful candidacy. Senator Gore declined to run, claiming that his son's serious auto accident demanded that he spend more time with his family. In July, with the president's approval rating approaching 75 percent, Gephardt declared that he was too busy attending to the nation's business as Speaker of the House to be a candidate.

Other national figures within the party were similarly reluctant to run. Texas senator Lloyd Bentsen, who had distinguished himself as the vice presidential candidate in 1988, and New York governor Mario Cuomo both made it clear on repeated occasions in early and mid-1991 that they were not interested in running. New Jersey senator Bill Bradley had frequently been mentioned as a presidential candidate. Bradley's academic and athletic achievements were noteworthy and enhanced his reputation as a thoughtful member of the Senate. But he had barely held on to his Senate seat in a very close 1990 election. He felt it would be better to secure his New Jersey base and pay attention to Senate business, rather than contend for the Democratic nomination, which by the summer of 1991 seemed as though it might be of little value.

At the very time that major figures within the party were expressing their reluctance to run, there were two encouraging signs for the Democrats. First, after losing three presidential elections by running on liberal social values, often important to Democratic constituencies but of lesser importance to the nation at large, Democratic leaders were focusing more on economic issues. In July 1991 Zell Miller, the liberal Democratic governor of Georgia, delivered a speech to southern Democrats meeting in North Carolina. The speech was widely circulated within Democratic circles. "For too many presidential elections," said Miller, we have had things backward. We have chosen to fight on social issues rather than to run on the economic issues that shape the daily lives of American families. When the average American family stays up late into the night, they are not worrying about whether school prayer should be voluntary or mandatory, they are worrying about how to balance the checkbook and where they will find the money for Junior's college education. Our party grew up around the economic issues that concern working Americans most deeply, and this is the common bond that unites us. But instead of rallying around those basic unifying economic issues, we have allowed ourselves to be distracted by social issues that not only divide us but defeat us.[43]

Miller went on to indict what he called "the elitists" of the Democratic party "who demand that we run on their issues." Among those impressed by Miller's speech was Bill Clinton. Clinton discussed Miller's speech with him at length, learning that parts of it had been written with the help of consultants James Carville, Paul Begala, and Bob Shrum. Miller's approach was exactly the approach that the Democratic Leadership Council, which had named Clinton its national chairman in 1990, was urging on the party.

As party leaders discussed the future, moving closer to the positions that Clinton held, yet a second encouraging sign for Democrats was taking place. During July 1991, though Bush's approval remained in the 70–75 percent range, for the first time in months, polls were showing that more than half the country believed that the nation was headed down the "wrong track."[44] The nation's economic recession was beginning to take its toll on the administration, and nowhere were growing economic problems being felt more strongly than in the nation's first primary state, New Hampshire.

As these signs might serve to encourage Democrats, candidates began to step forward. In September and October 1991 Virginia governor Douglas Wilder, the highest elected black officeholder in the nation, U.S. Senators Bob Kerrey of Nebraska and Tom Harkin of Iowa and former California governor Edmund G. (Jerry) Brown all announced their candidacies. On 3 October Arkansas governor Bill Clinton also announced his candidacy for the presidency. Significantly, none of these five candidates, or Tsongas, was a major national figure. Quickly dubbed the "six pack," it was a group without an obvious favorite.

Although three of the six Democratic candidates were incumbent or former U.S. senators, all ran as Washington outsiders. Wilder, Kerrey, and Clinton tried to emphasize that theme in their announcement addresses by delivering them in their respective statehouses. Tsongas and Harkin announced from locations that had personal significance for each of them. Brown chose to announce from Philadelphia's Independence Hall, suggesting that in the past government worked for Americans and his administration would make it once more work for Americans.[45]

Clinton used his announcement address to focus on what would become the biggest issue of the campaign, the very issue that centrist Democrats were urging their party to develop—the economy. Claiming that "we are losing America's leadership in the world because we're losing the American Dream right here at home," Clinton sketched out his differences with President Bush in such areas as financing public education, health-care financing, providing middle-class tax relief, demanding that the nation provide those on welfare with skills and then remove them from welfare, and encouraging greater domestic investment and less foreign investment by corporations. Clinton concluded that his campaign "would be a campaign for the future, for the forgotten hardworking middle-class families of America."[46]

Clinton's speech was well received. It was a clever effort to maintain his standing as a mainstream Democrat, while at the same time distinguishing him from the unpopular positions of his party. The stress was on economic issues, not social issues. Clinton advocated a middle-class tax cut and reduced government spending in areas like welfare. His attack on corporate America was based on his claim that by globalizing, many corporations were ignoring their responsibility toward America's working class. Shortly after his announcement address, Clinton delivered three other speeches. All of them elaborated on aspects of his announcement address. Speaking with other Democratic candidates to Democratic activists in Washington, Los Angeles, and Chicago, Clinton was better received than Tsongas, Harkin, and Brown as he attacked Bush and offered an alternative program for Democrats to run upon.[47] State party leaders at the Chicago speech were particularly impressed with Clinton.[48]

In short order, as the candidates descended on New Hampshire for the nation's first primary, Senators Kerrey and Harkin, and Governor Clinton became what the press called "first tier" candidates. The distinction between these three and the other three candidates was clear. Each of the other three candidates had some characteristic that seemed fatal to their campaigns. Wilder was little known outside Virginia and had never held federal office. Moreover, no black had ever been successful at the national level. Tsongas was easily characterized as yet another Massachussetts liberal, similar to Michael Dukakis, whom the country had rejected four years earlier. By 1992 Jerry Brown, in 1976 and 1980 a serious candidate for the Democratic nomination, was often thought of as "Governor Moonbeam," a nickname he had received for his host of unusual behaviors during and after his governorship. As governor, he had rejected the governor's mansion, living in an apartment that was furnished with nothing more than the mattress on which he slept. After leaving the governorship, this one-time Catholic seminary student studied Buddhism in Japan and then worked for Mother Teresa, only to reappear in California running for the Democratic state chairmanship.

In contrast to Brown, Tsongas, and Wilder, the remaining three candidates were perceived as plausible presidential candidates, though in most years they would have more likely contended for the vice presidency while more accomplished and nationally known figures like Cuomo, Gore, Jackson, Bradley, Gephardt, and Bentsen fought for the presidential nomination. Kerrey, Harkin, and Clinton had been elected to statewide office, though the states were not New York, or Texas, or even New Jersey, but rather Nebraska, Iowa, and Arkansas. Kerrey was relatively liberal, but his military service in Vietnam, where he had lost a leg and won the Congressional Medal of Honor, distinguished him from most liberals on many military and foreign-policy issues, likely making him invulnerable to Republican attacks in these areas. Furthermore, he was an articulate candidate who seemed to get along well with the press. Iowa senator Tom Harkin was the lone true liberal in the field. As such he could command the support of many of the traditional Democratic interest groups, including much of big labor. Both had served in the Senate and were well acquainted with national issues. Clinton was perceived, at this early stage, as an engaging, bright, innovative governor whose stress on economic issues rather than social issues had earned him the support of many Democratic activists who were tired of losing. He had been speaking on national issues and been active in national Democratic party organizations.

As 1991 ended and the focus of the nomination struggle turned to the New Hampshire primary, Clinton was fast becoming the Democratic leader. He had been itching to run for at least four years and was quick out of the starting gate. His initial speeches had helped lay to rest skepticism that he was an Arkansas lightweight. His organization spent $50,000 to secure his victory in the December Florida State Democratic Convention straw poll.[49] Clinton was able to hire James Carville and Paul Begala, who were fresh from helping Democrat Harris Wofford win an upset victory over Richard Thornburgh in a special election for the Pennsylvania Senate seat that was opened when Senator John Heinz was killed in an airplane crash.

In that campaign, Wofford, who had never run for public office though he had at one time served as associate director of the Peace Corps and had been serving in the cabinet of Democratic governor Robert Casey, who appointed him to a brief term replacing Heinz prior to the special election, had come from 47 points behind to defeat Thornburgh. Thornburgh, a popular former Pennsylvania governor, had been recruited by Pennsylvania Republicans to leave his position as the attorney general in the Bush administration and defend the Republican Senate seat held by Heinz. Drawing heavily on Carville and Begala's advice, Wofford focused on issues such as higher education and health care. He argued that in areas such as these the federal government should provide greater economic relief to middle-class Americans.[50]

Carville and Begala were recruited by all the top-tier Democratic candidates, Kerrey, Harkin, and Clinton. They ultimately decided to work for Clinton. "Neither of us," claims Carville, "had any sense of destiny about hooking up with Bill Clinton. He just seemed like a good guy, someone we could work for."[51] Nevertheless, the fact that the hottest Democratic consultants had chosen to work for Clinton contributed to the Arkansas governor's growing status.

The Wofford victory had caught the attention of political professionals on both sides of the aisle. A close Bush ally had been beaten by a comparative unknown. The issues used by Wofford were ones that could be transferred to a national race. The architects of that victory were now working for the individual who was fast becoming the leading Democratic contender for the nomination. What was more alarming, Republican polls, taken shortly after that race, indicated that only 41 percent of the public felt that Bush deserved reelection. All of a sudden, the Democratic nomination, which many party leaders had once seen as hopeless, was becoming viable.

Clinton had also added skilled advisers to his own staff, most notably George Stephanopoulos. Like Clinton a former Rhodes scholar, Stephanopoulos had worked on several congressional staffs and by 1991 was working for House Majority Leader Richard Gephardt. When Gephardt determined not to run, the ambitious Stephanopoulos began to look for another candidate. Stephanopoulos spoke to Kerrey but came away from the meeting unimpressed with both the candidate and his staff. He then interviewed with Clinton. He found Clinton "smart and ready."[52] Like many in Washington's political and press communities, Stephanopoulos was aware of Clinton's reputation as a womanizer. However, by the fall of 1991 Stephanopoulos believed that Clinton was no longer cheating on his wife, that he and his wife had resolved their problems, and that they had a strong marriage.[53] As he built his staff, Clinton also worked diligently to line up some of the Democratic party's premier fundraisers on his behalf. By the end of 1991, Clinton had almost $3.5 million dollars in the bank, more than any of his challengers.[54] His growing prominence within Democratic circles, his stress on key issues, the talented campaign team he had assembled, and his strong financial position had all put Clinton in a formidable position by December 1991.

Because Harkin was from Iowa, none of the Democrats chose to mount a serious challenge in that state's early caucuses. Hence, the New Hampshire primary would prove to be the first test of the campaign. It would likely winnow the Democratic field.

Former senator Paul Tsongas, from the neighboring state of Massachusetts, was the early favorite in New Hampshire. Much of New Hampshire received its news from Massachussetts media. Hence Tsongas was almost a favorite-son candidate, well known and well liked by many New Hampshire Democrats. A victory in New Hampshire would no doubt help Tsongas, but his natural advantages in the state would not make such a victory fatal for those candidates who finished closely behind him. Rather, if any of them could run a strong race against him, those candidates would likely move to the next primaries with Tsongas. For Bill Clinton, a strong second would be a good showing in a state that was partial to a neighboring state's senator and far from Arkansas.

Clinton's early support in New Hampshire was drawn from a small group of the state's party activists who had formed a New Hampshire chapter of the Democratic Leadership Council. His campaigning skills and moderate liberalism quickly made inroads with New Hampshire's Democratic voters. Throughout December 1991 Clinton divided his time between visits to New Hampshire and twenty-six fundraising events.[55] In early January the campaign began to run a simple television ad in which Clinton faced the camera and discussed his plans for the economy. Pollster Stan Greenberg reported that the ad had helped vault Clinton into a lead of 12 percent over Tsongas.[56] A strong showing in New Hampshire would likely provide Clinton's campaign with considerable momentum as the race shifted to other parts of the country, including the Clinton-friendly south. Clinton was clearly becoming the leader of the "six pack."

The issue that had dissuaded Clinton from running in 1988 had not gone away. Frank Greer, the Washington-based consultant who had done Clinton's television commercials in prior campaigns and was on board for his presidential race, had come to realize during the summer of 1991 that in Little Rock, Clinton had "an incredible reputation around town" for womanizing. He realized that the candidate would have to have a strategy ready for dealing with the issue. Far too many members of the local and national press, as well as too many political operatives, knew of Clinton's philandering for it not to be raised as an issue during the campaign.

Greer arranged for both Clintons to be invited to the Sperling Breakfast in September 1991. The Sperling Breakfast is an opportunity for major national political correspondents to talk informally with political figures. It was first hosted by Godfrey Sperling of the *Christian Science Monitor*. It would be a place where the Clintons could address the question directly and get a sense of the press reaction.

Clinton arrived in Washington the weekend before the breakfast. He was scheduled to meet with supporters to lay the groundwork for his candidacy. Several of them asked him about the adultery rumors. He used these questions as an opportunity to rehearse what became known as his "nobody's perfect" defense. He rehearsed it again in a long meeting attended by both Clintons as well as pollster Stan Greenberg, personal friend Bruce Lindsey, and Greer the night before the Sperling Breakfast. Greer was blunt. He wanted to know how Clinton would assure the political press that his campaign would not implode like that of Gary Hart.[57] Clinton told the group that the issue engendered an enormous amount of hypocrisy. A politician who divorced his wife had no problems, but one who tried to work out his problems with his wife was subjected to these attacks. He and Hillary had worked things out. They should not be penalized, while those who divorced were in effect rewarded. This approach, that he was not perfect, that he had had problems, but that he and Hillary had worked out the problems in their marriage and were committed to their marriage would be the essence of his response.[58]

The next morning Bill and Hillary Clinton were the guests of honor at the Sperling Breakfast. Greer had encouraged Gloria Borger of *U.S. News and World Report* to ask about Clinton's philandering. About half an hour into the meeting, she diplomatically reminded Clinton that he had talked about "a zone of privacy" concerning his personal life and asked if he would talk about that.[59] Clinton opened his answer by claiming that this was the sort of trivia that people obsessed about while Rome was in decline. However, he then stated, as he had the previous evening, that he and Hillary had been together for nearly twenty years and though their relationship "has not been perfect or free from difficulties," he and Hillary "believe in our obligation to each other, and we intend to be together thirty or forty years from now, whether I run for president or not."[60] Jack Germond and Jules Witcover, two major figures in the Washington political press establishment, observed that

> what Clinton was counting on was an adherence by the news media to the time-honored journalist code of reporting verifiable facts, not rumors or unproven allegations. At least the mainstream press, that is, as opposed to such embarrassments to the mainstream press as the supermarket gossip tabloids, to which nothing was sacrosanct. What he didn't figure on was that after the Gary Hart experience of the previous presidential election, important elements of the presumably more responsible news media had developed an itchier trigger finger on reports of personal misconduct by celebrated individuals in public life.[61]

On Thursday, 16 January 1992, advance copies of that week's edition of the supermarket tabloid the *Star* became available in New Hampshire. The *Star* featured a page-one story by former Little Rock newsperson and nightclub singer Gennifer Flowers claiming to have been involved with Clinton for twelve years. Almost immediately the *New York Post* and the *New York Daily News* picked up the story. The *Post* ran the story under the headline "Wild Bill," while the *Daily News* headlined it "I'm No Gary Hart." Though the Clinton campaign staff and the candidate tried to contain the story, they could not do so.[62] That week, in the midst of a televised debate between the Democratic candidates, ABC News and National Public Radio's Cokie Roberts asked Clinton about the concern of many Democrats that the allegations of his womanizing and the possibility that the Republicans would find a credible woman to testify against Clinton could cost the Democrats women voters.

The fact that a respected reporter for two of the nation's leading news organizations, NPR and ABC, had utilized the story as part of a televised political debate made it difficult for other mainstream news organizations to ignore it. The next week, the *Star* ran another article. Under the headline "They Made Love All Over Her Apartment," Flowers provided details of her twelve-year affair. The *Star* also claimed that Flowers had provided them with tapes of conversations between herself and Clinton, including one that took place as recently as the previous September. Even those media outlets reluctant to carry the story could not now avoid reporting that the Democratic front-runner's campaign was being disrupted by allegations of a twelve-year affair.[63] Clearly Clinton needed to respond. The allegations could no longer be ignored.

THE SPEECH

There was never any doubt in the minds of anyone associated with the Clinton campaign that the response to these accusations would be made by both Bill and Hillary Clinton. They had responded together at the Sperling Breakfast and, as their staff worked to find the proper setting for a response to Gennifer Flowers's accusations, it was understood that both Clintons would be involved. Indeed, the first effort of their staff was to line up an appearance on ABC's *Nightline* for the Clintons. That did not materialize because weather made it impossible for Hillary to get out of Atlanta and fly to New York, where she was to have met Bill for the show.[64]

As the *Nightline* appearance was falling through, George Stephanopoulos was suggesting to CBS that the Clintons appear on *60 Minutes* that Sunday, immediately after the Super Bowl. CBS accepted. The show and the campaign staff then negotiated the terms of the Clinton appearance. The mutual agreement of *60 Minutes* and the Clintons was critical to the rhetorical and political success of the Clinton apologia.

Rhetorical theorists and critics have thoroughly examined the genre of political apologia. Rhetoricians have found six characteristics of successful political apologias.[65] First, such addresses are more effective if they are done in a situation where the candidate does not appear to be in control of the situation. Hence, a forum such as that provided by *60 Minutes* would, from a rhetorical standpoint, be ideal for the Clintons. *60 Minutes* is perceived as the premier investigative newsmagazine of the air. It is known for its hard-hitting reporting and for the fact that its interviewers pull no punches when they confront their subjects. Rhetorically, it was precisely the kind of situation the Clintons needed.

In addition, a special edition of *60 Minutes* after the Super Bowl would provide the Clintons with an exceptionally large audience. They could speak directly to tens of millions of voters. If such an audience largely accepted the Clinton apologia, then presumably this issue would, once and for all, be behind the candidate. But, as Stephanopoulos observed, there was a potential political downside.

> *60 Minutes* offered us airtime right after the Super Bowl—the biggest audience of the year. If we accepted, the first thing most Americans would know about Bill Clinton was that he had some association with a lounge singer. But our situation was so serious that the only hope was the media equivalent of experimental chemotherapy. *60 Minutes* was strong enough to cure us—if it didn't kill us first.[66]

Politically, the Clinton campaign needed the large audience an appearance on the special edition of *60 Minutes* offered.

The Clintons prepared thoroughly for their appearance. Carville and Begala prepared a memo for the Clintons prior to their two preparation sessions. The longer session, held late Saturday evening before the Sunday interview, involved the Clintons, Stephanopoulos, Begala, Carville, Greer, pollster Stan Greenberg, Mandy Grunwald (the Clinton media consultant who had represented them effectively several evenings earlier on *Nightline*), and Hillary's close friend and scheduler, Susan Thomases. A second brief session was held Sunday morning before the interview. It involved only the Clintons, Stephanopoulos, and Carville.

In these meetings the Clintons and their staff determined what they were going to say and how they were going to say it. Clearly the goal of *60 Minutes* interviewer Steve Kroft would be to get Clinton to admit to adultery with Flowers. Mandy Grunwald pointed out that Kroft was doing the interview, not Mike Wallace or Morley Safer, the best known of the *60 Minutes* personalities. This was a chance for him to become a star. He was being handed the biggest audience *60 Minutes* would likely have all year. He would be aggressive in questioning. Clinton insisted that the Flowers story was not true, and so he would deny any affair with her. However, both Clintons agreed that he would make a general admission of adultery. Much as they had done at the Sperling Breakfast months earlier, they agreed that Clinton would not use the term *adultery,* but would acknowledge having created problems in his marriage that were now behind him and Hillary. At one point in their preparation, Clinton claimed that they would say that they "have had difficulties in our marriage and we don't think that we have to say any more." He went on to add "people get it."[67]

Though Stephanopoulos and others initially argued for using the term *adultery,* believing it would show that Clinton was being completely candid with the public, both Hillary and Bill were adamant about not using that term. They and others argued that it was too grating, too harsh, and that euphemisms such as *problems* or *difficulties* in our marriage would make the same point. Moreover, aware that Gennifer Flowers was holding a press conference on Monday, the day after the broadcast of the *60 Minutes* interview, several in the room claimed that an explicit admission of "adultery" would seem to confirm her story.

Having determined how to answer the critical question that interviewer Steve Kroft was likely to ask, the meeting then focused on other points the Clintons wished to make in the interview. Among the points that the Clintons determined they would try to make were

- This election should be about the nation's future, not the past of one candidate.
- The Clintons had a "real" marriage. Hillary was a woman of substantial accomplishment who truly loved her husband. She had not been forced into staying with Clinton just because he is a powerful political figure and she would have a greatly diminished life without him. They were together because they both truly love each other.
- The Clintons are sad about Gennifer, not angry. They do not know why she has made these accusations now, since she denied them in the past.[68]

Though it is highly unlikely that any of those involved in these sessions were familiar with the scholarly literature concerning apologias, instinctively the Clinton team was developing almost precisely the strategies that rhetoricians would recommend.

The interview that was broadcast ran only eleven minutes, though approximately an hour of questioning was taped. The interview was conducted in a suite of Boston's Ritz-Carlton Hotel. The Clintons were seated side by side on a couch across from Kroft in a room with a fireplace that looked like a study or library more than a hotel room. Throughout most of the interview, when the camera showed the two of them, Hillary had her arm around Bill's shoulders, or they were holding hands.[69]

In placing themselves in a vulnerable situation by making their apologia on *60 Minutes,* the Clintons followed the first strategy recommended by rhetoricians. The apologia was presented in an environment in which the speakers appeared to have little control. The second strategy recommended by rhetoricians is to deny the "alleged facts, sentiments, objects, or relationships that give rise to the charge."[70] Kroft opened the interview by observing that Gennifer Flowers "is alleging and has described in some detail in a supermarket tabloid what she calls a twelve-year affair with you."[71] Clinton immediately responded, "that allegation is false." When Kroft continued, attempting to establish the nature of the relationship between Clinton and Flowers, Clinton observed that he knew her from her days as a TV reporter in Little Rock, but that her story was total fabrication. As the interview continued, Kroft provided Clinton an additional opportunity to deny the affair. "I am assuming from your answer," said Kroft, "that you are categorically denying that you ever had an affair with Gennifer Flowers." Viewers saw Clinton vigorously nodding his head affirmatively as Kroft spoke and then declaring "I said that before."

Clinton was clearly denying the alleged affair with Flowers, but he did not deny the possibility of having had other affairs. At one point, in response to Kroft's persistent questioning about his alleged infidelities, Clinton observed, "I have caused pain in my marriage." Thus, Clinton denied the specific allegations concerning Gennifer Flowers, but he did not issue a blanket denial of infidelity. As both Clintons responded to Kroft's questions, they utilized most of the remaining strategies suggested by rhetoricians.

The third strategy frequently utilized in apologias has been called "bolstering." Rhetoricians B. L. Ware and Wil Linkugel define "bolstering strategies" as attempts by the candidate to identify "with something viewed favorably by the audience."[72] Both Bill and Hillary made use of bolstering when they attempted to make a virtue of Clinton's inability to totally deny the charges of his philandering. Clinton claimed, "I have acknowledged wrongdoing. I have acknowledged causing pain in my marriage." Clinton then went on to argue that he was being totally candid with the public.

Hillary reaffirmed what her husband was claiming. "Here's a guy who is leveling with us. There isn't a person watching us who would feel comfortable sitting on this couch detailing everything that ever went on in their life or their marriage and I think it's real dangerous in this country if we don't have a zone of privacy for everybody." Toward the end of the interview, Hillary made the point yet again. "We've gone further than anybody we know of and that's all we're going to say."

The Clintons were attempting to bolster their case by displaying character traits that they believed the public would view favorably. Their repeated claims of openness and candor, and their repeated suggestions that they were willing to let the public decide, were all attempts to bolster their image by linking them with virtues that the public admired. To the extent that the Clintons could make their candor and honesty the focus of audience attention, rather than the infidelity that gave rise to the need for such candor and honesty, they were likely to successfully bolster their case.

The very presence of Hillary Clinton, much less her active participation in defending her husband, also contributed to the couple's fulfilling the bolstering functions. When Senator Gary Hart had to deal with accusations of infidelity four years earlier, his wife Lee Hart remained sequestered and refused to speak with reporters. Finally, she gave a brief interview to a few selected reporters. She stated, "I do not ask Gary what he is doing every moment of his life nor does he ask me." She added that "my support today is as strong today as I have always given to him," though in reference to the weekend he had spent with Donna Rice, she then observed that "if I could have planned his weekend schedule, I think I would have scheduled it differently."[73] Hillary was playing a much bigger role in her husband's defense and in doing so was suggesting that they had a solid marriage that had endured stress.

By indicating that, though there had been stressful moments, their marriage was strong, the Clintons were identifying with something the audience likely viewed favorably. This critical bolstering strategy was most evident in the interview when both Clintons responded to Kroft's characterization of their marriage.

Kroft: I think most Americans would agree that it's very admirable that you've stayed together, that you've worked your problems out, that you seemed to have reached some sort of an understanding and an arrangement.

Bill Clinton: (jumping in immediately as Kroft finished): Wait a minute, wait a minute. You're looking at two people who love each other. This is not an arrangement or an understanding. This is a marriage. That's a very different thing.

Hillary Clinton: You know I'm not sitting here like some little woman standing by my man like Tammy Wynette. I'm sitting here because I love him, I respect him, and I honor what he's been through and what we've been through together.

Repeatedly Clinton suggested that he was part of a strong marriage. "My wife and I," he observed, "have a stronger marriage than most people who have never had to survive the trials and tribulations of a challenging marriage." As the Clintons portrayed themselves as people who had successfully resolved troublesome issues in their marriage, they were bolstering their own case by identifying themselves with a second set of qualities admired by most Americans, the determination and ability to work through troubled relationships.

The fourth rhetorical strategy often used in successful apologias is differentiation. This strategy is to separate "some fact, sentiment, object, or relationship from some larger context in which the audience presently views that attribute."[74] Clinton repeatedly tried to differentiate the questions about his infidelity and subsequent honesty from the context in which it was being viewed, namely as a measure of his presidential fitness, into the context of press responsibility.

The press, Clinton claimed both explicitly and implicitly, was violating his family's right to privacy. If the public saw the press inquisitiveness about his personal life in this context and not as a legitimate attempt to examine a measure of presidential fitness, clearly Clinton would benefit. He claimed that the tabloid press was not legitimate in offering money for news, pointedly observing that "it was only when money came out, when the tabloid went down there offering people money to say they had been involved with me that she [Flowers] changed her story." Clinton worked to differentiate the context in which these accusations were perceived. He hoped to make the public view them in the context of an irresponsible press, rather than in the context of a candidate unfit for office.

Kathryn M. Olson has observed that attacks on the press should be considered a "strategy near last resort." But, she has observed, candidates can more freely suggest that journalists have made what she terms "role imbalance attacks."[75] Candidates can suggest that journalists have gone beyond legitimate objective journalist reporting and treated them in a harsh and unfair adversarial fashion, thereby exacerbating and exaggerating the charges against the candidate. Essentially that was what the Clintons did with their attempt to differentiate. Hillary claimed everybody deserved a "zone of privacy" and the interview concluded on that note with Bill claiming "this will test the character of the press. It is not only my character that is being tested." In attempting to move the questions about his marital infidelity out of the context of presidential fitness and into the context of privacy rights, the Clintons were forced to question the press.

The fifth strategy found in political apologias is what Ware and Linkugel have called transcendental strategy. This strategy "cognitively joins some fact, sentiment, object, or relationship with some larger context within which the audience does not presently view that attribute."[76] Though the Clintons made no explicit effort here, the combined effect of their strategies served this purpose. If public reaction to the interview was largely to think about the courage the Clintons displayed in appearing on *60 Minutes*, their honesty in confessing to difficulties in their marriage, their perseverance in resolving the difficulties in their marriage, and the way the press seemed to be invading their privacy and behaving in an adversarial role rather than in an objective role, then these issues, and not Clinton's infidelity and what that might say about fitness for office, would be the focus of attention.

The sixth and final strategy rhetoricians have identified as common in successful political apologias is to confess. If the candidate is guilty, a quick confession is likely to put a quick end to the issue and allow the campaign to progress to other issues. The controversy becomes old news because there is nothing more to report on it.

The effectiveness of confession was illustrated during the 1984 Democratic primaries when Jesse Jackson's attitudes toward Jews became the focal point of fourteen days' worth of news coverage at the outset of the critical first primary in New Hampshire. The *Washington Post* reported that Jackson had used the derogatory term "Hymie" and characterized New York City and its large Jewish population as "Hymietown." Not only did such remarks suggest that Jackson was prejudiced against a significant number of Americans, but it also called into question his presidential fitness, for it suggested an inability to treat all citizens equally. After fourteen days of controversy swirling around his campaign, Jackson rejected the advice of many of his advisers and confessed. He spoke to a Jewish audience at Temple Adath Yeshurun in Manchester, New Hampshire, acknowledged that he had made the derogatory remarks that had given rise to the controversy, and observed that "however innocent and unintentional, it was insensitive and it was wrong." After his confession, the issue died. There was simply nothing more to be written. Jackson had put the issue behind him and was finally able to return to other issues. Moreover, it never surfaced in Jackson's later campaigns.[77]

However, confession was not an option for Clinton. When his name had first been linked with Flowers, well before the tabloid *Star* story, both Clinton and Flowers had denied it. He could scarcely now confess. Rather, he denied the *Star* story that he had a twelve-year affair with Flowers but never flatly denied having had extramarital affairs.[78] Most audience members, as well as interviewer Steve Kroft, interpreted his remarks about having caused "pain" in his marriage as essentially a confession of infidelity.

Having so confessed, there was little more that the press could pursue on this story.

EFFECTS

George Stephanopoulos clearly suggested the critical importance of the Clintons' *60 Minutes* apologia when he observed "we bet the whole campaign on a single interview."[79] Stephanopoulos was not exaggerating. Charges of womanizing and infidelity had destroyed the presidential campaign of Gary Hart four years earlier. Similar charges combined with questions raised by his involvement in a fatal car accident had destroyed the presidential ambitions of Senator Edward Kennedy. The public careers of a long list of lesser officials such as Congressman Wilbur Mills had also been ended or badly damaged by such charges. As we have seen since, the political careers of men such as Newt Gingrich and Robert Livingston have also been largely destroyed by such charges. It is no exaggeration to suggest that if this interview had gone badly, Bill and Hillary Clinton would have soon returned to Arkansas.

Though the Clintons left the interview feeling that it had gone well, they were dismayed that evening when they watched the broadcast. The segment was much shorter than what they expected. The one-hour interview had been edited down to little more than ten minutes. Clinton felt that the most emotional parts, where he and Hillary came across as most believable, had been edited out. He could not sleep that evening and the next morning told people "it was a screw job. They lied about how long it was going to be. They lied about what was going to be discussed. They lied about what the ending would be. It couldn't have been worse if they had drawn black X's through our faces."[80]

The following afternoon, Gennifer Flowers held a press conference at which she played tapes of phone conversations between Clinton and herself. Though her conference was televised by CNN, the audience was a mere fraction of that drawn by the *60 Minutes* interview in prime time after the Super Bowl. Flowers reiterated her claim to have been Clinton's lover for twelve years, though she acknowledged having lied about the relationship in the past. She then played audiotapes made in 1990–91. Investigations subsequently indicated that the conversations had been edited and only about twelve minutes of what Flowers claimed to be over an hour's worth of material was played. There was little doubt that Clinton's voice was on the tapes and the nature of the conversations suggested a high degree of familiarity. What was especially telling was that at several points Clinton suggests that if they were ever questioned about their relationship, Flowers could simply deny everything and then nothing could be proven.[81]

The Clintons had already acknowledged that he had been unfaithful. Moreover, the Clintons had skillfully suggested that they had overcome these difficulties and should be admired for working to preserve their marriage. They had skillfully suggested that they had leveled with the public to an unprecedented extent. They had skillfully suggested that the press was not treating them fairly. Flowers's allegations in no way diminished these claims.

One of the effects of the Flowers scandal was to clearly thrust Hillary Clinton into the limelight. Not only did she participate in the first major defense of her husband on *60 Minutes*, but she was continually thereafter involved in defending him. Reiterating many of the same arguments they had used on *60 Minutes*, Hillary appeared by herself on *Prime Time Live* four days after the *60 Minutes* interview. Interviewer Sam Donaldson characterized Hillary as Bill's "primary defensive shield."[82] It was an entirely appropriate characterization and remained so throughout the campaign.

Intuitively, the Clintons and their aides had mapped out an interview strategy that worked. Following most of the principal strategies that rhetoricians recommend for someone facing this type of speech, they made a formidable presentation on *60 Minutes*. Monday evening, twenty-four hours after the Clinton interview and about six hours after the Flowers press conference, a Boston TV poll indicated that Clinton was still ahead in New Hampshire. That same evening ABC's *Nightline* reported that 80 percent of the nation felt Clinton should stay in the race.[83] When the New Hampshire primary was over, Clinton had received 25 percent of the vote, running second to Paul Tsongas, who received 33 percent of the vote and had started the race as a much better-known New England favorite-son candidate. It is important to note that no other candidate came close to the top two. Kerrey received 11 percent of the vote, Harkin 10 percent, Brown 8 percent and a write-in effort for Mario Cuomo garnered him 4 percent. The remaining votes were split among a variety of lesser candidates.[84]

Tsongas had won, but Clinton had survived. Clinton was able, on election eve, to aptly describe himself as "the Comeback Kid" and in effect claim victory. A relatively unknown small-state governor from the South, he had faced serious obstacles during the New Hampshire campaign and overcame them to defeat every candidate except a New Englander who was almost a favorite-son candidate in New Hampshire. Clinton's showing effectively made it a two-man race. Unable to attract much over 10 percent of the vote, Kerrey, Harkin, and the other candidates soon did not have the financing necessary to continue and dropped out.

Clinton had survived New Hampshire, and his showing would no doubt encourage continued support throughout the coming primaries. It is impossible to ascribe his success exlusively to the interview the Clintons had given on *60 Minutes*. However, more than any other effort at defending themselves, this effort was critical. The timing and the size of the audience suggest its importance. The fact that the Clintons had prepared thoroughly and utilized many of the same arguments throughout the rest of the campaign give it added significance. Had he not done well in New Hampshire, William Jefferson Clinton's ultimate triumph in the struggle for the Democratic nomination, and his subsequent victory over President Bush and third-party candidate Ross Perot in the general election, would likely never have happened.

NOTES

1. On Clinton's early preparation for a 1988 White House bid, see Charles F. Allen and Jonathan Portis, *The Comeback Kid* (New York: Birch Lane Press, 1992), pp. 116–18; and Roger Morris, *Partners in Power* (New York: Henry Holt, 1996), pp. 431–32.
2. Allen and Portis, *Comeback Kid*, p. 119.
3. For a detailed account of Hart's difficulties, which also focuses heavily on the role of the press in treating the private lives of public figures, see Jack W. Germond and Jules Witcover, *Whose Broad Stripes and Bright Stars? The Trivial Pursuit of the Presidency 1988* (New York: Warner Books, 1989), pp. 169–214.
4. See Morris, *Partners in Power*, p. 436, for an account of this meeting, which was evidently provided to Morris in confidential interviews.
5. Joyce Milton, *The First Partner: Hillary Rodham Clinton* (New York: William Morrow, 1999), p. 185.
6. Morris, *Partners in Power*, p. 437; and Milton, *First Partner*, p. 185.
7. The quotations and details of this conversation come from a 1999 interview with Wright conducted and reported by Gail Sheehy. See Sheehy, *Hillary's Choice* (New York: Random House, 1999), pp. 176–77. Milton reports the same conversation, and the same outcome, though she does not include the details. See Milton, *First Partner*, p. 185. Donnie Radcliffe's admiring biography, *Hillary Rodham Clinton: A First Lady for Our Time* (New York: Time Warner Books, 1993), p. 218–19, also implies that Clinton's abrupt decision not to run surprised even his mother and was due to his fear that his presidential candidacy would result in an exposure of his infidelities. David Maraniss, the *Washington Post* reporter who won the 1993 Pulitzer prize for national reporting, confirms Sheehy's account, based on three interviews he had with Wright. See David Maraniss, *First in His Class: A Biography of Bill Clinton* (New York: Simon and Schuster, 1995), p. 441.

8. On Wagner and Cohen's recollections, see Sheehy, *Hillary's Choice*, p. 177; and Maraniss, *First in His Class*, pp. 441–42.

9. Clinton is quoted in Sheehy, *Hillary's Choice*, pp. 177–78. A picture of Hillary crying at the announcement can also be found in Sheehy.

10. Sheehy reports that both Betsy Wright and Dick Morris perceived her to be furious and devastated at his failure to capitalize on what both of them took to be perhaps his best opportunity for the White House. See Sheehy, *Hillary's Choice*, p. 179. Morris claims that people close to the Clintons tell several versions of what happened between them but that all versions concur that her reaction was "bitter." See Morris, *Partners in Power*, p. 437.

11. Allen and Portis, *Comeback Kid*, p. 5.

12. Ibid., p. 9.

13. These details of Clinton's early life can be found in most good biographies. Robert E. Levin, *Bill Clinton: The Inside Story* (New York: S.P.I. Books, 1992), includes a timeline that places the major events of Clinton's life in the context of national affairs. The picture of Clinton shaking hands with Kennedy can be found in most of his biographies and was featured in his campaign advertisements in 1992. Among the biographers who trace his interest in a political career to this moment are Allen and Portis, *Comeback Kid*, p. 9; and Levin, *Bill Clinton*, p. 35.

14. The marriage between Virginia and Roger was tumultuous. They were eventually divorced and remarried. On several occasions the police were called in to help settle disputes. In addition to his alcoholism, or perhaps because of it, Roger was largely unsuccessful at business. This evidently caused Virginia to work long hours out of the home, often at night. She had become a nurse anesthetist. This specialty no doubt paid her more than a normal nursing position but meant that she frequently had to leave home at all hours, whenever a doctor needed her aid for surgery. Nevertheless, both her sons recall that Virginia made every effort to provide them with a stable home life.

15. A bibliography of literature on children of alcoholics is given in Maraniss, *First in His Class*, pp. 38–39.

16. Roger Clinton, Jr., *Growing Up Clinton* (Arlington, TX: Summit, 1995), pp. 2–3.

17. Maraniss, *First in His Class*, p. 43.

18. The incidents mentioned in this paragraph are discussed in Maraniss, *First in His Class*, p. 48.

19. Clinton is quoted in Levin, *Bill Clinton*, p. 35.

20. In addition to his good grades and recommendations, Clinton evidently excelled in the scholarship interview. He recalls that while waiting in the airport on the way to his final interview, he found a copy of *Time* magazine and read an article about the world's first heart transplant. One of his interview questions concerned heart transplants. See Levin, *Bill Clinton*, p. 54.

21. All the details concerning the Clintons' initial meetings found in this paragraph can be found in Joyce Milton, *First Partner*, pp. 47–49, and are confirmed

in most other biographies, including Maraniss, *First in His Class,* and Sheehy, *Hillary's Choice.*

22. See Maraniss, *First in His Class*, p. 289.

23. Ibid.

24. See Radcliffe, *Hillary Rodham Clinton*, pp. 148–49, for details on the Clinton wedding.

25. The details in the preceding two paragraphs concerning Clinton's first term as governor are drawn primarily from Jim Moore, *Clinton: Young Man in a Hurry* (Fort Worth, TX: Summit Group, 1992), pp. 54–62.

26. The preceding details of Clinton's career can be found in any biography. See, for example, Moore, *Clinton*, pp. 69–180; Levin, *Bill Clinton*, pp. 123–83; and Allen and Portis, *Comeback Kid*, pp. 41–152. Levin also offers a chronology of Clinton's career. See especially pp. xxvi-xxvii. Paul Greenberg, *No Surprises: Two Decades of Clinton Watching* (Washington: Brassey's, 1996), is especially informative on Clinton's Arkansas career. Greenberg was the editorial page editor of the *Pine Bluff Commercial* and an editor and columnist at the *Arkansas Democrat-Gazette* throughout Clinton's Arkansas years. This book is a collection of Greenberg's columns and editorials, reprinted as they first ran.

27. On Clinton's 1990 race, see Maraniss, *First in His Class*, pp. 454–457.

28. Ibid., p. 460.

29. See Sheehy, *Hillary's Choice*, pp. 24–25.

30. On the jobs, as well as Dorothy Rodham's recollections, see Morris, *Partners in Power*, p. 116.

31. See Sheehy, *Hillary's Choice*, pp. 19–39; Radcliffe, *Hillary Rodham Clinton*, pp. 23–52; Morris, *Partners in Power*, pp. 112–24; and the first chapters of Norman King, *Hillary: Her True Story* (New York: Carol, 1963), for details about Hillary Rodham's family, early political beliefs, and early education.

32. See Radcliffe, *Hillary Rodham Clinton*, pp. 36–39; Milton, *First Partner*, pp. 17–24; and Morris, *Partners in Power*, pp. 116–18, on her high school years.

33. Virtually every study of Hillary Clinton mentions the influence of Jones. For a particularly informative explanation of Jones's "University of Life," see Radcliffe, *Hillary Rodham Clinton*, pp. 44–49.

34. Maraniss, *First in His Class*, pp. 255–56.

35. Milton, *The First Partner*, p. 32.

36. Rodham is quoted in Milton, *First Partner,* p. 33.

37. Ibid., pp. 45–46.

38. Sheehy, *Hillary's Choice*, pp. 85–86.

39. Ibid., p. 86.

40. Sheehy claims that in an interview with her, Bernard Nussbaum, Hillary's supervisor on the House Judiciary Committee Impeachment staff, recalled a conversation in which she claimed that Clinton would be president of the United States. When Nussbaum expressed his strong skepticism, Rodham replied, "You asshole. Bernie, you're a jerk. You don't know this guy. I know this guy. So don't

pontificate to me. He is going to be president of the United States." Quoted in Sheehy, *Hillary's Choice*, p. 91.

41. Bush was challenged in the Republican primaries by former Nixon aide and political commentator Patrick Buchanan. Buchanan ran surprisingly well in the New Hampshire primary, winning 37 percent of the vote. More important, Buchanan exploited Bush's apparent indifference to the economy, an issue that Democrat Bill Clinton and independent Ross Perot would use against him even more effectively in the general election. See Jack Germond and Jules Witcover, *Mad As Hell: Revolt at the Ballot Box 1992* (New York: Warner Books, 1993), pp. 147–52.

42. On Tsongas's early candidacy, see Germond and Witcover, *Mad As Hell*, p. 83.

43. Ibid., pp. 87–88.

44. Ibid., p. 90.

45. Bertram W. Gross, "The Announcement Speeches of Democratic Candidates for the 1992 Presidential Nomination" (Paper presented at the Speech Communication Association Annual Convention, Chicago, Illinois 29 Oct. 1992, pp. 1–8.

46. See Clinton's announcement address in Bill Clinton and Al Gore, *Putting People First* (New York: Times Books, 1992), pp. 187–98.

47. See Germond and Witcover, *Mad As Hell*, pp. 100–101.

48. *Newsweek, Special Election Issue* (Nov.-Dec. 1992), p. 30.

49. Ibid.

50. See Germond and Witcover, *Mad As Hell*, pp. 63–74, for details about the Wofford-Thornburgh Senate race.

51. Mary Matalin and James Carville, *All's Fair: Love, War, and Running for President* (New York: Random House, 1994), p. 9.

52. George Stephanopoulos, *All Too Human* (Boston: Little, Brown, 1999), pp. 29–30.

53. Ibid., p. 32. Stephanopoulos also believed that Clinton had laid the issue to rest with the press at the Sperling Breakfast, discussed in the following pages.

54. Christine M. Black, *The Pursuit of the Presidency 1992 and Beyond* (Phoenix: Oryx Press, 1994), pp. 26–27.

55. Ibid., p. 27.

56. Germond and Witcover, *Mad As Hell*, p. 171.

57. See Maraniss, *First in His Class*, pp. 460–61, for details of the strategy meeting at which the Clintons prepared for the Sterling Breakfast. Maraniss's discussion is informed by his interviews with Greer.

58. Ibid., p. 461.

59. Germond and Witcover, *Mad As Hell*, p. 169.

60. Clinton is quoted in Maraniss, *First in His Class*, p. 461, but it is not entirely clear whether Maraniss was relying on Greer for his quote. Clinton's statements at this meeting are slightly different in the version of the meeting presented in Germond and Witcover, *Mad As Hell*, p. 169. They report that after some pre-

liminary remarks, Clinton gets to the heart of Borger's question by saying "what you need to know about Hillary and me is that we've been together nearly twenty years. It has not been perfect or free from problems, but we're committed to our marriage and its obligations—to our child and to each other. We love each other very much." Germond and Witcover do not identify their sources nor do they indicate whether they were present at the meeting.

61. Germond and Witcover, *Mad As Hell*, p. 171.

62. For insiders' accounts of these efforts, see Stephanopoulos, *All Too Human*, pp. 56–62, and Matalin and Carville, *All's Fair*, p. 104.

63. See Germond and Witcover, *Mad As Hell*, pp. 171–83, for an account of how the mainstream press treated this story.

64. Clinton surrogate Mandy Grunwald went on in their stead and did an excellent job, making some of the points that the Clintons would later make themselves. See Matalin and Carville, *All's Fair*, p. 103.

65. See the first chapter of Dennis D. Cali, *Generic Criticism of American Public Address* (Dubuque, IA: Kendall Hunt, 1996), for a discussion of the premises underlying genre theory and criticism. See Judith S. Trent and Robert V. Friedenberg, *Political Campaign Communication: Principles and Practices* (Westport, CT: Praeger, 2000), pp. 235–42, for a review of literature and illustrations of genre criticism applied to political apologias.

66. Stephanopoulos, *All Too Human*, p. 62.

67. The account of the preparation sessions found in this paragraph and the next two paragraphs are drawn primarily from Stephanopoulos, *All Too Human*, pp. 64–67, and Matalin and Carville, *All's Fair*, pp. 108–11.

68. Carville claims that "our prep had been good and there were no surprises" in the *60 Minutes* interview. See Matlin and Carville, *All's Fair*, p. 110. These points are drawn from the acounts of Carville and Stephanopoulos, who were involved in all the planning sessions for the *60 Minutes* interview.

69. The following analysis of the interview is patterned after a briefer earlier analysis done by the author that appears in Judith S. Trent and Robert V. Friedenberg, *Political Campaign Communication: Principles and Practices* (Westport, CT: Praeger, 2000), pp. 237–41.

70. B. L. Ware and Wil A. Linkugel, "The Spoke in Defense of Themselves: On the General Criticism of Apologia," *Quarterly Journal of Speech* 59 (Oct. 1973): 275.

71. This quotation and all subsequent quotations from this interview have been transcribed directly from a videotape of the *60 Minutes* broadcast of 28 January 1992.

72. Ware and Linkugel, "They Spoke in Defense of Themselves," p. 277.

73. See Germond and Witcover, *Whose Broad Stripes*, pp. 193–202, for Lee Hart's limited role in this matter. The Hart marriage had long been a difficult one. At one time they were separated.

74. Ware and Linkugel, "The Spoke in Defense of Themselves," p. 278.

75. Kathryn M. Olson, "Exploiting the Tension Between the News Media's Objective and Adversarial Roles: The Role of Imbalance Attack and Its Use of the Implied Audience," *Communication Quarterly* 42 (Winter 1994): 36–56.

76. Ware and Linkugel, "The Spoke in Defense of Themselves," p. 280.

77. On Jackson's 1984 confession, see *Newsweek Election Extra,* Nov.–Dec. 1984, p. 52, and Jack W. Germond and Jules Witcover, *Wake Us When It's Over: Presidential Politics of 1984* (New York: Macmillan, 1985), p. 159.

78. Clinton was no doubt aware that Flowers was holding a press conference the following day at which she would play what she alleged were tapes of phone conversations with Clinton. In January 1998, as part of a sworn deposition in the Paula Jones case, Clinton acknowledged having had a sexual relationship on one occasion with Gennifer Flowers. His defenders observed that in 1992 he had denied a twelve year affair and claimed that his 1998 statement made under oath did not contradict his 1992 claim.

79. Stephanopoulos, *All Too Human*, p. 66.

80. *Newsweek Election Extra*, p. 34.

81. For Flowers's statement to the press and the tape transcripts, see Floyd G. Brown, "*Slick Willie*" (Annapolis, MD: Annapolis Publishing, 1992), pp. 149–59.

82. See Norman King, *Hillary* (New York: Carol Publishing, 1993), pp. 153–58, on Hillary's *Prime Time Live* interview.

83. Stephanopoulos, *All Too Human*, p. 69.

84. Germond and Witcover, *Mad As Hell*, p. 208.

Chapter Six

2000—George W. Bush

> I believe the presidency—the final point of decision in the American government—was made for great purposes. It is the office of Lincoln's conscience and Teddy Roosevelt's energy and Harry Truman's integrity and Ronald Reagan's optimism. For me, gaining this office is not the ambition of a lifetime, but it is the opportunity of a lifetime.

Throughout his adult life, George W. Bush had struggled with being the first son, the namesake, of his famous father. In most outward respects, he had emulated his father. He had followed in his father's footsteps at Andover and Yale. At both schools the father excelled, while the son had modest success. The father had volunteered for flight training during World War II and returned home a hero. The son enlisted in the Air National Guard during the Vietnam War era and never flew in combat. The father refused the offer of a secure future working in the family investment and banking concerns on the East Coast. Instead, he charted a path of his own, settling in Midland, Texas, and subsequently Houston, Texas, making his own fortune in the oil industry. The son too turned down opportunities that were available to him by virtue of being a Bush, returned to the town of his earliest memories, Midland, worked hard, and made a comfortable living, but not a fortune, in the oil industry. While his father became a national figure during the 1970s and 1980s, ultimately elected to the presidency in 1988, George W. Bush moved from job to job with modest success.

Bush always seemed to be emulating his father, yet he never quite attained the success of his father. Throughout George W. Bush's life he had been a heavy social drinker. Known as partyer since his college days, Bush liked to drink what he called the four Bs, beer, bourbon, and B & B. Bush was not an alcoholic. He did not drink daily, nor did he drink during working hours. Rather, on those occasions when he did drink, he seemed to drink excessively. His friends called him a "spree or binge drinker." For when he did start, as his close friend and now cabinet member Don Evans has said, "he couldn't, didn't shut it off. He didn't have the discipline." Bush has acknowledged that his drinking had reached a disturbing level by the mid-1980s. "I realized that alcohol was beginning to crowd out my energies and could crowd, eventually, my affections for other people. . . . When you're drinking it can be an incredibly selfish act."[1]

By the mid 1980s, now married for almost a decade and the father of twin four year olds, Bush had become an active member of his wife Laura's Methodist church, even teaching, as had his father, Sunday school classes. In early 1985 he began a series of conversations with Billy Graham. Graham joined the Bush family at one of their summer retreats. The famous evangelist was a close friend of the Bush family and saw much in George W. that he had seen in his own son Franklin. Franklin had been a hard-drinking partyer as a youth, eventually giving it up to settle down and work in his father's ministry. Graham told Bush that if he was to commit his life to Christ, he would likely have to give up drinking.[2]

Bush has acknowledged that Graham's influence was "like planting a mustard seed. It took time to grow, and I began to change."[3] Bush has always been defensive about the role his wife has played in his change. "If I were a totally irresponsible person she wouldn't have married me," he has claimed. Nevertheless, he gives her credit for "bringing a lot of stability, a lot of common sense to our relationship."[4] Others claim that she had been urging him to give up alcohol for years.[5] Thus, by the summer of 1986, George W. Bush was renewing his faith and was on the verge of giving up his drinking.

Bush's religious faith is more important to him than people typically recognize. He claims that his religion "gave me a different perspective on what matters. I don't fear failure, nor do I fear success. If things don't work out, they just don't work out. My religion provides a sense of security. I'm secure in the knowledge my family will love me either way."[6] Bush finds his religious beliefs to be a refuge from the cynicism that he feels has become pervasive in American life since the 1960s.[7]

By all accounts, the change came on 28 July 1986. George and Laura Bush, their longtime friends Don and Susie Evans, Joe and Jan O'Neill (who had introduced George to Laura), Penny Royal (a good friend who was in the process of separating from her husband), and George's brother Neil had gotten away for a weekend celebration at the Broadmoor Hotel in

Colorado Springs to mark the fortieth birthdays of Bush and several of the others. The drinks flowed, though none of those present felt that they flowed to any greater excess that night than on many other occasions. Bush woke up with a hangover and began his morning run.

But unlike many other mornings when he woke with a hangover, Bush had decided that he would no longer drink. Bush did not make a big production about his decision. Laura recalled that "he just said 'I'm going to quit' and that was it. We joked about it later, saying he got the bar bill and that's why." Jan O'Neill recalled that as Bush's friends learned of his decision "I didn't get the sense at all that it was anything momentous at the time. I think it was a big turning point in his own mind, but these things never take on momentous meaning until you follow through."[8]

Though his decision to stop drinking may not have appeared momentous to others, O'Neill's observation was correct. It was a major decision for Bush. He later called the morning he stopped drinking and the related renewal of faith that his talks with Billy Graham had provided him "the defining moments" of his life.[9] While the immediate impetus for these changes might well have been his conversations with Graham and with his wife, and perhaps his feelings when he awoke after the fortieth birthday celebration, it would not be unreasonable to surmise that at least two other factors influenced Bush's decision.

First, by the summer of 1986 his father's presidential campaign was gearing up. It was clear that Bush would play a critical role in his father's organization. Joe O'Neill felt that Bush's decision was motivated at least in part by the launch of his father's presidential campaign. O'Neill's explanation of Bush's abrupt decision to cease drinking indicates the admiration that the son had for the father whose footsteps he never seemed quite able to fill. O'Neill claims that Bush "looked in the mirror and said, 'someday, I might embarrass my father. It might get my dad in trouble.' And boy, that was it. That's how high a priority it was. And he never took another drink."[10]

Second, Bush's decision was made at a fortieth birthday celebration. If Bush was to accomplish something of real significance in his life, something comparable to that which his father had accomplished, it was time to start. Excessive drinking, even if only occasionally, was not the way to accomplish anything. Bush had been born into a family that provided him with many advantages. Moreover, he had a number of talents. Perhaps the recognition that his life was likely half over provided yet another impetus for his decision. Regardless of the reasons, on 28 July 1986 George W. Bush gave up alcohol and launched himself on the path that fourteen years and one week later would take him to the Republican party's nomination for the presidency of the United States.

THE SPEAKER

George W. Bush claims that

> I have never plotted the various steps of my life, certainly never campaigned for one office to try to position myself for the next. I am more spontaneous than that. I live in the moment, seize opportunities, and try to make the most of them.

For most of his life, that judgment seems accurate. Still, as we will see, Bush's drive to the White House began prior to his last race for the governorship of Texas. That race was used to position Bush for a presidential race. Nevertheless, Bush's observation is largely correct. For most of his life he seemed to act spontaneously, living in the moment, seizing the opportunities presented to him.

George W. Bush was presented with unusual opportunities. His great-grandfather, Samuel P. Bush, was raised on the East Coast but moved to Columbus, Ohio, where he became a leader in the steel and railroad industries. He was a charter member of the U.S. Chamber of Commerce, a director of the Federal Reserve Bank in Cleveland, and a close adviser to President Herbert Hoover. Prescott Bush, George W. Bush's grandfather, grew up in Columbus but was sent east to be educated at eastern prep schools and Yale. He had a skill that his grandson inherited and which served both of them well in their political careers, the ability to memorize names.[11] Prescott had a highly successful career on Wall Street and had been prominent in local Connecticut politics for two decades prior to running for the U.S. Senate in 1950.[12] Though he lost a close race to incumbent William Benton, two years later he was elected to the Senate from Connecticut, the same year that his son George was serving as the Eisenhower for President chairman in Midland County, Texas.[13]

George Bush had settled in Midland, Texas, after serving as a pilot in World War II and graduating from Yale. In 1941 he had met Barbara Pierce at a Christmas dance. She was a descendent of President Franklin Pierce and the granddaughter of the president of McCall Publishing Company. On 6 July 1946, while his father was studying at Yale, George W. Bush was born. With his father's 1948 graduation from Yale, the Bush family moved first to Odessa, Texas, and then to Midland, Texas. George Bush was working for Dresser Industries, a holding company that provided drilling rigs to oil firms. The move was a dramatic one for the Bushes, for George could have moved into a lucrative career on Wall Street, following in his father's footsteps. Barbara Bush later recalled that "we wanted to get out from under the parental gaze, be on our own!"[14]

Life in Midland was pleasant for the young George W. Bush. His father was prospering and Bush's days were filled with school and sports, particularly baseball. Three years after George W. Bush's birth, on 20 December 1949, the Bushes had their second child, Pauline Robinson (Robin) Pierce Bush, named after her maternal grandmother. The family grew yet again when in February 1953 John Ellis, soon known as Jeb, was born. But within months of Jeb's birth, Robin was diagnosed as suffering from leukemia. Though the Bush's quickly took her to New York's Sloan-Kettering Institute, within six months of the diagnosis she died.

Robin's death was, for her older brother George W., "the starkest memory of my childhood, a sharp pain in the midst of an otherwise happy blur."[15] Bush recalls that "others have said I tried to cheer up my parents, told jokes and even stayed inside the house after school for weeks because I was worried about my mother, but I don't remember much of that. I remember being sad."[16] His parents had hidden the serious nature of Robin's illness from their son, so that her death came as a total surprise to him. But the death did have one positive consequence. It tightened the bond between George W. and his mother. Barbara Bush claimed that during this period she heard George telling a friend that he couldn't come out to play because he had to play with his mother who was lonely.[17] The entire Bush family was profoundly affected by Robin's death. Young George had nightmares for months afterward.

Robin's death affected Bush in a multitude of ways, but most observers center on two of its effects on the development of George W. Bush. First, it provided him with a sense of fatalism. As an adolescent, Bush would tell friends, "You think your life is so good and everything is perfect: then something like this happens and nothing is the same."[18] As we have seen, Bush claims to live his life in the present, to seize the opportunity of the moment and not worry about tomorrow. That attitude might well, at least in part, trace to the experience of his sister's death. Second, in drawing him close to his mother, Robin's death may have caused him to pick up many of her personality traits. Bush has been frequently described as a more intuitive and natural politician than his father. Those observations reflect his outspokenness, his irreverence, his quick-witted personality. Family friends and relatives all feel that characteristics such as these are far more descriptive of his mother than of his more guarded and dignified father.

As Bush grew up in Midland, his father's business became more and more successful. The family moved into nicer housing. The eldest son seemed to always be the center of attention among his friends. But Midland was too small a stage for the elder Bush. His business was prospering and when his son finished seventh grade at Midland's San Jacinto Junior High, where he had been elected class president, the Bushes moved to Houston. George Bush had become a millionaire and his business was becoming more and more involved with offshore drilling. The move was a natural progression for a couple that had been raised in the urban East. They enrolled their eldest son in the Kinkaid School, perhaps the most prestigious college preparatory school in Houston.

But though he would not return to Midland for many years, Midland stayed with George W. Bush. He claims

> Midland was a small town, with small-town values. We learned to respect our elders, to do what they said, to be good neighbors. We went to church. Families spent time together, outside, the grown-ups talking with neighbors while the kids played ball or with marbles and yo-yos. Our homework and schoolwork were important. The town's leading citizens worked hard to attract the best teachers to our schools. No one locked their doors, because you could trust your friends and neighbors.[19]

George W. Bush fit in naturally at the Kinkaid School. He was quickly elected a class officer and developed a large circle of friends. But in the fall of 1961, at the end of ninth grade, his parents decided that he should attend Phillips Academy in Andover, Massachusetts. It was one of the most exclusive schools in the country and his father's alma mater. At Phillips, Bush was once more among the most popular of students. He seemed able to recall everyone's name. He became the head cheerleader and though he was not an outstanding athlete or an honor student, he nevertheless soon became comfortable at Andover. He was always impulsive and a natural prankster. By his senior year he had become high commissioner of the school stickball league. Bush made the most of it, passing out favors, making rulings—and in doing so mimicking Boss Tweed and the infamous New York political machine that he headed. Bush's friends soon took to calling him "Tweeds." Bush's father had excelled as a student athlete. Bush made his mark as head cheerleader and stickball commissioner. The father's pursuits were ones that demanded hard work and discipline. The son's pursuits were ones that required the ability to motivate people, persuade them, and to some degree entertain them. Bush's political skills were developing.

During Bush's senior year at Andover, Senator Barry Goldwater spoke at Andover and Bush read Barry Goldwater's *Conscience of a Conservative*. His roommate at the time, John Kidde, recalls that "we didn't have any time to read anything extracurricular. If we did, you would read a novel. But George seemed honestly interested in the book. He said his parents had asked him to read it. I remember him telling me what Goldwater stood for."[20]

Bush applied to both Yale and the University of Texas as he was finishing at Andover. Though his friends at the time don't recall that he had any specific career ambitions, the Andover experience had given Bush considerable confidence. "Andover taught me independence," he later recalled. "I recognized the value of the education it provided. Most of all, though, at Andover, I learned how, as the old saying goes, to bloom where I was planted. I would never again feel isolated. One of the most valuable lessons of Andover was what I learned about myself."[21] For a young man whose father seemed to be such a dominant influence, it was no small lesson.

Continuing in his father's footsteps, Bush arrived at Yale in the fall of 1964. As Bush set foot on campus, his father was locked in a close Senate race with incumbent Democrat Ralph Yarborough. Bush ran exceptionally well, but Yarborough had the benefit of fellow Texan Lyndon Johnson's coattails and won.

Shortly after the election was over, Bush had an experience that typified much of what he would find at Yale. One of his father's contemporaries at Yale was the Reverend William Sloane Coffin, who at that time was serving as Yale's chaplain and would later win fame for his antiwar activities. The elder Bush suggested to his son that he look up Coffin. Coffin greeted him "I knew your father and your father lost to a better man."[22]

Bush seemed to adhere to the old traditions, the Yale of his father, rather than the changing Yale. He was comfortable with fraternities, eventually winning election to the presidency of Delta Kappa Epsilon, known as the jock fraternity. He was an enthusiastic partygoer. He was tapped for Skull and Bones, a secret society to which his father had belonged. After his freshman year, he lived with the same group of friends, many of whom he had known at Andover. Contemporaries remember Bush as a "a fraternity guy, but he wasn't Belushi in *Animal House*." He did nothing, they recalled, that would embarrass him today as president.[23]

But Yale was changing. The Vietnam era witnessed a host of campus protests and changes. Bush was not one for protest and rebellion. Yet he conversed easily with those that were and seemed to maintain friends among many of the politically and socially diverse groups at Yale. Classmates such as Lanny Davis, who later served as special counsel to President Clinton, recall that Bush had excellent "analytical people skills."[24] Other classmates recall that Bush reached out beyond his normal social circle. One recalls that "he moved seamlessly among all the different groups."[25] During the Christmas break of his junior year, Bush and Cathy Wolfman, a student at Rice in Houston, became engaged. Though finishing their education in different cities, they stayed close for a year. But the wedding was delayed and eventually called off. Doug Hannah, a Houston friend, claims that Bush took it very hard.[26]

As Bush finished at Yale, the Vietnam conflict was dividing the country. Bush's views were no doubt affected by the public position his father, now a congressman from Houston, had taken in favor of the war. Bush's position was clearly the unpopular one at Yale. Bush stood his ground on the issue and was frequently criticized for doing so. Indeed, by the time he graduated in the spring of 1968, Bush believed that the antiwar left that he encountered at Yale included a great many intellectually arrogant snobs.

On 27 May 1968, with the Vietnam War at its height, Bush interviewed for a position with the Texas Air National Guard. He was quickly sworn in. When asked why he wanted to join the Texas Air National Guard, Bush responded, "I want to be a fighter pilot because my father was."[27] The way in which a variety of political leaders, George W. Bush among them, responded to Vietnam has been closely examined. Certainly the Texas Air National Guard was subject to political pressure during this era. With a congressman father who was supporting the war, Bush's application might well have benefited from that pressure. However, it appears that no overt pressure was brought to bear on Bush's behalf. Perhaps, depending on the political sensitivity of the Texas Air National Guard officials, none was necessary. Certainly, Bush was not the only politically connected young man to join the Texas Air National Guard at that time. Lloyd Bentsen's son was placed in the same guard unit slightly earlier than Bush and the sons of other Texas political figures fulfilled their service obligation with the Texas Air National Guard as well.[28]

Bush impressed his flight school classmates as an excellent pilot. He graduated near the top of his class and all the public portions of Bush's military record indicate that that he received exemplary ratings throughout his training.[29] Bush spent slightly over a year, from November 1968 to December 1969, in training at Moody Air Force Base in Valdosta, Georgia. When he graduated from flight training, his father pinned on his second lieutenant wings. He was then assigned to Ellington Air Force Base in Houston, where he learned to fly F-102 jets. Bush claims that his time in the guard taught him respect for the military.[30]

Living in Houston during the early 1970s as he completed his National Guard obligations, Bush accepted a management trainee position with Stratford of Texas, a Houston-based agricultural company run by an old Bush family friend. Bush found the job dull. By 1972 he was ready to move on. He was not the only Bush ready to move on. President Nixon had offered his father a position as head of the Republican National Committee. The elder Bush accepted and moved the family to Washington. Meanwhile, George W. was accepted at the Harvard Business School.

To start in the fall at Harvard, Bush needed to receive an early release from his National Guard duty, which he received. He served five years and four months of his six-year obligation to the Texas Air National Guard. There was nothing unusual in Bush's early release. Early releases were common, and since Bush's unit was phasing out the F-102s, the plane Bush was trained to fly, his services were no longer needed. Bush was transferred to a reserve unit in Boston for the remaining months of his guard duty.[31] Bush began at Harvard in September 1973 as the first stirrings of Watergate were under way.

Bush was not the typical Harvard Business School student. He had graduated from Yale five years earlier and had worked in several endeavors while fulfilling his military service obligation. In addition to his management trainee position with Stratford, he had worked in several political campaigns and held a wide variety of summer jobs. Bush later observed that "Business school was a turning point for me. By the time I arrived, I had a taste of many different jobs but none of them had ever seemed to fit."[32]

Bush's classmates did not perceive him as fitting the Harvard Business School mold. First, he was not sure what he would do with his business degree. Many of his peers were headed for Wall Street or similar employment. Bush simply was not sure what he wanted to do upon graduation. Second, he certainly did not live up to the stereotypes that many of his classmates had when they learned that he was the son of the chairman of the Republican National Committee. He drove a spray-painted Oldsmobile Cutlass and dressed in old, but comfortable, clothing. "One of my first recollections of him," claimed one classmate, "was sitting in class and hearing the unmistakable sound of someone spitting tobacco. I turned around and there was George sitting in the back of the room in his [National Guard] bomber jacket spitting in a cup. You have to remember this was Harvard Business School. You just didn't see that kind of thing."[33]

As he had at Yale, Bush seemed to withdraw from much of campus life. He found a few good friends, and socialized with them and with his extended family in the Boston area. His aunt, Nancy Ellis, who lived in Boston, remembers Bush's difficulties at Harvard during the Watergate scandal. "You know Harvard Square and how they felt about Nixon. But here was Georgie, his father head of the Republican National Committee. So he came out a lot with us just to get out of there."[34] Bush took his studies at Harvard more seriously than he had at Yale. Classmates remember that Bush enjoyed his Harvard classes and found them engaging. He was exceedingly interested in learning about how organizations worked and how people worked in organizations.[35]

The lessons of a business school are not those of a liberal arts college, or a law school, or a journalism school. The press have largely ignored Bush's years at Harvard Business School, but those years are important if one is to understand him.[36] They help account for his relative skepticism of history and his focus on the future. They help account for his nuanced personal skills. They help account for the importance he places on human resource management and placing the right people in the right jobs. These characteristics would subsequently contribute appreciably to his electoral successes.[37]

In February 1975, Bush's last year at Harvard, the business school released a study that indicated that the highest-paying jobs of the previous year's graduates were in the petroleum industry. Indeed, the study suggested that energy sector salaries were likely to be two to three times as high as salaries for Harvard Law School or Harvard Ph.D. graduates. Never happy in the Northeast, Bush spent part of his spring break visiting old friends in Midland. Bush learned that the oil boom was for real. "I could smell something happening," he later recalled. "All of a sudden it dawned on me that this is entrepreneurial heaven. This is one of the few places in the country where you can go without portfolio and train yourself and become competitive. The barriers to entry were very low in the oil sector. I can't tell you how obvious it was."[38] Though almost two-thirds of Bush's Harvard Business School classmates would move into positions with large corporations, Bush was headed back to Texas. Like his father, he would seek success in the oil industry.

Before settling in Midland, however, George W., his brother Marvin, and sister Dorothy, would spend part of the summer in China. Their father had been named the first American ambassador to China. The Bush children spent several weeks touring a nation where any American presence was rare.

Bush returned to Midland in the fall of 1975. His work at Harvard seemed to have given him focus and he was ready to be a success in the oil business. Bush did not want to work for anyone. Rather, he was interested in becoming what in the oil fields was known as "a land man," the middleman who discovered who was drilling where and then attempted to obtain nearby land from the farmers and ranchers who owned it and hustle up investors to attempt to exploit it. It seemed like the perfect opportunity for a man like Bush whose greatest successes—cheerleader, stickball commissioner, fraternity president—involved motivating and persuading people. He named his company Arbusto, Spanish for Bush.

Two years later, the struggling land man's close friends Joe and Jan O'Neill introduced him to one of Jan's oldest friends, Laura Welch, a librarian who had grown up in Midland. For both of them, it was a case of love at first sight. The O'Neills had tried to get them together on several occasions, but were not sure whether their opposite personalities would jibe. As Bush tells it, the O'Neills had nothing to worry about.

> Laura is calm; I am energetic. She is restful; I am restless. She is patient; I am impatient. But our differing styles exaggerate our differences. We share the same basic values. . . . We both love to read, we both love spending time with our friends, and we both, very quickly, fell in love with each other.[39]

Within three months Bush had asked Laura to marry him. On 5 November 1977 she did.

THE FIRST CAMPAIGN

When Bush returned to Midland, it was the major population center in a congressional district that had been represented for more than forty years by a conservative Democrat, George Mahon. By 1977 Mahon was the most senior member of the Congress, with forty-three years of service. That February, Mahon announced that he would not seek reelection. In 1976 Mahon had been challenged by Jim Reese, a local television personality and mayor of Odessa. Reese had given Mahon a good fight, winning 45 percent of the vote. Most observers expected Reese to be the Republican nominee again. But two weeks after Mahon's announcement, George W. Bush announced that he would be a candidate for the Republican congressional nomination.

For two years, Bush had worked as an entry-level land man, never able to put together the one big deal that every land man sought, the deal that could make him rich. But by 1977 he was an experienced political campaigner. He had worked in three of his father's campaigns and he had held responsible positions in the campaigns of two Republican U.S. Senate candidates, Edward J. Gurney's Florida race in 1968 and Nixon cabinet member Winton Blount's 1972 Alabama race. Though an experienced campaign operative, Bush was not necessarily prepared to be a congressman. Years later he would make the observation that the opportunity to run outweighed his preparedness. Bush no doubt recognized that the 1978 election might be his best shot at winning a Texas congressional seat for many years.[40]

The primary fight between Bush, Reese, and retired Air Force officer Joe Hickox was hotly contested. Bush had a large circle of friends who were drawn to his winning personality and conservative philosophy. But Reese started with many of the allies that had enabled him to mount a serious challenge to Mahon just two years earlier. The fact that Reese was closely allied with Ronald Reagan, one of Bush's father's foes, added additional drama to the primary campaign. If there had been any doubt about Bush's abilities as a campaigner, they were soon dispelled. He was a natural. Not only was he an articulate and outgoing candidate, he was relentless. He worked the district, Midland, Odessa, Lubbock, and all the points in between. The three-way primary did not produce a clear winner, and Bush and Reese were forced into a runoff election.

Reese tried to define Bush as an easterner and claimed he was a liberal Rockefeller Republican. In conservative West Texas Reese had the added advantage of help from Ronald Reagan. Bush received considerable financial support from his father's network of contributors, but he claims that on balance, being his father's son was not much of an advantage in this race. Reese's charges that he was really not a Texan, but a transplanted liberal easterner, were largely based on Bush's family background and education. Nevertheless, Bush won the runoff election by 1,400 votes.

Bush faced State Senator Kent Hance, a Lubbock native, in the general election. Most Republicans recognized that Bush had an uphill race. The district had elected a conservative Democrat to Congress in twenty-two straight elections, and in Kent Hance the Democrats had nominated another conservative Democrat who had proven his popularity in a large part of the district that had elected him state senator. Former governor Allan Shrivers told Bush, "Son, you can't win. This district is just made for Kent Hance. It's rural, conservative, and Democrat, and he's a rural, conservative Democrat."[41]

Hance immediately attacked Bush, much as had Reese, claiming that he was not really a Texan. Though raised in Texas, Bush had been born in the East and had attended school in the East. In contrast, Hance had lived his entire life in Texas, graduating from Texas Tech in Lubbock. Moreover, Hance charged that Bush had never had any real success on his own and was hoping to be elected because of his family name. Hance contrasted Bush's life with his own life, concluding that his family of farmers had never given him the advantages that Bush's family had been able to provide their son.

Bush attempted to run on issues, but Hance would not let him. Bush, with the help of his friends and those of his father, had raised $400,000 for his campaign, much of it from out of state. Hance was able to use this as yet more evidence that he could better represent the district than could Bush. Hance was also able to mobilize many of the fundamentalist churches against Bush when one of Bush's own volunteers ran an ad in the Texas Tech school paper inviting students to a "Bush Bash" with free beer. When Hance went after Bush because of the "Bush Bash," Bush chose not to respond in kind. Bush's staff had learned that Hance leased land he owned to a bar called Fat Dogs, which served Texas Tech students. Bush refused to use this information in the campaign. In sum, Hance effectively portrayed Bush as an outsider who likely did not share the heritage and values of the district. Hance, a conservative Democrat who did not differ dramatically from Bush on many issues, carried the district with 53 percent of the vote.[42]

Though he lost, several good things came out of Bush's first campaign for public office. First, as Bush describes it, the campaign was "an extended honeymoon." It was, he later reflected, "a wonderful way to spend our first year of marriage. We were united on a common mission; we spent lots of time together."[43]

Moreover, George W. Bush learned two critical lessons from this election. First, as a conservative Republican, he had to pay attention to the religious right of his party. The attacks precipitated by the "Bush Bash" hurt Bush among an important constituency. In the future he would not ignore this constituency. Second, he could never allow an opponent to define him. Bush felt that the principal reason he lost was that Hance had been successful in defining him as an outsider.[44] Both lessons were remembered years later when Bush ran for more important offices.

1979–1994: THE MAKING OF A TEXAN

Though Bush had been raised in Texas and had never felt comfortable in the East, Hance had effectively defined him as an easterner. During the next fifteen years, Bush's activities put an end to any doubts about his Texas roots. After his unsuccessful race for Congress, Bush turned his full attention to Arbusto Energy, Inc., his company. Bush quickly established a reputation as a knowledgeable and fair man with whom to deal. That reputation, his family ties, his Ivy League credentials, and his Wall Street connections all helped to provide him with investors. Increasing oil prices during the late 1970s and early 1980s and favorable tax laws also contributed to attracting investors in the oil industry.

Bush was attracting investors, but the firm had a lackluster performance record. Drilling for oil is a risky business. By 1985 Arbusto had been involved in the drilling of ninety-nine oil wells and about half of them had hit oil or gas. Bush's investors had put $4.66 million into his firm. They had received back only $1.54 million. On the other hand, investors in the right tax brackets saw their investments with Bush yield tax savings of almost $3 million.[45]

In 1984, as the Reagan-Bush reelection campaign seemed headed toward a landslide victory, the principals in Spectrum 7, an oil exploration firm, approached Bush about a merger. Bush ultimately acquired 16 percent of the merged company, still called Spectrum 7. Cincinnati businessmen William Dewitt, whose family had long been owners of major league baseball franchises, and Mercer Reynolds III, were Spectrum 7's principal owners. They were interested in the merger because while Spectrum 7 had invested in the oil industry, they had never operated wells in the oil fields, as had Bush and Arbusto. They also recognized that the Bush name would certainly help in attracting investors.[46] Bush was named CEO of Spectrum 7 and received a $75,000-a-year salary.

Within two years, by the winter of 1986, Spectrum 7 was in trouble. The dramatic decline in the value of oil, which had fallen from a price of $25 per barrel to $9, had sharply diminished the value of the firm's wells, land, and drilling rights. The forty-year-old Bush, now the father of twin daughters, was contemplating a major cutback in the operations of his company, hoping to hold on until oil prices increased. But Spectrum 7, an oil exploration and drilling firm in distress, was precisely the type of firm that Harken Oil and Gas, a large Dallas-based firm, had been acquiring. In acquiring Spectrum 7, for a total cost of $5.3 million, Harken gambled that it could withstand the fall in oil prices until the industry recovered. In addition to the existing leases held by Spectrum 7, the firm had oil and gas reserves that were projected to be able to ultimately produce $4 million or more in revenue. Bush was given a seat on the Harken board, $300,000 worth of Harken stock with options to purchase more, and a consulting contract with the company. The latter left Bush with free time to work on his father's campaigns. By 1986 Bush had a decade of experience in the oil industry. He had an excellent reputation as a knowledgeable, hardworking, honest manager who was witty and likable, though his firms had never lived up to their promise. In purchasing Spectrum 7, one of Harken's directors observed that "we saw an opportunity to buy a company at an attractive price." Harken was also aware that it was purchasing the services of George W. Bush and that "he was somebody who had been in the oil patch, somebody who had experience, although his status as the [U.S.] vice president's son was not a fact you could ignore."[47] With the sale to Harken completed, George W. Bush would no longer work on a daily basis in the oil industry.[48]

Bush claimed that he learned a great deal during his years in the oil industry. Those years taught him the risks associated with entrepreneurship and the importance of keeping in mind long-term goals. They gave him experience in managing large enterprises. During those years he sharpened his interpersonal skills, both in evaluating others and working with them.

Moreover, they provided Bush with a sense of responsibility. He developed a growing sense of responsibility for his family, for his employees, and for those who had invested in his businesses.[49]

Bush was now in a financial position that enabled him to turn his full attention to his father's presidential campaign.

In 1988 and again in 1992, George W. served as a senior adviser with two principal functions in his father's campaigns. First, he served as a surrogate. More important, he was his father's "loyalty thermometer." He believed, said Samuel Skinner, later chief of staff in the first Bush White House, "that if a guy brought you to the dance, you went home with him. You didn't leak to the media, you didn't waver and you didn't feather your own nest."[50] During the 1988 campaign Bush worked closely with Lee Atwater, an outstanding Republican political operative.

With the election of George Bush to the presidency, his son could turn to other projects. His friends recognized that he was interested in elected office, but they advised him that he needed to do something totally on his own. Therefore, when he was approached by his old partner, William DeWitt, about joining a group of investors to purchase the Texas Rangers baseball team, he jumped at the opportunity. Bush was a lifelong baseball fan. His political mentor, Karl Rove, was among those who urged Bush to become involved. Rove recognized that being an owner of the Texas Rangers "anchors him clearly as a Texas businessman."[51]

Bush's investment in the Texas Rangers was modest compared to those of several other investors, but Bush would be the public face of the ownership group. In that capacity he spoke on behalf of the team throughout Texas and led the drive for a new stadium. It was the perfect job for a Texas political candidate in waiting. It clearly identified him as a Texan. It constantly kept him in the public limelight.

He and his partners did a fine job with the Rangers. The team improved on the field and as a business they flourished. Revenues rose from slightly under $30 million a year at the time the Bush group bought the franchise to more than $120 million a decade later.[52] Bush spearheaded a successful drive to build the team a new stadium, which also greatly enhanced its value.

In 1992 the elder Bush was defeated in his bid for reelection. George W. Bush was no longer in his father's shadow. The Texas Rangers were doing well, prospering on the field and financially. The new stadium was scheduled to open the following year. Bush, a 10 percent owner, was in a position to make a substantial profit if he sold his interest in the team. As Rove had anticipated, he had become a well-known Texas businessman. In the spring of 1993 Bush and Rove began to meet with Republican leaders and other potential supporters throughout the state. While incumbent governor Ann

Richards was personally popular, the Bush camp felt that her policies were not.

Bush claims "I vividly remember the night I first thought I might run for governor." That was the evening of 1 May 1993, a special election day in Texas. Texans were voting to replace Democratic senator Lloyd Bentsen, who had become secretary of the treasury in the Clinton administration. Also on the ballot was a school-funding proposal that Governor Richards had strongly backed. Critics had named Richards's plan the "Robin Hood" plan, for essentially it took local taxes from wealthy school districts and redistributed them to poorer school districts. George and Laura had gone to the election eve headquarters of Republican candidate Kay Bailey Hutchison to watch the returns and support her. Bush recalled that "Kay and I are longtime friends, and when the time came for her to speak, she asked me to introduce her. I walked up on the stage and the crowd of activist Republicans started hollering, 'Run for governor,' and 'Governor Bush.' I was surprised but not completely so.' "[53]

By that summer Bush was putting together a campaign team. He hired people like Rove who would be loyal to him, not to their careers. Still sensitive to the likelihood of being called an outsider, he avoided national figures, particularly those associated with his father. Most important, Bush had himself determined the approach that the campaign would take. He told Rove, "We're never going to attack her because she would be a fabulous victim. We're going to treat her with respect and dignity." But Richards's policies would be an entirely different story. Bush clearly wanted an issue-oriented campaign.[54]

Bush had good reason to want an issue-oriented campaign. A year before the 1994 election, a Texas poll indicated that though the majority of Texans liked Ann Richards personally, they were not happy with her job performance. They had rejected her scheme for financing the public schools. They were not happy with the $2.7 billion tax increase she had signed after making a campaign promise that she would not raise taxes. Nor was she able to deliver on her campaign promise to bring Texas teachers' salaries up to the national average.

The nature of the campaign was forecast early when Bush observed that "Ann hasn't been defined very much. She's gotten a free ride. I haven't read too many editorials on her failure to lead on the educational issue. She's kind of ducked. So it may require a campaign to define her." Richards responded by quoting the famed Texan who had served many years as the speaker of the House. "You know, Sam Rayburn used to say that any jackass can kick down a barn, but it takes a carpenter to build one."[55] Bush would define Richards by focusing on the differences between the two of them on four issues: education, welfare, juvenile justice, and tort reform. Richards engaged him on those issues, but her comments on the issues were largely overshadowed by her personal attacks.

Richards consistently referred to Bush sarcastically as "shrub" or "young George." In late August she referred to him as "some jerk." When she subsequently denied having said it, KDFW in Dallas replayed a clip illustrating that she had. Bush responded by laughing and claiming "I couldn't remember being called names like that since I went to grade school at Sam Houston Elementary." Not only did Bush's reaction dramatize the childishness of Richard's remark, but it reminded everyone of his Texas roots. In addition to the demeaning language, Richards attacked Bush by claiming that that he was simply capitalizing on his name and had been a failure in his business ventures.[56]

Richards had no central message. By the last weeks of the campaign she seemed focused more on attacking Bush personally than on offering voters real reasons to vote for her. Bush remained highly focused on his four key issues throughout the campaign. He proved himself to be an exceptionally adept campaigner. Personable when meeting people one to one and disciplined in his public speeches, Bush dictated the issues of the campaign. Richards and Bush held one debate during the campaign. There was little newsworthy that came out of the debate. When copies of it were sent to Washington for operatives at the Democratic National Committee to examine, though, they were startled. Bush was articulate. Bush never let Richards fluster him. Most important, Bush stuck to his message and repeatedly got his basic themes across. This was not a candidate to underestimate.[57]

If Bush was disciplined in the debate, he was also disciplined on the campaign trail. By the end of the campaign he seemed to be working harder than Richards. Moreover, he refused to engage in the personal attacks that became the focal point of the last eight weeks of Richards campaign. As the polls showed her support diminishing, Richards focused more and more on her perceptions of Bush's shortcomings and less and less about her plans for Texas. In contrast, Bush refused to attack Richards. His positive approach distinguished him from virtually every major Republican candidate in 1994, including his brother.

Bush was personally inclined to run a positive campaign and he perceived Richards as a popular figure who might effectively portray herself as a victim of his attacks. His refusal to go negative against her was born both out of personal inclination and out of political expediency.[58] On election day Bush carried 54 percent of the vote. Meanwhile, in Washington, the Democratic party was stunned by losing the House of Representatives for the first time in forty years. As the final vote came in from Texas, opposition researchers, with an eye to the future, were jotting down their explanation for Bush's upset of one of the most personally popular Democratic governors in the country.

First and foremost, they concluded, was Bush's remarkable ability to remain disciplined. It was, they noted, not simply the message discipline that enabled him to stay focused on his core issues, but it was the personal discipline that enabled him to ignore the sarcasm and taunting of Richards. He did not lose his temper or respond in kind as many Democrats expected he might. He had proven himself a formidable campaigner.[59]

PREPARING FOR THE PRESIDENCY: BUSH AS GOVERNOR

Texas governor George W. Bush delivered on most of his major campaign promises during the first half of his first term. Working closely with Democrats, he reformed the Texas welfare system, putting a time limit on welfare assistance. He imposed other requirements on welfare recipients, designed to make them better able to support themselves. As he had promised during the campaign, he imposed more stringent juvenile justice laws, most notably by lowering the age at which a juvenile could be tried as an adult for murder. He had campaigned on court reform. He and the pro-business Texas legislature placed a ceiling on punitive damages that a court could award and made it more difficult to sue doctors and government workers acting in their official capacities. With one exception, the major planks of Bush's campaign were largely enacted early in his administration.[60]

Bush had presented himself to voters as a governor who would be concerned with education. Financing public education in Texas had been a difficult issue for his predecessor. Tests indicated that when Bush took office fully 25 percent of Texas students could not pass basic reading tests. Almost 100,000 Texan youth were still unable to read by fourth grade. Bush perceived reading as the key to all education and so focused his efforts on developing the reading skills of Texas children. Bush takes credit for directing approximately $70 million of resources to this problem through what became known as the Texas Reading Initiative. Special reading academies were established within schools, teacher training focused on reading, Texans were urged to volunteer as reading tutors in their local schools. Thousands did so as many Texas business firms adopted schools and aided in their reading programs. Success in teaching reading became a criterion used to help distribute educational funding. While the Bush administration was helping to strengthen the effort of Texas schools, they were careful not to usurp local control of those schools.[61] Ultimately, these reforms increased the reading ability of Texas children and had a positive impact throughout their educational experience.[62]

It is significant that Bush recognized that in order to be an effective governor, he would have to work closely with the Democratic leaders of the Texas legislature. He quickly began a regular series of breakfast meetings with the Democratic lieutenant governor Bob Bullock and the Democratic speaker of the Texas House, Peter Laney. Bush is effusive in his praise of these two Democratic leaders, claiming that throughout his two administrations they worked closely with him for the good of Texas.

As Bush's largely successful first term as governor drew to a close he began to gear up for a second race. But this was no ordinary governor seeking reelection. This was the governor of the third-largest state, heir to a political dynasty, and himself a veteran political operative in two presidential campaigns. Bush and those around him well knew that his second race for the governorship could be the launching pad for a presidential bid. Indeed, his reelection quickly became the first step in a plan to win the White House.[63]

Bush's team recognized that any presidential ambitions he had would be shattered if he did not win reelection impressively. They were aided by the fact that Bush had proven to be a popular first-term governor, that many Democrats in the legislature spoke highly of him, and that the Democratic party had trouble offering a strong alternative. Some Democrats, especially Bob Bullock, felt that the state party would be better served by letting Bush run unopposed. Believing that Bush was clearly going to win a second term, they felt it would be wiser to utilize resources on other more competitive races rather than an ill-conceived race for the governorship.[64]

But the national leadership of the Democratic party did not want Bush to run unopposed. By early 1998 it was apparent that Bush had national aspirations. Throughout 1998 Bush was meeting with several policy experts drawn largely from the administrations of his father and Ronald Reagan. Virtually all of them agreed that Bush was presidential material. He was bright. He had good judgment. He asked good questions. He was engaging. Curiously, most felt that not only could he be president, but the president he reminded them of was not his father, but Ronald Reagan.[65] It did not take a crystal ball to determine that George W. Bush was thinking beyond his reelection as governor. The national Democratic party did not expect to defeat him, but they did want him tied to Texas with a reelection campaign, rather than free to develop a national constituency beyond Texas.

Thus, Texas land commissioner Gary Mauro, against the advice of some of his closest mentors in Texas including Bob Bullock, was ultimately persuaded to run against Bush. Mauro had become friendly with Bill Clinton in

1972 when both had worked on the McGovern campaign. He was encouraged to run by the Clintons, who wanted Bush forced to raise money for a Texas race and tied down campaigning in Texas. Nevertheless, though he might have support in the White House, Mauro had little support where it counted, in Texas. Over a hundred Democratic officeholders in Texas broke ranks with their party to endorse Bush, including the highest Democratic officeholder in the state, Lieutenant Governor Bullock.

Had Bullock's advice been followed, and the Democrats not run a candidate against Bush, it is possible that several other elements of the Bush plan for winning the presidency might not have materialized. For if winning reelection decisively was the first element in Bush's plan to win the White House, Bush and his team felt that he had to accomplish two other tasks in the 1998 Texas elections to maintain his viability for the Republican presidential nomination. The second step in their plan was to do well among minority voters. Doing well with the Latino and black voters of Texas would enable Bush to position himself as a Republican who had broad appeal to minorities, distinguishing him from most other likely contenders for the Republican nomination.

Third, they perceived it as critical that most of the other Republican statewide candidates also win, particularly the candidate for lieutenant governor, Rick Perry. Bullock was in failing health and stepping down as lieutenant governor. If Bush ran for the presidency and had to leave Texas, and Rick Perry did not win, it would mean turning over the governorship of one of the nation's largest states to the Democrats. Bush could be accused of sacrificing his party's interests to his own if he ran for the presidency—unless Perry won.

Finally, the Bush organization deemed it critical that his brother Jeb win the Florida governorship. With both Texas and Florida clearly supportive, Bush would enter the primaries with the third- and fourth-largest states already in his corner. Hence, George W. Bush sent some of his most reliable political operatives to Florida to help his brother and many of his Texas contributors provided financial support to Jeb.

On election eve 1998 it was clear that George W. Bush was rapidly becoming a serious contender for the 2000 Republican presidential nomination. Bush won reelection with 69 percent of the vote. It was the most decisive statewide victory by a Republican in Texas history. He carried El Paso County, the most Hispanic area of the state, as well as Austin, the most traditionally Democratic area of the state. Bush won 49 percent of the Hispanic vote and 27 percent of the black vote, enabling him to position himself at the national level as a Republican with broad minority appeal. Moreover, all fourteen statewide Republican candidates, including Rick Perry, won in a total Republican sweep of the statewide offices. Bush had secured his base and would not be vulnerable to charges that he was placing himself above his party if he sought national office. Finally, Jeb Bush won decisively in Florida. He had been the recipient of approximately a million dollars of campaign contributions that were directed to his campaign by George W.'s Texas fundraisers. Jeb's most effective ads, charging Democratic candidate Buddy McKay with being a typical tax-and-spend Democrat and ending with the phrase "He's Not My Buddy," had been written by consultants who had previously worked for his brother.[66] As 1998 closed, George W. Bush was clearly positioned to run on a larger stage than that offered by Texas.

SECURING THE 2000 REPUBLICAN PRESIDENTIAL NOMINATION

As 1999 opened, most Republicans could readily recall that in 1996 a divisive primary campaign had weakened their candidate, Senator Robert Dole, in his bid against incumbent Bill Clinton. In early 1999 it seemed likely that Vice President Albert Gore would not be seriously challenged for the Democratic nomination and that he would head a unified Democratic party. The Republicans did not want to weaken their candidate's general election efforts in a series of costly primaries, as had happened in 1996. The Republican party was therefore looking for a strong front-runner who could sweep the primaries and unite the party for the fall election.

When George W. Bush announced, in March 1999, that he was forming a presidential exploratory committee, many Republicans believed that they had found their candidate. Within weeks, key Republicans from around the country were traveling to Austin for meetings and interviews with the governor. Invariably, these long private meetings were followed by press conferences in which the visiting dignitaries would announce their support of Bush's candidacy. Although these meetings appeared to be relatively spontaneous, or initiated by those who visited, in fact Bush's campaign team headed by Karl Rove was orchestrating them.[67] Within months, sixteen other Republican governors endorsed him. By the end of May, with the help of Texas Congressman Henry Bonilla, Bush had been endorsed by 222 of Bonilla's fellow Republican congressmen, almost 90 percent of the Republicans in that body.[68] Other potential candidates, such as Arizona senator John McCain, former cabinet member Elizabeth Dole, former vice president Dan Quayle, Congressman John Kasich of Ohio, and conservative activists such as Steve Forbes, Gary Bauer, and Allan Keyes, soon found themselves attempting to win the nomination of a party whose elected leadership was already overwhelmingly committed to Bush. Bush's strong base in Texas and Florida, his overwhelming name recognition, and his ability to attract minority votes seemed to make him the ideal candidate for Republicans who wanted to avoid a divisive primary season.

As icing on the cake, by the end of 1999, Bush reported to the Federal Election Commission that he had raised $37 million and would not accept federal matching funds.[69] Bush's reluctance to accept federal matching funds arose from the fact that to do so meant that he would have to accept the spending limitations entailed by accepting those funds. Dole had done that in 1996 and had been hurt in the primaries by wealthy publisher Steve Forbes. Forbes had rejected federal money and without any limitation on his spending had used his own money to attack Dole relentlessly in several primaries. Dole had spent virtually all his money responding to Forbes. When the primaries were over, Dole did not have money left. Clinton, unopposed in the Democratic primaries, used the months between the end of the primaries and the general election to attack Dole, who did not have the resources to respond. Bush was determined not to make the same mistake. Moreover, perhaps alone among the Republican candidates, he had the fundraising network to sustain a major effort beyond the primaries and into the general election.

Bush's status as the clear favorite for his party's nomination took a big step forward in the Iowa caucus. Republican candidates, except for McCain, had been busy in Iowa during the months preceding the caucus. By January 2000 they had all campaigned in Iowa, been involved in candidate forums, and were running advertisements. On the evening of 25 January 2000, party activists caucused throughout Iowa. They gave Bush a respectable 41 percent of the vote. Conservative publisher Steve Forbes received 30 percent, and the remainder was divided among Alan Keyes, who received 14 percent, Gary Bauer, who received 9 percent, John McCain, who received 5 percent and Orrin Hatch, who received 1 percent.[70] Though Bush had solidified his position as the front-runner, at least two elements of the caucus results tempered the enthusiasm of his supporters. First, the total votes for social conservatives such as Forbes, Keyes, Bauer, and Hatch not only exceeded those for Bush, but constituted a majority of the Iowa caucus vote. Forbes, who had used his own money to support a major advertising campaign against Dole in the 1996 primaries, had focused his 2000 attack on Bush. But Forbes's attack was shorter, more restrained, and less damaging to Bush than was his comparable attack on Dole four years earlier.[71] Nevertheless, if the conservative vote unified behind one candidate it posed a threat to Bush. Second, Arizona senator John McCain, who was perceived to be Bush's most serious rival for the nomination, had not seriously campaigned in Iowa as had Bush and the others; his low vote did nothing to negate his candidacy. After Iowa, the first real confrontation between Bush and McCain would be in New Hampshire.

McCain loomed as the most formidable challenger to Bush. Known as a maverick in the U.S. Senate, McCain had differed with his party on a range of issues, most notably campaign finance reform. Now he was trying to derail the campaign of the candidate that the vast majority of his party's leaders had endorsed. McCain's biography made him appealing to many voters. He was a third-generation navy officer. Both his father and grandfather had been admirals. As a navy pilot, McCain had been shot down over North Vietnam. Captured by the North Vietnamese, he was a prisoner of war for more than five years. During that time he had suffered repeated beatings, likely made all the worse by the North Vietnamese knowledge that his father was commanding American naval forces arrayed against them. Upon his release, McCain underwent medical treatment but never regained the full range of motion in his arms, lacking the ability to raise them above his shoulders. Eventually elected to the U.S. Senate from Arizona, where he became best known for championing campaign finance reform, he hoped to use public dismay with the influence of money on politics as his key issue in the campaign.

In New Hampshire, yet another issue quickly distinguished him from Bush. In addition to their differences over campaign reform, they differed over tax policy. Bush favored a massive tax cut that would reduce taxes for all who paid them. As McCain cruised throughout the Granite State in his campaign bus, "The Straight Talk Express," he often sounded more like Democrat candidates Al Gore and former senator Bill Bradley than like a Republican. He proposed to protect most federal entitlement programs and argued for smaller targeted tax cuts.[72] Whether it was because of his issue positions, or because of his ethos as an open and honest war hero, McCain quickly began to receive highly favorable press coverage.[73] More important, his standing in the New Hampshire polls began to rise and his crowds were growing. As the New Hampshire primary approached, McCain was giving pause to those who perceived Bush's nomination as inevitable. The Bush camp knew it was in trouble. But, consistent with the candidate's practices in prior elections, during the closing days of the campaign he rejected those of his advisers who urged him to attack McCain. "Our object is to win a nomination that is worth having," said Bush strategist Rove when questioned about Bush's failure to attack.[74]

On Tuesday, 1 February, the Republican voters of New Hampshire gave John McCain 49 percent of their vote and George Bush only 30 percent. No other candidate received more than 6 percent.[75] The *New York Daily News* characterized the results with the editorial, "New Hampshire Rattles the

Race."[76] The momentum that had been building for Bush was indeed rattled when voters had their first real opportunity to react to him in New Hampshire. Bush had proven himself to be the favorite of the party leaders and major contributors. Also, in the Iowa caucus, where a very limited number of party activists participated, he had done well. But in New Hampshire, a large number of voters participated in the primary and they had decisively rejected Bush.

The next seriously contested primary was in South Carolina. It was now critical. Bush's strength was based on the fact that he was a winner. But if voters outside Texas continued to reject him, his campaign would end quickly. Though he had upset Bush in New Hampshire, McCain did not have the finances or organization to sustain a protracted series of primary races. All of that could change if he could follow up his victory in New Hampshire with a second one in South Carolina. Such a victory would strongly suggest that McCain had more voter appeal than did Bush and give enormous impetus to all his campaign efforts.

South Carolina's primary on 19 February would be the next major contest. But on 8 February Delaware held its primary. Neither candidate spent much time or much money in Delaware. Bush won 51 percent of the vote and all 12 of the state's convention delegates. McCain's won 25 percent of the vote with the remainder split between the other candidates.[77] This primary was indicative of the problem McCain faced. With the Republican state organizations working on Bush's behalf, McCain could not win a state unless he was able to mount a strong effort there.

Both candidates had nineteen days between the New Hampshire and the South Carolina primary. Both would mount a strong effort. Bush and his team went to work immediately. On the flight to South Carolina, the morning after the New Hampshire primary, Bush made himself accessible to the press, much in the manner that McCain had been doing on his "Straight Talk Express." He attacked McCain, claiming that in New Hampshire, McCain "came at me from the left." It was clear that in conservative South Carolina, Bush would come at McCain from the right. Bush was "on message" throughout the next nineteen days, from his very first South Carolina speech, delivered at Bob Jones University. The venue itself, a highly conservative Christian university that banned interracial dating, as well as the fact that Bush used the term *conservative* twelve times in the first two minutes of his speech, signaled which portion of Bush's compassionate conservative message would receive the greatest attention in South Carolina.[78]

Within a day of its arrival in South Carolina the Bush organization had developed its campaign plan. Bush would attack McCain on the issues. His more conservative positions would hopefully have considerably more appeal to South Carolina's conservative brand of Republican voters than they did to New Hampshire's more moderate Republicans. Moreover, the Bush organization would now attack McCain. They would characterize McCain as a Washington insider, chairman of the Senate Commerce Committee. Worse yet, they would claim, he was a double-talking insider who champions campaign finance while accepting large contributions from business lobbyists and executives, many of whom were affected by the actions of the Senate Commerce Committee.[79] Bush never liked to make negative personal attacks, but this attack was clearly linked to McCain's big issue. That fact and the importance of South Carolina no doubt caused Bush to attack.

Outside groups that supported Bush, including the National Right to Life Coalition, Americans for Tax Reform, and the National Rifle Association, also recognized the critical nature of the South Carolina primary. They supplemented the Bush campaign with a flurry of radio and television advertisements as well as a massive phone-bank effort and literature drops, all on Bush's behalf. South Carolina voters were also exposed to a smorgasbord of smear attacks on McCain by such groups. McCain's wife was described as a drug addict, and racial attacks were made on McCain and his wife because of his dark-skinned adopted Bangladeshi daughter.[80]

Moreover, McCain faced a Catch-22 situation as he campaigned in South Carolina. He was calling for campaign finance reform, but his victory in New Hampshire had made him an object of affection of many lobbyists. Campaigning in the midst of the South Carolina primary, McCain attempted to capitalize on his growing popularity. He held a massive fundraiser at Washington's Willard Hotel. Most of those who bought the high-priced tickets were Washington, D.C. lobbyists and corporate executives. The irony of this event caused it to be covered by a great many media outlets and caused renewed press investigations of McCain's campaign financing. For most U.S. senators, the fact that thirty-three of the forty-six members of their principal fundraising committee were Washington lobbyists would not be newsworthy. But for John McCain, who portrayed himself as the foe of what he called "the Iron Triangle of lobbyists, big money and legislation," such revelations seemed to confirm the precise charges that George W. Bush was making about him in South Carolina.[81]

Whether it was Bush's emphasis on the contrast between his conservative positions and the more liberal positions of McCain, the smear campaign, or the perception that McCain's campaign suffered from many of the same problems that he decried in others, South Carolina's Republican voters gave Bush a big win. Bush won South Carolina with 54 percent of the vote and 34 of the state's convention delegates. McCain carried 42 percent of the vote and 3 delegates.[82]

Bush had the Republican organization in most states working on his behalf. He had a massive campaign treasury. McCain lacked both. He had hoped that by defeating Bush decisively in New Hampshire and South Carolina he could dramatically change the dynamics of the Republican primaries. But after South Carolina he faced a string of Republican primaries where both the state Republican organization and the Republican governor were clearly working for George W. Bush. Moreover, Bush would be able to outspend him. Though there would be other battlegrounds, perhaps most notably Michigan the following week, South Carolina severely hurt McCain's challenge. On 22 February McCain won Michigan. Had that been his third straight victory, McCain might well have been able to mount a serious challenge. But the following week Bush won Virginia and North Dakota, effectively negating McCain's victory in Michigan, much as his victories in South Carolina and Delaware nullified McCain's New Hampshire victory. On 7 March Bush won seven of the eleven primaries held, including the three largest, California, New York, and Ohio.[83] The campaign for the Republican presidential nomination was effectively over.

GEORGE W. BUSH'S ACCEPTANCE ADDRESS

For many Americans George W. Bush's nationally televised acceptance address to the Republican National Convention would be their first real opportunity to evaluate him. His opponent, Vice President Al Gore, had twice gone through national campaigns. For the preceding eight years, if not longer, Gore had been a well-known public figure. In contrast, Bush advisers recognized that many voters would be getting their first sustained look at Bush in this speech. For that reason, they felt that this speech was critical.

The Bush campaign could not ignore the rhetorical situation in which this speech would be delivered. Rhetorical critic Ray Dearin, who has studied each of the last four Republican acceptance addresses, describes the contemporary Republican acceptance speech as "a tightly framed media event in which the candidate articulates a personal vision of the American Dream while rallying Republicans and beginning the process of coalition-building with non-Republicans."[84] Dearin finds that Bush was able "to articulate what appears to be a more expansive concept of the American community than his predecessors [Republican presidential candidates] had set forth, but that, in fact, both his rhetorical strategy and unique interpretation of the American *mythos* are solidly grounded in the tradition of these speeches."[85]

Mike Gerson, Bush's principal speechwriter, was well versed in the tradition of prior Republican acceptance addresses. While working for about two months on the early drafts of the speech, he had read scores of prior convention speeches, watching many of them on tape, and evaluated the reactions they provoked. He spoke at length with Bush and several of Bush's top advisers before largely isolating himself for ten days in College Station, Texas, home of the George Herbert Walker Bush Presidential Library, outlining and re-outlining the speech. During the Memorial Day weekend, Bush and Gerson, as well as aides Karl Rove and Karen Hughes, worked over the outlines. As the speech began to take shape, Bush was an active participant, working over each line of the speech. Gerson observed, "when he gets up there to speak he will have touched every word of this speech one way or another." Bush himself kept making changes. Ultimately it went through fifteen drafts. Bush told his staff not to bother with the conclusion. He did not want their help with that portion of the speech.[86] He then began practicing his delivery several weeks before the convention.

As he stood backstage, moments before the speech, Bush was nervous. He was fearful that he would start to cry early in the speech when he reached the passages in which he thanked his family. Bush recalled that

> I walked out on that stage, and I mean, it was—it's hard to describe the feeling. The place just erupted. I just needed to get through that part about my family, then I knew it would be clear sailing. I was praising my dad and my mother, you know, my wife and kids. I don't want to get too emotional. . . . I think when I get a little high-strung or tired my emotions well up inside of me. I can be touched easily. I can be. I love deeply.[87]

Once Bush had glanced at his family and finished with his opening observations about them, he relaxed as he progressed into the body of his speech.

Communication scholars have noted that while the functions of acceptance addresses have not changed since those of Goldwater and Nixon discussed earlier, new strategies have been developed as a consequence of changes in the electorate. Like those earlier acceptance addresses, contemporary addresses still serve four basic functions. They are the means by which the candidate formally assumes the role of candidate and party leader. Second, they should function to generate a strong positive response from the immediate audience. Third, they should function to unify the party. Finally, they should function as a strong partisan persuasive message.

To fulfill these functions, contemporary candidates, as in the past, use four strategies. They frequently use simplified partisan statements. They lament the present and celebrate the future. They stress the crucial nature of this election. Finally, they typically seek support from the entire constituency. However, as communication scholar Kurt Ritter and others have argued, with the declining importance of political parties, candidates face a voting public who will judge them not so much on the basis of their political party as on their personal appeal on television. As a result, recent acceptance addresses typically involve not only the four traditional strategies, but also two additional strategies. First, contemporary candidates utilize their biographies to provide support material for the positions and arguments they make in their addresses. Second, contemporary acceptance addresses much more frequently involve personal comparisons between candidates.[88] George W. Bush's acceptance address to the 2000 Republican National Convention made use of all six of these strategies, though one was used only minimally.

First, Bush does use simplified partisan statements. Ritter has suggested that while partisan statements can still be found in acceptance addresses, consistent with the lessening importance of political parties, such statements are of diminishing importance in acceptance addresses.[89] Ritter's observation seems borne out in Bush's address.[90] Though Bush is critical of the Clinton-Gore administration, it is a muted criticism. In his only direct reference to Clinton, Bush observes that "our current president embodied the potential of a generation. So many talents. So much charm. Such great skill. But, in the end, to what end? So much promise to no great purpose." Similarly, when he talks of the accomplishments of the current administration, Bush repeatedly finds that "this administration had its moment. They had their chance. They have not led. We will." He uses this refrain repeatedly to indict the foreign policy, the educational programs, the Social Security policies, and the Medicare policies of the administration. It is not so much harsh partisan criticism as it is a statement of wistful regret.

When Bush turns directly to Vice President Albert Gore, his criticism is again gentle. He never mentions Gore by name but accuses him of practicing the "politics of the roadblock, the philosophy of the stop sign." Then, Bush uses one of Gore's pet phrases to make his point.

> If my opponent had been there at the moon launch, it would have been a "risky rocket scheme." If he'd been there when Edison was testing the light bulb, it would have been a "risky anti-candle scheme." And if he'd been there when the Internet was invented, well . . . I understand he actually was there for that. He now leads the party of Franklin Delano Roosevelt. But the only thing he has to offer is fear itself.

Bush is critical. But consistent with the move away from harsh partisan statements, Bush's criticism is gentler, relying on humor and regret. Moreover, it should be noted that except for these two passages, Bush makes virtually no mention of Vice President Al Gore or the Clinton-Gore administration.

The reduction of purely partisan statements is also evident in the targets of Bush's criticism. Bush never criticizes the Democratic party by name. Nor does he ever attack it. Rather, to the extent that he criticizes, he focuses his disparagement on the Clinton-Gore administration. He indicts that administration for doing nothing during eight years of increasing need. At one point he observes, "we will write, not footnotes, but chapters in the American story," implying that the Clinton-Gore administration has accomplished little. Moreover, when he does criticize, it is not simply of Democrats, but rather of "Washington." He claims that "I don't have enemies to fight. And I have no stake in the bitter arguments of the last few years. I want to change the tone of Washington to one of civility and respect." These remarks apply to both political parties, who have been at one another's throats during the second Clinton administration. To clinch the point, moments later, in contrasting his accomplishments in Texas to the gridlock in Washington, Bush observes, "I don't deserve all the credit, and don't attempt to take it. I worked with Republicans and Democrats to get things done. A bittersweet part of tonight is that someone is missing, the late Lieutenant. Governor of Texas, Bob Bullock. Bob was a Democrat, a crusty veteran of Texas politics, and my great friend." Clearly, the level of partisanship evident in Bush's acceptance address is substantially less than that found in those of early presidential candidates.

A second strategy characteristic of acceptance addresses, particularly those of challenger candidates such as Bush, is that they tend to lament the present and celebrate the future. Typically, challengers claim that incumbents have abandoned fundamental American values, but that if they are elected they will return to those values and hence provide America with reason to celebrate the future. Bush follows the formula in his acceptance address. After suggesting that the current administration did nothing, accomplished little, indeed squandered many opportunities, Bush observes that "our generation has a chance to reclaim some essential values." He then observes that "greatness is found when American character and American courage overcome American challenges." He offers examples of character and courage overcoming challenges during the Revolutionary era, World War II, and the civil rights movement. He concludes that "We will add the work of our hands to the inheritance of our fathers and mothers—and leave this nation greater than we found it."

Similarly, the conclusion of the speech, which Bush evidently wrote without aid, laments the present and the loss of American values but celebrates the future. As he does throughout the speech, in the conclusion

Bush's criticism of Democrats, President Clinton and Vice President Gore is restrained. He simply observes that "our country is ready for high standards and new leaders . . . an era of tarnished ideals is giving way to a responsibility era." Turning to the future, he concludes that

> My friend, the artist Tom Lea of El Paso, captured the way I feel about our great land. He and his wife, he said, "live on the east side of the mountain. It is the sunrise side, not the sunset side. It is the side to see the day that is coming, not the side to see the day that is gone." Americans live on the sunrise side of the mountain. The night is passing. And we are ready for the day to come.

Clearly, Bush hopes that his audience regrets the past but is optimistic about the future.

Typically, candidates stress the urgency of this election. They invariably find that they are running at a significant moment in American history. But for all intents and purposes Bush does not stress the urgency of this election. Among the common strategies found in acceptance addresses, this is the least developed in Bush's speech. Early in the speech he does observe that "this is a remarkable moment in the life of our nation. Never has the promise of prosperity been so vivid. But times of plenty, like times of crisis, are tests of American character." With the country at peace and prosperous Bush does not stress the urgency of this election to the degree of many past candidates.

The fourth strategy characteristic of acceptance addresses is to call on all members of the immediate and secondary audience to unify behind the nominee to secure victory in the general election. Candidates typically use acceptance addresses to reach out beyond their own party to the general electorate. The entire Republican convention was an attempt to reach out to the general electorate. It was a convention at which comparatively few politicians spoke. It was a convention in which the Republican party let women, Hispanics, and blacks take center stage to an unprecedented degree. Since the convention was orchestrated by Bush and his staff, it is no surprise that his speech included clear efforts to broaden his Republican base into the general electorate. Moreover, Bush made specific appeals to voter blocs such as Hispanics, blacks, and the elderly. These were groups with whom he had had success in Texas, though his party had not had great success in the rest of the country.

At various points in his speech, Bush spoke of "extending the promise of prosperity to every forgotten corner of this country"; improving "our highest poverty schools" where "seven in ten fourth graders cannot read a simple children's book"; strengthening "Social Security and Medicare for the greatest generation, and for generations to come"; ending "the soft bigotry of low expectations" in which "too many American children are segregated into schools without standards, shuffled from grade-to-grade because of their age, regardless of their knowledge"; abolishing "the death tax"; moving "people from welfare to work"; and working "with Republicans and Democrats to get things done." All these remarks seem targeted at the general electorate, particularly groups that had not been traditional Republican voters.

Perhaps nowhere was this appeal more evident in Bush's speech than at the point, slightly over halfway through the speech, where Bush utilized his longest example. Bush spoke about visiting a juvenile jail in Marlin, Texas, and described a conversation he had with one of the young inmates.

> A small voice, but it speaks for so many. Single moms struggling to feed the kids and pay the rent. Immigrants starting a hard life in a new world. Children without fathers in neighborhoods where gangs seem like friendship, where drugs promise peace, and where sex, sadly, seems like the closest thing to belonging. We are their country, too.
>
> And each of us must share in its promise, or that promise is diminished for all. If that boy in Marlin believes he is trapped and worthless and hopeless—if he believes his life has no value, then other lives have no value to him—and we are ALL diminished.
>
> When those problems aren't confronted it builds a wall within our nation. On one side are wealth and technology, education and ambition. On the other side of the wall are poverty and prison, addiction and despair. And my fellow Americans, we must tear down that wall.

At this point and at many other points in his speech, Bush was attempting to move beyond his own party and unify the nation behind his leadership.

The candidate-centered contemporary campaign, in contrast to the party-centered older campaign, has caused contemporary candidates to stress elements of their own biography in acceptance addresses and to compare themselves personally with their opponents to a greater degree than earlier candidates. Bush certainly made use of biographical elements, and though he did at some points compare himself to Gore, that was not a major strategy.

Rather, Bush simply chose to stress his own biography. After accepting the GOP nomination, Bush thanked his running mate Dick Cheney, thanked John McCain and the others he had defeated in the primaries, and then reached the portion of the speech that he was concerned about. "I am especially grateful to my family." At this point he spoke briefly about Laura, his daughters, and his parents.

Having acknowledged his family roots, Bush later acknowledged his Texas roots. "But I come from a different place [not Washington] and it has made me a different leader. In Midland, Texas, where I grew up, the town motto was 'the sky is the limit' . . . and we believed it." Bush then goes on to discuss the values he learned growing up in Midland. In doing so he describes the American dream, "a basic conviction that, with hard work, anybody could succeed and everybody deserved a chance." Bush also draws on his biography when he discusses his leadership style and accomplishments as governor of Texas.

It is Bush's policies he contrasts to those of Gore rather than their biographies. On occasion he does use implied contrasts between his biography and that of his opponent. But he does not explicitedly utilize his biography for that purpose other than in one brief passage:

> For me, gaining this office is not the ambition of a lifetime, but it is the opportunity of a lifetime. And I will make the most of it. I believe great decisions are made with care, made with conviction, not made with polls. I do not need to take your pulse before I know my own mind. I do not reinvent myself at every turn. I am not running in borrowed clothes. When I act, you will know my reasons. . . . When I speak, you will know my heart.

This passage does imply contrasts between himself and Gore.

Although both men had fathers who held high public office, Gore was largely raised in a hotel suite in Washington, D.C., and Bush was raised in Texas. Moreover, Gore always seemed to be thinking about high public office. Gore had first seriously run for the presidency in 1988. Bush was scarcely a public figure at that time, working in his father's campaign. Gore was being widely discussed as Clinton's successor from the very outset of their administration in 1992. As of 1992 Bush had never held any public office. As we have seen, Bush seemed to be largely undirected until he reached his forties. At a comparable age, Gore was serving in Congress and being mentioned as one of the bright young presidential prospects of his party. Though clearly both campaigns made use of polls, the Clinton administration was well known for being the most poll-driven administration in history. Certainly Bush would no doubt use polls, but Gore's reputation for being part of an intensely poll-driven administration made him somewhat vulnerable to Bush's suggestion that his decisions would be largely poll-driven. Moreover, the fact that Gore had reinvented his campaign persona on several occasions, even switching wardrobes at the advice of consultants, facilitated Bush's implied contrast.[91] Bush did not compare and contrast himself directly with Gore. His contrasts were largely indirect.

Rather, he spent his time indicating what he believed and what his policies were. Bush had to introduce himself to much of the public. That was the focus of his efforts.

On balance, Bush delivered an acceptance address that to some degree utilized five of the six principal strategies of contemporary acceptance addresses. His speech made use of simplified but muted partisan statements. He laments the present, claiming that under Clinton-Gore we have lost our way. He suggests that he will use basic American values to help us reclaim our heritage and thus create a bright future. More than most candidates, Bush made a sustained effort throughout this speech to unite both his immediate and particularly his secondary audiences behind his leadership. Bush utilized his personal story in introducing himself to the nation. He included long passages about his family, about growing up in Midland, about his accomplishments and leadership in Texas. Bush uses one passage to draw personal contrasts between himself and Gore, but he does not make a major point of this. Last, he makes virtually no effort to stress the critical nature of this election. Artistically, this was a solid effort that developed many of the principal themes that rhetorical critics and the public alike have come to expect in contemporary political acceptance addresses.

EFFECTS

Evaluating the effects of a single speech, given at the end of a four-day political convention that takes place in the midst of a long national campaign, is difficult. Nevertheless, by most measures, this speech seems to have been highly successful. Bush had three closely related goals that he hoped to fulfill with this speech. First was to illustrate that he was up to the task of being a strong national leader. Second, the speech required a critique of the Clinton-Gore years. Finally, Bush wanted to create an image of himself that distinguished him from Al Gore and the ordinary run of political candidates.[92]

Throughout the Republican convention, others spoke of Bush's leadership ability. During this speech, Bush appeared presidential. He likely reduced the concern about his leadership abilities and his ability to serve as president but he did not eliminate them. The "gravitas" question, whether Bush had the experience and intelligence to serve effectively, though diminished, was not entirely eliminated by this speech. Rather, though diminished, it persisted until the general election debates. Those debates, more than this speech, largely nullified that potential obstacle to Bush's election.[93]

That some reservations remained about Bush's abilities is not an indictment of Bush's performance in this speech. Rather, it is primarily a function of the difference between a single political speech and a series of political debates. It is harder to prove one's intellectual ability and readiness to lead by presenting a speech that can be written and rehearsed for weeks in advance than by responding to questions and an opponent in a group of political debates. While the latter are also often well prepared and rehearsed, the very fact that the questions are not known in advance and that the response of the opponent is not known in advance make debates more challenging. The campaign debates against Al Gore, more than this speech, tended to reduce reservations about Bush's leadership abilities and presidential stature.

Second, Bush wanted to use this speech to critique the Clinton-Gore years. This critique could not be an old-fashioned slashing partisan political attack. As we have seen, the general citizenry was tiring of such an approach, and partisanship among the general electorate has diminished in recent years. Nevertheless, this was an acceptance address to an immediate audience that had partisan feelings. Bush was skillful in attacking the Clinton-Gore administration in this address. He referenced the Clinton-Gore years in regret and sorrow rather than in harsh partisan anger. His first reference to President Clinton and the Clinton-Gore years well characterized his remarks about them. "Little more than a decade ago, the Cold War thawed and, with the leadership of Presidents Reagan and Bush, that wall came down. But instead of seizing this moment, the Clinton/Gore administration has squandered it." Bush sounded more like a regretful citizen who had seen his nation waste an unprecedented opportunity than a harsh uncompromising partisan. "They have had their chance. They have not led," was virtually the most partisan refrain in Bush's entire speech.

Bush attempted to distinguish himself from Vice President Gore and most other politicians in two ways. First, he stressed his programs. He would be a compassionate conservative. He indicated what he had in mind with regard to education, Medicare, Social Security, taxes, and the military. He stayed with the same themes that had won him the nomination. He clearly distinguished himself from Gore and attempted to do so in a humorous fashion by noting, at the end of his discussion of issues, that "every one of the proposals I've talked about tonight, he has called a 'risky scheme,' over and over again." Bush was effective in distinguishing himself from Gore by sticking to the message of compassionate conservatism that had won him the nomination. His willingness to try new methods, such as utilizing vouchers for the parents of students in poorly performing schools, utilizing individual investment accounts as part of Social Security, urging a major tax cut that would provide some degree of relief to virtually all taxpayers, and rebuilding the military, all distinguished him from Gore.

In addition to policy distinctions, the section of the speech where Bush discussed himself distinguishes him from Gore. Bush portrayed himself as a westerner, a Texan. "This background leaves more than an accent, it leaves an outlook. Optimistic, impatient with pretense. Confident that people can chart their own course. That background may lack the polish of Washington. Then again I don't have a lot of things that come with Washington." At this point, Bush indicates that Gore is a partisan Washington warrior and that he, Bush, is not. Thus, by stressing both his programs and his personal background, Bush distinguished himself from Gore.

On balance, the content of Bush's speech and the artistic merit with which it was presented seems sufficient to have accomplished at least two of his three likely goals. That he might not have achieved his third goal, indicating that he had the leadership ability necessary for the job, seems as much a function of the situation as of any Bush shortcoming.

Public and press reaction to this speech also suggests that Bush was successful. Bush's standing in the polls had been increasing throughout the Republican Convention. At the outset of the convention Bush had an 11 percent lead over Vice President Gore. The day after his speech, Bush jumped about 2 percent in public opinion polls, and in the following few days his lead increased another 4 percent, providing him with a 16–17-percentage-point lead. Polls showed Bush hovering right around 50 percent and Gore at about 32–34 percent.[94] Though the race tightened, ultimately becoming one of the tightest elections in American history, Bush seemed to largely accomplish his principal goals, and that was reflected in the jump this speech appears to have given him in the public opinion polls taken shortly after it was delivered.

Finally, it should be noted that Bush's speech was well received by the press. That conservatives such as columnist Peggy Noonan, or the *Chicago Tribune*, found Bush's speech praiseworthy should not be surprising.[95] But even the liberal press praised Bush. Perhaps part of the reason for that was best summarized by the *Washington Post*'s David Broder, who observed that three of the principal goals that Bush highlighted in his speech, "expanding and extending Medicare, reforming education and strengthening Social Security—come right out of the Democrats' playbook." Broder went on to add that the "unprecedentedly prominent role" given to Latino and African Americans throughout the convention week also indicates Bush's willingness to contest for traditional Democratic constituencies.[96]

George W. Bush faced a greater challenge than many candidates in accepting the nomination of his party. This was his first race for national office. He had first won public office only six years earlier. By his own admission, his accomplishments prior to turning forty were not equivalent to those of many men who seek the presidency. He was running against an experienced political figure who had been seeking the presidency for twelve years and held high public office well before that. He was running against an incumbent vice president who had served during a time of unprecedented prosperity and peace. Clearly, Bush's acceptance address presented him with an opportunity to introduce himself to much of the American public in a favorable light. Rhetorician Ray Dearin accurately characterized Bush's response to this opportunity as "a personal vision of America and its destiny that retained the distinctively Republican emphasis upon individual liberty and limitless opportunity, even as he stressed, more than any of his predecessors had done, the equally venerable tradition of America as the compassionate, welcoming, and benevolent community."[97] To the extent that the speech had artistic merit sufficient to accomplish his goals, to the extent that public opinion polls showed that Bush's standing increased immediately after this speech, and to the extent that the press reaction to the speech was generally favorable, it would appear that George W. Bush's acceptance address contributed positively to his winning what will certainly be long remembered as one of the most controversial presidential elections in American history.

NOTES

1. All the quotations and descriptions of Bush's early drinking in this paragraph are drawn from Lois Romano and George Lardner, Jr., "Bush's Life-Changing Year," *Washington Post*, 25 July 1999, p. A1. The article was also posted on the *Washington Post* Internet site, http://www.washingtonpost.com. Subsequent references are to the Internet version.

2. The precise advice that Graham offered is likely to remain unknown. However, all signs indicate that he suggested that Bush terminate his drinking. J. W. Hatfield, *Fortunate Son: George W. Bush and the Making of an American President* (New York: St. Martin's Press, 2000), pp. 71–72, quotes portions of their conversations but does not provide any sources, other than to indicate that the author had confidential interviews with members of the Graham organization. Virtually all Bush's biographers acknowledge the influence Graham had on Bush in the years immediately before he quit drinking. See, for example, Bill Minutaglio, *First Son: George W. Bush and the Bush Family Dynasty* (New York: Times Books, 1999), pp. 288–89.

3. Hatfield, *Fortunate Son*, p. 72.

4. Ibid., p. 60.

5. Minutaglio, *First Son*, p. 210.

6. Bush is quoted in Fred Barnes, "The Gospel According to George W. Bush," *Weekly Standard*, 22 Mar. 1999, p. 22.

7. The best short account of Bush's religious faith is Barnes, "The Gospel," pp. 20–22.

8. Laura Bush and Jan O'Neill are both quoted in Hatfield, *Fortunate Son*, p. 72.

9. Ibid., p. 72.

10. Minutaglio, *First Son*, p. 210.

11. For material on the Bush family history, see any of the better biographies of George W. Bush. On Prescott's memory, see Minutaglio, *First Son*, p. 19.

12. The Benton-Bush race is memorable because Democratic incumbent Senator William Benton used television commercials. It was the first use of television commercials in a major race.

13. On Prescott Bush's elections, see Elizabeth Mitchell, *W: Revenge of the Bush Dynasty* (New York: Hyperion, 2000), pp. 42–43.

14. Mitchell, *W*, p. 16.

15. George W. Bush, *A Charge to Keep* (New York: William Morrow, 1999), pp. 14–15.

16. Ibid, p. 15.

17. For a particularly insightful look at the mother-son relationship, see George Lardner, Jr., and Lois Romano, "Tragedy Created Bush Mother–Son Bond," *Washington Post*, 26 July 1999, p. A1. This article was also available on the *Washington Post* Internet site and subsequent references are to the Internet version.

18. John Kidde, a friend of Bush's since high school, recalls Bush making this statement when the two were students together. Quoted in Lardner and Romano, "Tragedy," p. 2.

19. Bush, *A Charge to Keep*, p. 18.

20. Hatfield, *Fortunate Son*, p. 30.

21. Bush, *A Charge to Keep*, p. 22.

22. This story has been widely repeated in Bush biographies, though Coffin denies any memory of the conversation, claiming that if it did happen he was no doubt making a joke. See Lois Romano and George Lardner, Jr., "Bush: So-So Student but a Campus Mover," *Washington Post*, 27 July 1999, p. A1, http://www.washingtonpost.com, and subsequent references are to the Internet version.

23. Ibid., p. 4. The quote is from Calvin Hill, the Yale All-American football player who was a Bush fraternity brother.

24. Romano and Lardner, "Bush: So-So Student," p. 5.

25. Ibid.

26. See Minutaglio, *First Son*, p. 123.

27. Ibid., p. 120.

28. Ibid., pp. 120–22.

29. Hatfield, *Fortunate Son*, pp. 44–45.

30. Bush, *A Charge to Keep*, p. 55.

31. George Lardner, Jr., and Lois Romano, "At Height of Vietnam, Bush Picks Guard," *Washington Post*, 28 July 1999, p. A1, http://www.washingtonpost.com, and subsequent references are to the Internet version.

32. Bush, *A Charge to Keep*, p. 59.

33. Lardner and Romano, "At Height of Vietnam," p. 7.

34. Quoted in Hatfield, *Favorite Son*, p. 51.

35. See Minutaglio, *First Son*, p. 157.

36. James Higgins, "What Bush Learned at Harvard," *Weekly Standard,* 19 Feb. 2001, pp. 14–16. Higgins claims that the press does not understand the most important part of Bush's education, his MBA years at Harvard. He claims that the press's lack of understanding accounts for those years being treated as "a sideshow."

37. Ibid., pp. 15–16. Higgins, writing during the first days of Bush's administration, also finds that these skills account for many of Bush's initial successes.

38. Minutaglio, *First Son*, p. 161.

39. Bush, *A Charge to Keep,* p. 80.

40. Lois Romano and George Lardner, Jr., "Young Bush, A Political Natural, Revs Up," *Washington Post*, 29 July 1999, p. A1, http://www.washingtonpost.com, and subsequent references are to the Internet version.

41. Shriver is quoted in Bush, *A Charge to Keep*, p. 173. Ironically, once in Congress, Hance changed his party affiliation.

42. The preceding account of the 1978 congressional election is based on Bush, *A Charge to Keep*, pp. 172–76; Romano and Lardner, "Young Bush," pp. 1–7; Minutaglio, *First Son*, pp. 179–80; and Mitchell, *W*, pp. 153–60.

43. Bush, *A Charge to Keep*, pp. 82–83.

44. Ibid., p. 193.

45. George Lardner, Jr., and Lois Romano, "Bush Name Helps Fuel Oil Dealings," *Washington Post*, 30 July 1999, p. A1, http://www.washingtonpost.com, and all subsequent references are to the Internet version.

46. Ibid., p. 7.

47. Jeffrey Laikind, a member of the Harken Board of Directors, quoted in Lardner and Romano, "Bush Name," pp. 7–8.

48. The preceding account of Bush's career in the oil industry is based on Minutaglio, *First Son*, pp. 195–214; Lardner and Romano, "Bush Name," pp. 3–10; Mitchell, *W*, pp. 184–207; and Bush, *A Charge to Keep*, pp. 61–65.

49. Bush, *A Charge to Keep*, pp. 64–65. When Bush's firms merged, he invariably went out of his way to see that his employees were treated well by the new firm or were able to find some satisfactory alternative.

50. Quoted in Hatfield, *Favorite Son*, p. 75.

51. Quoted in Lois Romano and George Lardner, Jr., "Bush's Move Up to the Majors," *Washington Post*, 31 July 1999, p. A1, http://www.washingtonpost.com, and all subsequent references are to the Internet version.

52. Romano and Lardner "Bush's Move Up," p. 5.

53. Bush, *A Charge to Keep*, p. 24. Bush is being a bit disingenuous here when he claims this was the first time he had ever thought of running for governor, though this may well have been the first public demonstration on his behalf.

54. Romano and Lardner, "Bush's Move Up," p. 7.

55. Bush and Richards are quoted in Hatfield, *Favorite Son*, p. 121.

56. Ibid., p. 141.

57. See Minutaglio, *First Son*, p. 286.

58. Barnes, "The Gospel," p. 22.

59. On the Democratic National Committee's reactions to Bush's victory, see Minutaglio, *First Son*, p. 293.

60. See Hatfield, *Favorite Son*, pp. 155–61, for a discussion of Bush's accomplishments during his early years as governor.

61. Bush's pride in this program is evident. See *A Charge To Keep*, pp. 73–78. For other accounts, all of which are favorable, see Minutaglio, *First Son*, p. 303; and Mitchell, *W*, p. 317. Even Bush critics such as Molly Ivins and Lou Dubose acknowledge that though his claims may be exaggerated, "education is one area where George W. Bush deserves real credit." See Molly Ivins and Lou Dubose, *Shrub: The Short But Happy Political Life of George W. Bush* (New York: Random House, 2000), p. 122.

62. For specific details of the success of the Texas reading initiative, see Bush, *A Charge to Keep*, p. 78.

63. The following discussion of Bush's four-step plan to win the White House is drawn largely from Hatfield, *Favorite Son*, pp. 237–44.

64. Bullock was concerned that, if challenged, Bush would have an excuse to raise and spend millions of dollars to help the entire Republican ticket. See Hatfield, *Favorite Son*, p. 234.

65. Evan Thomas and *Newsweek's* Special Projects Team, "The Inside Story: What a Long, Strange Trip," *Newsweek*, 20 Nov. 2000, pp. 50–51.

66. On the results of the 1998 election in Texas, see Hatfield, *Favorite Son*, pp. 244–46.

67. Fred Barnes, "George W.'s Brain," *Weekly Standard*, 5–12 Apr. 1999, p. 13.

68. Hatfield, *Favorite Son*, p. 262.

69. Ibid., p. 291.

70. "Iowa Caucus Results," *Columbus Dispatch*, 25 Jan. 2000, p. 1A.

71. Fred Barnes, "Steve Forbes, Mr. Nice Guy," *Weekly Standard*, 24 Jan. 2000, pp. 9–10.

72. David Brooks, "The McCain-Bush Tax Wars," *Weekly Standard*, 24 Jan. 2000, pp. 10–12.

73. The press seemed so enamored with McCain, likely because of his personality, his accessibility, and his issue positions, that his campaign staff, only partly in jest, began to refer to them as "the base." *Newsweek* characterized press coverage of McCain in New Hampshire as "fair to fawning." See Thomas, "Inside Story," p. 56.

74. Michael Duffy, "What It Took," *Time*, 20 Nov. 2000, p. 131.

75. www.politics1.com/primaries/.

76. "*New York Daily News*, 2 Feb. 2000, p. 36.

77. www.politics1.com/primaries/.

78. Thomas, "The Inside Story," pp. 57–58.

79. See Duffy, "What It Took," p. 131; and Thomas, "Inside Story," p. 58.

80. Duffy, "What It Took," p. 132; and Thomas, "Inside Story," p. 60. Duffy, Thomas, and others who have examined this campaign describe it as exceedingly nasty but conclude, as Thomas does, that "most of the smear campaign was impossible to track, and the discernible footprints do not reveal what was organized, what was freelance, what was scripted and what was merely street gossip."

81. On McCain's fundraising, see Matt Labash, "Lobbyists for McCain," *The Weekly Standard*, 21 Feb. 2000, pp. 15–16.

82. www.politics1.com/primaries/.

83. For a full breakdown of the 2000 primary results, see www.politics1.com/primaries/.

84. Ray Dearin, "George W. Bush in the Tradition of Republican Acceptance Speeches" (Paper presented at the Central States Communication Association Annual Meeting, Cincinnati, OH, Apr. 2001), p. 2.

85. Ibid., p. 3.

86. On the development of this speech, see "Inside Politics," *Washington Times*, 31 July 2000, www.washtimes.com/inpolitics.htm/. See also Fred Barnes, "Prime Time Bush," *Weekly Standard*, 7 Aug. 2000, pp. 10–12; and Duffy, "What It Took," p. 135.

87. Thomas, "Inside Story," p. 74.

88. On the rhetorical strategies utilized in contemporary acceptance addresses, upon which the following analysis is based, see Judith S. Trent and Robert V. Friedenberg, *Political Campaign Communication: Principles and Practices* (Westport, CT: Praeger, 2000), pp. 218–25. Trent and Friedenberg's analysis of more contemporary acceptance addresses is particularly indebted to the work of communication scholars Kurt Ritter and William L. Benoit.

89. Ibid. On the lessening importance of partisan statements, also see Sharon E. Jarvis, "Partisan Campaign Rhetoric of Al Gore and George W. Bush" (Paper presented at the annual convention of the National Speech Association, Seattle, WA, Nov. 2000).

90. All references to George W. Bush's acceptance address are drawn from the text of that address as found at www.georgewbush.com. This was the official site of the Bush campaign.

91. Most Gore biographies stress how his parents prepared him for public service and his growing desire for the presidency. See, for example, the early chapters of David Maraniss and Ellen Nakashima, *The Prince of Tennessee: The Rise of Al Gore* (New York: Simon and Schuster, 2000). Also see Bill Turque, *Inventing Al Gore* (Boston: Houghton Mifflin, 2000). Turque's use of the term *inventing* is particularly revealing, for a central theme of his biography is that Gore has often changed both his policy positions and aspects of his personal life, reinventing himself, to facilitate gaining the presidency, much as Bush's statement implies.

92. Barnes, "Prime Time Bush," p. 10.

93. See Robert V. Friedenberg, "The 2000 Presidential Debates," in Robert Denton, ed., *The 2000 Presidential Campaign: A Communication Perspective* (Praeger, in press). Publication is expected in late 2002.

94. For a compilation of polling results, see www.pollingreport.com/election/. The shifts reported in this paragraph are drawn from NBC, *Newsweek*, Reuters/Zogby, and CNN/*USA Today* polls reported at this web site.

95. Noonan claimed that "George W. Bush's speech was good, and a success. It did what it had to do with verve and persuasive power." See Peggy Noonan, "A Breakthrough Convention," *Wall Street Journal*, 4 Aug. 4, 2000. Found at http://opinionjournal.com/columnists/pnoonan/. The *Chicago Tribune* analysis story claimed that Bush "made a powerful rhetorical case, and did so with a vigor that Clinton's two GOP foes, including Bush's father in 1992, demonstrably lacked." Author Michael Tackett called Bush's speech "inspired in tone and unusual in content" and added that Bush has some of Ronald Reagan's sunny optimism and some of Clinton's dive-in-the-crowd warmth.

96. David S. Broder, "Challenging Democrats on Their Turf," *Washington Post*, 4 Aug. 2000, p. A1.

97. Dearin, "George W. Bush in the Tradition," p. 12.

Bibliographic Essay

Sources for texts of each of the speeches examined in this study can be found in the endnotes to each chapter. Sources that were helpful in providing critical tools for the analysis of individual speeches can also be found in the endnotes that accompany each chapter.

PROLOGUE: 1840—WILLIAM HENRY HARRISON

The best study of the campaign of 1840, particularly for those seeking a communication perspective, is Robert Gunderson, *The Log-Cabin Campaign* (Westport, CT: Greenwood Press, 1977). Harrison has not been the subject of any recent biographies, though Dorothy Goebel, *William Henry Harrison: A Political Biography* (Indianapolis: Indiana Library and Historical Department, 1926), Freeman Cleaves, *Old Tippecanoe: William Henry Harrison and His Time* (New York: Charles Scribner's Sons, 1939), and James A. Green, *William Henry Harrison: His Life and Times* (Richmond, VA: Garrett and Massie, 1941), are all helpful.

The best collections of Ohio newspapers that covered the 1840 election, including many of those issued by both Whigs and Democrats, can be found at the Ohio Historical Association in Columbus. The Harrison collection at the Cincinnati Historical Society library is also very useful. It contains a great many campaign-related materials as well as an 1835 biography that may have been the first written about Harrison.

1960—JOHN F. KENNEDY

The 1960 election has been the subject of intensive study. The contemporaneous account by journalist Theodore White, *The Making of the President 1960* (New York: Pocket Books, 1961), remains the definitive account of the campaign. Also very useful on Kennedy's campaigning and speaking are the many works by such Kennedy associates as Kenneth P. O'Donnell and David F. Powers, *Johnny, We Hardly Knew Ye* (New York: Pocket Books, 1972), and Theodore C. Sorensen, *Kennedy* (New York: Harper and Row, 1965).

Kennedy's approach to the pragmatic problem of electing a Catholic first became public in "Can Catholic Vote Swing an Election?" *U.S. News and World Report*, 10 Aug. 1956, pp. 41–46. Dan B. Flemming, Jr.'s, *Kennedy vs. Humphrey, West Virginia 1960: The Pivotal Battle for the Democratic Presidential Nomination* (Jefferson, NC: McFarland, 1992), provides insight into how the Catholicism issue was handled in what is widely considered to be the most critical primary. Also see Hermann G. Stelzner, "Humphrey and Kennedy Court West Virginia," *Southern Speech Communication Journal* (Fall, 1971): 21–33.

A fine account of Kennedy's preparation for this speech and his activities immediately preceding it are in Susan Dewine, "John Fitzgerald Kennedy Speaks on Catholicism September 12, 1960" (Unpublished M.A. thesis, Miami [Ohio] University, 1967). Stephen R. Goldzwig and George N. Dionisopoulos, *"In a Perilous Hour": The Public Addresses of John F. Kennedy* (Westport, CT: Greenwood Press, 1995), provides an excellent examination of Kennedy's speaking career, including this speech. Kathleen Hall Jamieson, *Packaging the Presidency: A History and Criticism of Presidential Campaign Advertising* (New York: Oxford University Press, 1984), helps to illustrate how this speech was utilized during the campaign by the Kennedy organization.

1964—BARRY GOLDWATER

The rise of conservative Republicanism has been examined in such works as David W. Reinhard, *The Republican Right since 1945* (Lexington: University of Kentucky Press, 1983), and Nicol C. Rae, *The Decline and Fall of the Liberal Republicans from 1952 to the Present* (New York: Oxford University Press, 1989).

Biographies of Goldwater include such early and generally highly favorable efforts as those of Jack Bell, *Mr. Conservative: Barry Goldwater* (Garden City, NY: Doubleday, 1962), and Stephen Shadegg, *Barry Goldwater:*

Freedom Is His Flight Plan (New York: Fleet, 1962). More recent biographies include Lee Edwards, *Goldwater: The Man Who Made a Revolution* (Lanham, MD: Regnery, 1995); Peter Iverson, *Barry Goldwater: Native Arizonan* (Norman; University of Oklahoma Press, 1997); and Rick Perlstein, *Before the Storm: Barry Goldwater and the Unmaking of the American Consensus* (New York: Hill and Wang, 2001).

Journalists and scholars have published a library full of accounts of the 1964 campaign. Among the best of them are Theodore H. White, *The Making of the President 1964* (New York: Pocket Books, 1965); Charles McDowell, *Campaign Fever: The National Folk Festival, from New Hampshire to November, 1964* (New York: William Morrow, 1965); Karl A. Lamb and Paul A. Smith, *Campaign Decision-Making: The Presidential Election of 1964* (Belmont, CA: Wadsworth, 1968); Milton C. Cummings, Jr., ed., *The National Election of 1964* (Washington: Brookings Institution, 1966); and John H. Kessel, *The Goldwater Coalition: Republican Strategies in 1964*, (Indianapolis: Bobbs-Merrill, 1968). For an insightful work that places the presidential race in context, see Jon Margolis, *The Last Innocent Year: America in 1964* (New York: William Morrow, 1999).

Many of the activists who were involved in the Goldwater campaign have written about it. Particularly insightful are the accounts of F. Clifton White, *Suite 3505: The Story of the Draft Goldwater Movement* (Ashland, OH: Ashbrook Press, 1992); and Stephen Shadegg, *What Happened to Goldwater? The Inside Story of the 1964 Republican Campaign* (New York: Holt, Rinehart and Winston, 1965). In his later years Goldwater himself published several volumes of memoirs and observations. Most pertinent for this study is Barry Goldwater, *With No Apologies* (New York: Berkley Books, 1980).

Rhetorical studies of Goldwater include John C. Hammerback, "Barry Goldwater's Rhetoric of Rugged Individualism," *Quarterly Journal of Speech* (Apr. 1972); 175–83, and Ernest J. Wrage's "The Little World of Barry Goldwater," *Western Journal of Speech Communication* (Fall 1963); 207–15.

1968—RICHARD M. NIXON

Formative influences on Richard Nixon have been examined by a wide variety of authors. Among the more valuable studies is Steven E. Ambrose, *Nixon: The Education of a Politician, 1913–1962* (New York: Simon and Schuster, 1987), the first volume of his multivolume study. Also helpful is Nixon's autobiographical writing, particularly *Memoirs of Richard Nixon* (New York: Grosset and Dunlap, 1978). On his early political career, see

Christopher Matthews, *Kennedy and Nixon: The Rivalry That Shaped Postwar America* (New York: Simon and Schuster, 1996). Studies that focus on Nixon's political comeback include Jules Witcover, *The Resurrection of Richard Nixon* (New York: G. P. Putnam's Sons, 1970); and William Safire, *Before the Fall: An Inside View of the Pre-Watergate White House* (Garden City, NY: Doubleday, 1975).

Perhaps the finest single volume on the 1968 campaign is Lewis Chester et al., *An American Melodrama: The Presidential Campaign of 1968* (New York: Viking Press, 1969). Other valuable studies of that campaign include Joe McGinnis, *The Selling of the President 1968* (New York: Pocket Books, 1970), and the appropriate sections of Steven E. Ambrose, *Nixon: The Triumph of a Politician, 1962–1972* (New York: Simon and Schuster, 1989).

The best single volume study of Nixon's speaking is Hal W. Bochin, *Richard Nixon: Rhetorical Strategist* (Westport, CT: Greenwood Press, 1990). Other informative works on Nixon's speaking include Ben Padrow and Bruce Richards, "Richard Nixon: His Speech Preparation," *Today's Speech*, Nov. 1959, pp. 11–25; and Craig R. Smith, "Richard Nixon's Acceptance Speech As a Model of Dual Audience Adaptation," *Communication Quarterly* (Fall 1971): 15–22.

1980—RONALD REAGAN

Reagan has been the subject of a variety of biographers. Two sympathetic biographers who also provide a great deal of insight on Reagan's early years are Lou Cannon, *Reagan* (New York: G. P. Putnam's Sons, 1982); and Dinesh D'Souza, *Ronald Reagan: How an Ordinary Man Became an Extraordinary Leader* (New York: Free Press, 1997). Also of interest on Reagan's early years and family life is Nancy Reagan's *My Turn* (New York: Random House, 1989). On Reagan's early years, also see his autobiography, *An American Life* (New York: Simon and Schuster, 1990).

The 1980 election has been examined by many scholars and journalists. Among the more insightful studies are Elizabeth Drew, *Portrait of an Election* (New York: Simon and Schuster, 1981); Richard Harwood, ed., *The Pursuit of the Presidency: 1980* (New York: Berkley Books, 1980); and Paul T. David and David H. Everson, eds., *The Presidential Election and Transition 1980–81* (Carbondale: Southern Illinois University Press, 1983).

Reagan's speaking has also been widely examined. Perhaps the two best book-length studies are Paul Erickson, *Reagan Speaks: The Making of an American Myth* (New York: New York University Press, 1985); and Kurt Ritter and David Henry, *Ronald Reagan: The Great Communicator* (Westport, CT: Greenwood Press, 1992). Kurt W. Ritter's "Ronald Reagan and 'The Speech': The Rhetoric of Public Relations Politics," *Western Journal of Speech Communication* (Winter 1968): 50–58, and Henry Z. Scheele, "Ronald Reagan's 1980 Acceptance Address: A Focus on American Values," *Western Journal of Speech Communication* (Winter 1984): 51–61, though not dealing directly with the speech studied here, are excellent studies of other critical speeches in Reagan's career that help to illustrate the relative consistency of his message throughout his public career.

1992—BILL AND HILLARY CLINTON

Few, if any, presidents, and fewer still first ladies, have been as controversial as the Clintons. Though there is a considerable body of biographical material available about William Jefferson Clinton and Hillary Rodham Clinton, dispassionate biographies and accounts of their activities, particularly at this early stage, only months after he has left the presidency, are surprisingly few. Perhaps the soundest overall biography is David Maraniss, *First in His Class: A Biography of Bill Clinton* (New York: Simon and Schuster, 1995). Roger Morris, *Partners in Power* (New York: Henry Holt, 1996), is also a judiciously written work. On Hillary Rodham Clinton, see Joyce Milton, *The First Partner: Hillary Rodham Clinton* (New York, William Morrow, 1999), and Gail Sheehy, *Hillary's Choice* (New York: Random House, 1999). Unusually valuable because of their perspectives are Roger Clinton, Jr., *Growing Up Clinton* (Arlington, TX: Summit, 1995); and Paul Greenberg, *No Surprises: Two Decades of Clinton Watching* (Washington: Brassey's, 1996). Roger Clinton's work provides valuable insight into Clinton's formative years and a sympathetic view, while Greenberg was an editor and columnist for two of Arkansas's largest papers throughout the Clinton years in that state. Among the more insightful books written by a Clinton associate is George Stephanopoulos, *All Too Human* (Boston: Little, Brown, 1999).

On the 1992 campaign, see Jack Germond and Jules Witcover, *Mad As Hell: Revolt at the Ballot Box 1992* (New York: Warner Books, 1993); Mary Matalin and James Carville, *All's Fair: Love, War, and Running for President* (New York: Random House, 1994); and Robert E. Denton, Jr., ed., *The 1992 Presidential Campaign: A Communication Perspective,* (Westport, CT: Praeger, 1994).

2000—GEORGE W. BUSH

As this is being written, within six months of the tumultuous end of the 2000 campaign, rhetoricians, historians, biographers, political scientists, and other academicians do not have the advantage of historical perspective in dealing with George W. Bush. As a consequence, at this point their studies are limited. No doubt that will change shortly. Journalists have produced many of the best existing works on Bush and the 2000 campaign. Perhaps the best biography of Bush is Bill Minutaglio, *First Son: George W. Bush and the Bush Family Dynasty* (New York: Times Books, 1999). J. W. Hatfield, *Fortunate Son: George W. Bush and the Making of an American President* (New York: St. Martin's Press, 2000), generated considerable controversy because of the accusations about Bush's drug usage, but it is nevertheless highly informative. Lois Romano and George Lardner, Jr.'s biographical series of articles for the *Washington Post*, 25–29 July 2000, provides a wealth of biographical detail about Bush. Bush's campaign autobiography, *A Charge to Keep* (New York: William Morrow, 1999) is also helpful. James Higgins, "What Bush Learned at Harvard," *Weekly Standard* (19 Feb. 2001), pp. 14–16, argues that most accounts of his life underplay the importance of Bush's years earning his MBA from Harvard.

This is being written prior to the publication of any book-length studies of the 2000 campaign. Evan Thomas and the *Newsweek* Special Projects Team's "Inside Story: What a Long, Strange Trip," *Newsweek*, 20 Nov. 2000, pp. 30–133, is among the more thorough accounts of the campaign currently available. For details concerning the immediate setting and circumstances surrounding this particular speech as well as biographical information concerning Bush, also see the extended coverage of the Republican National Convention in *Time*, 7 Aug. 2000, pp. 26–60. With most major newspapers now having a presence on the Internet, researchers can access a virtually unlimited supply of news accounts of contemporaneous events. The notes to this chapter will indicate those that the author found particularly helpful.

As indicated above, this is being written too early for a large body of work by scholars in political rhetoric and related disciplines to have appeared. However, two early studies that informed this work are Ray Dearin, "George W. Bush in the Tradition of Republican Acceptance Speeches" (Paper presented at the Central States Communication Association Annual Meeting, Cincinnati, OH, Apr. 2001), and Sharon E. Jarvis, "Partisan Campaign Rhetoric of Al Gore and George W. Bush" (Paper presented at the National Communication Association Annual Meeting, Seattle, WA, Nov. 2000). By the time this volume is in print it is likely that other academic works will also be available.

Index